SETTLERS OF THE LATROBE VALLEY

By the Same Author

Polish Immigrants in Britain: A Study of Adjustment (1956)

Immigrants in Australia: A Demographic Survey based upon the 1954 census (1960)

Immigrants in Australia: Statistical supplement (1960)

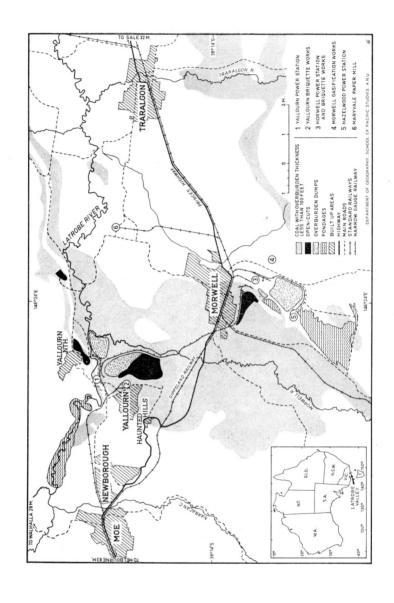

SETTLERS OF THE LATROBE VALLEY

A sociological study of immigrants in the brown coal industry in Australia

by
JERZY ZUBRZYCKI
Senior Fellow in Sociology, The Australian National University

THE AUSTRALIAN NATIONAL UNIVERSITY
CANBERRA

First published in 1964 by
THE AUSTRALIAN NATIONAL UNIVERSITY

Registered in Australia for transmission by post as a book
PRINTED IN AUSTRALIA BY HALSTEAD PRESS, SYDNEY

For the men and women of the Latrobe Valley,
who made it what it is today.

The Survey Team

Frank L. Jones
Phillip Boas
Estelle Carey
Tania Harris
Leon Mann
Rosemary Scouller
Evelyn Snow
Margaret Wallace
Jo Weetman

PREFACE

This book is about the immigrant men and their families who form a substantial proportion of the total workforce of the brown coal industry in the Latrobe Valley of Victoria. The immigrant workers whom one sees in the huge open-cuts where brown coal is mined, in the power stations, briquette factories, and in the various ancillary installations, are the principal *dramatis personae* of the study. The material that follows tells us how the immigrants adjust to their new environment, strike new roots, build their houses, raise families, how they spend their earnings. But the newcomers from Europe do not settle in a social vacuum; the stage on which we watch them as actors is not an empty one.

Throughout the process of adjustment the immigrants interact not only with other immigrants but also with Australians. We watch the immigrants name Australians as workmates and friends, visit their homes and enter their associations; we speak of the immigrants, again, absorbing the ideas and the values of Australian society through reading the Australian press, listening to radio, viewing television, and formally renouncing their former national allegiance at the time of naturalization.

The Australians on our stage are not the only factor in the process of immigrant adjustment. There is another, or perhaps a group of factors, of consequence which can be grouped under the environment. The importance of this environmental factor has been given due prominence in Chapters 1 and 2. This has been done deliberately, for the study of even the tiniest segment of the population of the Latrobe Valley would be meaningless unless accompanied by a full description of the wider setting in which the people live—the geography and the industry of the Valley, the towns and their amenities, the whole course of the development of the region past and present. Another reason for the emphasis given to the environmental factor is that it affects the lives of all the inhabitants in the Latrobe Valley, so that, although the present monograph is primarily a study of the immigrants employed in the brown coal industry, the findings and conclusions can be said to apply *mutatis mutandis* to other foreign-born people who live under the same environmental conditions.

The present volume is devoted mainly to the presentation of

the findings of the study. This follows closely the main factors affecting immigrant adjustment in the Latrobe Valley listed in a document prepared in June 1958 after two scouting expeditions in the field:

(a) The socio-economic background of the immigrant and the decision to migrate to Australia (Chapter 4).

(b) Occupational adjustment of the immigrant (Chapter 5).

(c) Standard of living (Chapter 6).

(d) The structure of the immigrant family (Chapter 7).

(e) The pattern of social and cultural participation with special reference to ethnic origin (Chapters 8 and 9).

Additional documentary material as well as the research instruments used in the present study have been presented in Appendices A-G.

The statistical material derived from the two field surveys constitutes the backbone of the report; case histories and field workers' reports serve to illustrate points to be made, and together form a basis for generalizations upon differences between ethnic groups. Thus, the extent to which certain patterns of behaviour are specific to, or characteristic of, a given ethnic group is the main point of statistical analyses,[1] often supported by examples derived from observations, personal documents, and newspapers. Other factors considered are the length of residence in Australia, age group, rural/urban pre-migration background, and present occupation.[2]

The frequent use in the text of the terms 'ethnic group' and 'ethnic origin', interchangeable with 'birthplace', may give rise to confusion in the mind of the reader. The adjective 'ethnic' denotes more than a single characteristic; for most scholars it stands for complex interweaving of physical, geographical, religious, linguistic, political, and other social characteristics. In this study, however, 'ethnic' is taken to be a less comprehensive category. When we speak of the ethnic origin of a collectivity of people we do not mean by it a group bound together and identified in terms of all the characteristics listed above. What we mean is a degree of broad cultural affinity associated with the geographical location of origin in Europe. This usage enables us to combine, firstly, certain composite groups of immigrants whose areas of origin cut across the boundaries of nation states such as 'Greece and Italy' and 'Baltic states'. Secondly, 'ethnic origin', so broadly defined, embraces all the regional groups within one birthplace in spite of possible and often very marked linguistic, religious, and other social differences. For example, the British Isles and Yugoslavia are identified as such birthplaces and the immigrants who were born in these countries are referred to as belonging to the British or Yugoslav ethnic groups. This is done in spite of the fact that there may not be much in common between, say, the Irish and the Scottish people, or the Serb and the Croat immigrants included in the study.

In emphasizing the usage adopted with regard to the terms 'ethnic origin' and 'ethnic group' no attempt is being made to gloss over possible, and often very important, differences arising from diverse regions of origin, that is, with ethnic divisions of a smaller scale than the nation state. Observations in the field suggest that these differences are very important in so far as they affect the process of immigrant adjustment. Yet—with the exception of a special sociometric survey of the Dutch and the Ukrainian populations reported in Chapter 9—the size of the sample used in the main survey was not large enough for such refinements.

This point should be understood lest the reader draw wrong conclusions about the precise nature of the relationship between 'ethnic origin', occupational adjustment, standard of living, social participation and other characteristics discussed in this study. For example, the circumstances of origin in a particular region of a country may affect the person's chances of acquiring better education, attaining a higher occupational status and so on. On the other hand it is equally possible that there may be other factors involved such as the circumstances of migration, family status, duration of residence in Australia. In all such instances, and when the size of the sample made a further analysis by regions of origin impracticable, resort was made to a considered judgment based on the author's knowledge of the situation. On these occasions the fact that a qualitative judgment was made is clearly stated.

One final point concerns the ultimate objective of this study. Throughout the following pages the aim has been to contribute to our understanding of the immigrant component of Australian society in the 1960s, and, indirectly, Australian society itself. This has been done not so much in the belief that new social uniformities will be discovered and therefore that new socio-logical hypotheses will be tested, though this in fact may occur.

The ultimate objective of this research can rather, perhaps, be expressed in the hope that it will throw light on that larger problem of unity of men and natural resources that David E. Lilienthal of TVA fame speaks about:

> Command nature not by defying her, as in that wasteful past, but by understanding and acting upon her first law—the oneness of men and natural resources, the unity that binds together land, streams, forests, minerals, farming, industry, mankind.[3]

ACKNOWLEDGEMENTS

A study of the kind reported in this volume is of necessity a co-operative venture and I am deeply indebted to all who helped me both in the field and during the analysis of the material. Dr Frank L. Jones, now my colleague in the Department of Sociology at The Australian National University but then my Research Assistant, was chiefly responsible for the organization of field work, the training of interviewers, and the supervision of operations in the field in January, February, and March of 1959. To him and to the group of eight students from the Department of Social Work in the University of Melbourne belongs the credit for the success of the major portion of my survey. Two members of the team, Estelle Carey and Margaret Wallace, returned to the Latrobe Valley for three months in 1961 to join me in the sociometric surveys of the Dutch and the Ukrainians. I am particularly grateful for their assistance and devotion to duty during the hottest months of the year. I must also thank Associate Professor Ruth Hoban, Director of the Department of Social Studies in the University of Melbourne, for her co-operation in putting at my disposal a team of such enthusiastic students and excellent interviewers. Other members of that Department who assisted me in this regard were Miss Lorna Hay, Miss Alice Hyde, Mrs L. O'Brien, and Miss Teresa M. Wardell.

The study would not have been possible without the kind co-operation of the State Electricity Commission of Victoria, who granted me access to their personnel records, allowed me to inspect their files relating to the recruitment policy, and gave the survey team every assistance during the interviewing. For all this I must thank the Secretary of the Commission, Mr D. H. Munro, and Brigadier J. Field, Works Superintendent at Yallourn. The following officers of the Commission in Melbourne, Morwell, and Yallourn helped in my research: Messrs T. Adams, A. L. Cross, T. B. Jensen, R. McDonnell, A. A. Mitchell, L. H. Robertson, J. W. Schulz, F. Sims, N. Taylor, and J. C. Turner.

The success of our field operations in 1959 and 1961, as well as of my frequent visits to the Latrobe Valley during the four-year period 1958-62, was largely due to the people of the Latrobe Valley, both the Australian- and the foreign-born, who generously gave their knowledge of the area, and maintained co-operating interest in our work. To many of them we owe a particular debt for entertaining us in their houses, so giving us an insight into problems of migration and assimilation from both the Australian and the immigrant angle. I am particularly indebted to Councillors H. Stoddard and A. McHardy of Moe, E. Scott of Newborough and J. Pettigrew of Morwell; Messrs F. A. Bartlett, Town Clerk of Moe, A. G. Holden, Secretary-Organizer of the Advance Latrobe Valley Association in Morwell, E. F. Greenwood, Headmaster of the Moe High School; Dr Alan McPhate of Warragul; Messrs Kevin Wakefield of the Newborough Chamber of Commerce, D. S. Manley of the Moe Chamber of Commerce; L. F. Le Get of the Good Neighbour Council in Moe, M. B. Peter of Moe, Dr Ric Bouvier of Morwell, Messrs Laurence F. Davey, Secretary of the Y.M.C.A. in the Latrobe Valley, R. Rundell of Moe, the Rev. H. Pilkington of Moe, Messrs R. Savige of Moe, L. G. Edwards of the Rotary Club in Moe, G. A. Evans of Yallourn, Miss Dorothy King, Secretary of the Y.W.C.A. branch in Newborough, Rev. Fathers P. Dwyer of Moe and F. Ruth of Newborough and Mr R. H. Milner of Apex Club, Morwell. I also owe much to all those settlers who helped me with life histories and translations and generally smoothed the way for the survey team. Many of them prefer to remain anonymous, but the following permitted me to give their names: Rev. and Mrs D. C. Bouma, Rev. J. A. Bouwmeester, Mr and Mrs M. Broeren, Mr R. van den Eijnde, Messrs G. Faith, J. Farrugia, M. Gajek, Mr and Mrs G. L. Goris, Mr F. Grixti, Mr and Mrs H. Gulbis, Mr A. van Houts, the late Mr D. Jongsma, Mr I. Karleusa, Mr and Mrs J. Krawec, Mr R. O. Lingley, Mr W. Luettjens, Mrs L. Makuch, Mr and Mrs K. Malek, Mr and Mrs F. Manicola, Mrs S. Masalski, Mr J. Mifsud, Mr and Mrs W. Nowak, Mr P. Pawlyszyn, Mr and Mrs K. Piorkowski, Mr G. Policronopoulos, Mr G. Poulos, Mr and Mrs J. Prokopiwskj, Messrs G. Rubino, V. Shehade, O. E. Singer, T. Smeale, Mrs M. Stearman, Mr and Mrs B. Sterkenburg, Mr and Mrs P. Sturk, Mr and Mrs A. Top, Mr and Mrs J. Vaniya, Mr C. G. Vella, Mr and Mrs H. Veenstra, and Mr and Mrs J. de Zaayer.

A factor of some importance in the success of survey operations was the congenial atmosphere of the places where the members of the team stayed in 1959 and 1961. The survey headquarters was at Fairfield House, Yallourn, whose licensee, Mr Rex Hamilton, proved a most helpful host. Mr Thorold Irwin, licensee of Moe Hotel in Moe, looked after the members of the team and gave us the benefit of his knowledge of the district.

For assistance in publicizing the survey amongst the local residents I must thank the Editor of the *Advocate*, Mr H. A. Forwood, the manager of Station 3TR in Sale, Mr G. Lewis, and the manager of Station 3UL in Warragul, Mr V. Ganley.

For continuing assistance and advice in facilitating contacts with migrant groups I have to thank Miss Thelma Jarrett, M.B.E., General Secretary of the Good Neighbour Council of Victoria. Other persons in Melbourne who arranged contacts with the migrant groups in the area included the Rt Rev. Bishop I. Prasko, Rev. A. Katkoff, M.I.C. and Father P. Bacinskas. Messrs A. Prestashewsky, Vice-President of the Federation of Ukrainian Associations in Australia, and B. Shemeth, President of the Association of Ukrainians in Victoria, were especially helpful in arranging contacts with the Ukrainian settlers.

Mrs L. Wilson, Mrs M. Gilson, Mrs H. Morley, and Mrs M. J. Salter assisted me in the tedious task of checking interview schedules, coding, and preliminary statistical analysis. Mr I. B. Johns of the I.B.M. helped me to draw up the tabulation programme. To Mrs N. Kuskie belongs credit for the bulk of the statistical analysis of the material finally incorporated in this volume. I wish to thank her for unswerving loyalty and devotion to duty.

Several of my academic colleagues read sections of this book. Professor Walter I. Firey and Professor Richard J. Hill, of the University of Texas, gave me the benefit of their advice and criticism during my term as Visiting Lecturer in that University in 1962-3. Professor Sj. Groenman, of the Sociologisch Instituut van de Rijksuniversiteit in Utrecht, as well as Professor E. W. Hofstee and Dr A. K. Constandse, of the Department of Rural Sociology in the Landbouwhogeschool in Wageningen, commented on the material presented in Chapter 9 during my visit to the Netherlands in June 1963. To others who patiently read successive drafts of my manuscripts and made many helpful suggestions I extend my warm thanks. I must especially mention my friend Dr C. A. Price, of The Australian National University, Professor M. G. Marwick of Monash University, Professor Kurt Mayer of Brown University, and Professor Frank E. Jones of MacMaster University. My colleagues at The Australian National University who commented on my MS. included Drs R. T. Appleyard, F. L. Jones, Norma McArthur, and J. J. Mol. To Professor W. D.

Borrie I owe a special debt for all the advice and encouragement he has given since the study began in 1958.

All these persons helped me to correct my errors and faulty interpretations but they are, of course, not to be blamed for the errors that remain and my occasional failure to heed their advice.

I wish to thank the Editorial Section of the Publications Committee of the University for the energy and time spent in improving my manuscript. I also gratefully acknowledge the help of Mrs D. K. Craft and Miss Ann Godfery in the typing of the text, and the services of Mr Hans Gunther, of the Cartographic Section of the Geography Department, for drawing my map.

Finally I must express my appreciation of the generous grant of the Nuffield Foundation which enabled me to carry out the surveys in the field.

J.Z.

Canberra,
July 1964

CONTENTS

	PAGE
Preface	ix
Acknowledgements	xiii
List of Tables	xix
Illustrations	xxi

PART I THE SETTING OF THE STUDY

1	Industry	3
2	Life and Labour	11
3	Sources and Methods of Gathering Information	33
	The Sample of Immigrants	33
	The Interview Schedule and the Training of Interviewers	34
	Field Survey, January to March 1959: Formal Interviews and Informal Participant Observation	38
	The Life History Material	41
	The Sociometric Survey, December 1960 to April 1961	42
	Other Sources	44
	A Note on the Statistical Tests	44

PART II THE SETTLERS

4	The Settlers' Backgrounds	51
	Mode of Migration	58
	Duration of Residence in Australia and the Demographic Characteristics	67
	Size of Family	69
5	Occupational Adjustment	73
	Migration and Change of Occupation	73
	Stability of Employment and Job Satisfaction	77
6	Standard of Living	90
	Income, Expenditure, and Savings	90
	Housing	97
	Ownership of Motor Vehicles and Consumer Durables	103

B

PAGE

7 The Immigrant Family 111
    Kinship Ties 111
    Family under Stress 113
    The Integrating Forces 118

PART III SOCIAL PARTICIPATION

8 Community Participation 129
    Factors Responsible for Participation 129
    Friendship Patterns 142
    Membership of Voluntary Associations 144
    Naturalization 156
    People Who Do Not Participate 158
9 Social Participation and Group Affiliation 167
    Case Studies of the Dutch in Moe and the
        Ukrainians in Newborough 167
    Social Integration in the Dutch and Ukrainian
        Populations 168
    Province of Origin and Social Participation 172
    Religious Affiliation 173
10 Creating Common Values 183
Appendix A   The Life History Schedule and the Histories 187
             The Life History Schedule 187
             The Life Histories 188
                From London to East Newborough 188
                From Haarlem to Moe 193
                The Story of a Maltese Trade Union
                    Official and Political Organizer 202
                From the Agony of War and Slave
                    Camp to Freedom and Peace in Aus-
                    tralia 211
                The Story of a Latvian Engineer 233
Appendix B   Sampling Procedure and Non-response 239
Appendix C   The Interview Schedule 245
Appendix D   Classification of Occupations 264
Appendix E   Problems of Interviewing (by Evelyn Snow) 267
Appendix F   Interview Schedule used in the Sociometric
             Survey 271
Notes and References 274
Bibliography 296
Index 301

LIST OF TABLES

In the text:

1	Population of the Latrobe Valley Sub-Region: Census Years 1891-1961	12
2	Population of the Latrobe Valley Sub-Region, by Birthplace, Censuses 1891-1961	14
3	Intercensal Comparisons of Overseas-born Persons in the Latrobe Valley, 1947-1961	16
4	Age Structure and Conjugal Condition, Latrobe Valley and Victoria, 1954 and 1961	17
5	Period of Residence, in Latrobe Valley and Victoria, of Persons Born Outside Australia, 1954 and 1961	18
6	Distribution of the Overseas-born Population in the Latrobe Valley: Censuses 1954 and 1961	25
7	Masculinity Rates in the Latrobe Valley and Victoria, Census 1954	26
8	Residential Distribution of Immigrants in the Latrobe Valley	52
9	Religious Distribution of Immigrants within each Birthplace	53
10	Pre-migration Socio-economic Status of the Immigrants	54
11	Mode of Migration	59
12	Period of Residence	68
13	Selected Demographic Characteristics of the Immigrants	68
14	Children in Family by Immigrant's Country of Birth (All Durations of Marriage): Catholics and Non-Catholics	70
15	Malta and Poland: Crude Birth-rates, 1930-1954	72
16	Comparison of Pre-migration and Present Occupations	74
17	Proportions of Unskilled, Skilled, and Semi-skilled Occupations Ranked by Birthplaces	76
18	Employment Stability by Birthplace	78
19	Satisfaction with Present Employment	79
20	Subjects' Assessment of Change in Occupational Status	81

21	Selected Economic Characteristics of the Immigrants by Birthplace	90
22	Selected Economic Characteristics of the Immigrants by Period of Residence in Australia	94
23	Privately-housed Immigrants: Statistical Summary	96
24	Statistical Association between Birthplace and Possession of a Motor Vehicle	105
25	Statistical Association between Birthplace and Possession of Selected Consumer Durables	106
26	Statistical Association between Birthplace and Factors bearing on Social Participation	130
27	English-language Publications Read by a Group of 594 Immigrants of Specified Birthplaces	136
28	Foreign-language Publications Read by Immigrant Households	139
29	Choice of Friends by Birthplace: Percentage Distribution	143
30	Membership of Voluntary Associations by Birthplace	145
31	Naturalization by Birthplace of Immigrants Resident in Australia Five Years and more	157
32	Frequency Distribution of Sociometric Choices by Dutch Adults in Moe and Ukrainian Adults in Newborough	169
33	Sociometric Choices of Members of the Moe Reformed Church (*Gereformeerde Kerk*) Congregation	176

In Appendix B:

I	Extent of Wastage from the Sample, Classified by Causes in conjunction with Country of Birth	241
II	Characteristics of Respondents who Refused to be Interviewed	241
III	The SEC Universe and the Planned and Obtained Samples	242

ILLUSTRATIONS

Map of the Yallourn Valley   *Frontispiece*

1   A Ukrainian family's shack at Yallourn North   10

    The family's permanent dwelling   10

    A shack in Old Newborough   10

2   Cross Street, Newborough   11

    A garage housing a Maltese family of six   11

    The Ukrainian Hall, Newborough, in 1961   11

3   The Ceremony of Saint Nicholas   26

    A 'Black Peter'   26

    Taking the Oath of Allegiance   26

4   The Ukrainian Community at Newborough welcomes
    a Catholic Archbishop of the Greek Rite   27

    A ceremony of baptism performed by a visiting
    Ukrainian Catholic Archbishop of the Greek Rite   27

PART I
THE SETTING OF THE STUDY

I
INDUSTRY

An account of the brown coal development in the Latrobe Valley is a story of the dramatic transformation of what was, forty years ago, a rich dairying region into Victoria's industrial power centre. Few members of the farming community knew then that beneath the rich green pastures lay still greater riches of brown coal. The systematic exploitation of this fuel, once regarded as almost worthless, has brought about revolutionary changes in the region.

A visitor approaching Yallourn from the direction of Melbourne at night can see the glare of lights as he drives from Newborough over the hills that surround the works and the town of Yallourn from three sides. On reaching the crest of the hill the floodlit sections of the open-cut, the trains running to and from the coal bunkers, the power station with its switchyards, and the briquette works can be seen, and in the quiet of the night a hum of activity from Yallourn can be heard for miles. In daylight the most conspicuous feature of the place is the tall chimney stacks of the power station and briquette works.

Latrobe Valley is a wide plain running through Gippsland on both sides of the Latrobe River. The Latrobe rises on the southern slopes of the Great Dividing Range and falls to the southeast until it reaches the Haunted Hills block which forms a land barrier separating the Moe swamp on its western side from the east Gippsland plains. The Latrobe has cut a deep gorge through the Haunted Hills in the vicinity of the present Yallourn open-cut. It then flows in an easterly direction through east Gippsland into Lake Wellington, approximately ten miles east of Sale.

Gippsland was first discovered in 1840 by the explorers James Macarthur and Paul Strzelecki and was named after Sir George Gipps, the Governor of New South Wales. The favourable account of the region given by the explorers soon attracted pastoralists, who moved in with their cattle from what was then known as the Port Phillip District of New South Wales. The Gippsland squatting district was proclaimed in September 1843. By 1844 all the open country in the Latrobe Valley was occupied.[1]

For the next thirty years or so the grazing industry flourished in the large runs of the Latrobe Valley, providing cattle for the Hobart and New Zealand markets. At that time the only port suitable for such export trade was Melbourne and this meant

3

that, until the railway to Melbourne was opened in 1879, cattle had to be taken overland.[2]

The construction of a road and rail link between Gippsland and Melbourne brought about a transition from grazing to dairying in the district. The rich pastures of the Latrobe Valley, within easy reach of the new railway towns that grew up in the seventies, were ideally situated for dairy farming; but even while dairying was still in its infancy a new source of wealth was discovered in the Valley. In the early 1870s gold seekers, who had been working on the alluvial in the mountain streams of Gippsland since 1853, reported outcrops of brown coal in the district,[3] so arousing periodic outbursts of public interest, and a Royal Commission in 1891.[4] There were one or two short-lived attempts to produce brown coal briquettes, notably that of the Great Morwell Coal Mining Company which came to an end four years after a disastrous fire in 1895.

Then, in 1912, came the decision to electrify the metropolitan railway system (the implementation of which would require considerable supplies of fuel) ; and a prolonged coal strike in the New South Wales coal fields in 1916 hardened Victorian opinion into a solid decision to develop Victorian coal resources. The former site of the Great Morwell Coal Mining Company was re-opened by the Victorian Mines Department in the emergency, and the Brown Coal Advisory Committee was established. This recommended that, in view of the increased demands which would soon be made on existing electrical services, an electrical generation and transmission scheme be established in the neighbourhood of Morwell, in conjunction with an open-cut, to meet the requirements of the power house for brown coal. In 1918 the State Electricity Commission of Victoria (known until 1921 as the Electricity Commissioners) was constituted by Act of the Victorian Parliament, with the primary object of developing the brown coal resources of the Latrobe Valley.

The Commission is a semi-government authority constituted for the purpose of co-ordinating the supply of electric power throughout the state of Victoria. 'It is vested with power to erect, own and operate electrical undertakings; acquire existing electrical undertakings; supply electricity retail to individual consumers or in bulk to any corporation or public institution; establish brown coal open-cuts; and own and operate briquette works.'[5]

During the four decades of its existence the growth of the State Electricity Commission (SEC) has been rapid. In 1921 Sir John

Monash was appointed chairman and continued during the important formative period until his death in 1931.[6]

The Commission acquired an area of 3,166 acres about five miles west of Morwell,[7] and here, early in 1921, work started on the stripping of the overburden—the surface layer of clay, sand, and gravel—in advance of coal winning. On the edge of what was to be known as the Yallourn Open-cut a power station and a briquetting plant were erected. A start was also made on a town to house the Commission employees. The town and the surrounding area was named Yallourn from the aboriginal words, *yaleen* (brown) and *lourn* (fuel).

The site chosen for the power station on the bank of the Latrobe River had numerous advantages. Adequate water was available for the station's requirements, land nearby provided a good town site, while, most important of all considerations, an area of one square mile adjacent to the proposed station contained proved reserves of brown coal totalling about 150 million tons with averages of 200 feet thickness and 40 feet overburden.

On 24 June 1924 power started to flow from Yallourn Power Station to Melbourne. From this historic day in the development of Victoria the SEC has progressed rapidly. Brown coal production in the Yallourn Open-cut grew from $0 \cdot 7$ million tons in the year 1925/6 to $11 \cdot 86$ million tons in 1960/1, and the generating capacity of the Yallourn Power Station was increased during the same period from 50,000 kW. to 501,000 kW. This rapid rate of progress has transformed fourteen square miles of scrub country into the industrial nerve centre of Victoria. The Yallourn enterprise today consists of one of the largest brown coal open-cuts in the world (together with a subsidiary open-cut at Yallourn North), a power station which is at present one of the largest steam power stations in the southern hemisphere, and Victoria's pioneer briquette factory. The briquette factories at Yallourn and Morwell are the only ones of their kind outside Europe.

The Yallourn undertaking also includes a secondary subsidiary open-cut at Yallourn North which lies on the north side of the Latrobe River. This open-cut was the original source of supplies for the Great Morwell Coal Mining Company from 1889 to 1899, and is located on a field of coal of less extent but with a significantly lower moisture content than the Yallourn field. An extension of the Yallourn North seam has been opened up about four miles east of the original Yallourn North open-cut. Output of Yallourn North and the extension is now mainly used for briquette-making and the coal is sold only to the Australian Paper Mills at Maryvale (three miles north of Morwell) and a few industrial users in the Latrobe Valley.

Yallourn brown coal in its natural state is a very low-grade fuel because of its high moisture content, amounting to about 66 per cent. It is because of the relative cheapness with which brown coal can be won in great quantities by machinery from not far beneath the surface of the ground, and the manner in which the damp coal is burned in special furnaces at Yallourn power station, that generating costs in Latrobe Valley power stations are among the lowest in Australia.

At Yallourn, brown coal lies under a shallow overburden of sand and clay about 40 feet thick; underneath lies a solid seam of coal 200 feet thick. The overburden is dug away by land dredgers and other types of mechanical excavators, and moved by rail traction (shortly to be replaced by conveyor belts) to the worked-out floor of the open-cut.

The uncovered coal is then mechanically won by huge dredgers that operate on four faces of the deposit; these are terraced cliffs of solid coal ranging in length from a quarter to nearly two-thirds of a mile and reaching down in giant steps nearly two hundred feet into the bottom of the open-cut. The dredgers load the coal into narrow-gauge rail trucks which take it direct to large bunkers situated on two levels of the open-cut; from there the coal goes through huge crushers and is then carried by conveyor belts to the top of the boiler houses of the Yallourn power station.

Coal won at Yallourn is also used for briquette manufacture. In the process of briquetting, the raw coal is converted to a high-grade fuel. The process consists of crushing, screening, drying, cooling, and pressing the coal into hard, durable blocks of compressed fuel with only 15 per cent of moisture and a calorific value —weight for weight—approximately treble that of the original raw coal.

The open-cut, power station, and the briquette works constitute, then, the three main branches of the Yallourn undertaking. In addition there are, of course, the various services, including workshops, maintenance unit, and an elaborate fire service organization. This last maintains an unceasing watch not only on the power station and the briquette works but above all on the open-cut. The reason for some of the elaborate firefighting installations in the open-cut is the highly inflammable nature of dry coal dust. Fires in the open-cut in the past have caused serious losses and interruptions to the production of electricity, hence it is necessary to have an elaborate grid system of spray lines to keep the coal surface moist and fireproof.

The potentialities of the brown coal deposits of the Latrobe Valley are enormous. From Yallourn eastwards the coal belt is practically continuous for forty miles, and for much of the distance is between five and ten miles wide. Boring at one point has revealed a seam of unbroken coal 757 feet thick at a depth of only eighty-nine feet below the surface. This is the thickest known coal seam in the world.[8] The region contains also what are believed to be the largest continuous deposits of brown coal in the world. Proved reserves of brown coal in the Latrobe Valley which could be economically won in large-scale workings by present open-cut methods are estimated at about 17,500 million tons, and it is probable that further deposits will be discovered as exploratory boring proceeds. In addition, there are immense quantities known to lie too deep for economic winning by present open-cut methods.

One of the richest deposits lies south of the town of Morwell and this has now become the centre of the State Electricity Commission's second major development of brown coal supplies in the Latrobe Valley. Known as the Morwell Power and Fuel Undertaking, this consists of a brown coal open-cut, the annual output of which will eventually more than double Victoria's brown coal production. A new power station operates in conjunction with briquetting works which have more than trebled Victoria's annual output of briquettes.

The reason for this emphasis on briquette production is of great interest for it is connected with important developments in the brown coal industry in the Valley. Ever since the very beginning of the brown coal industry in Victoria scientists have been attempting to produce synthetic gas and other important by-products from brown coal. These experiments were successful, and in 1951 the Gas and Fuel Corporation of Victoria established at Morwell, in anticipation of the SEC Morwell Project, a plant for the production of synthetic gas from brown coal briquettes by a process known as the Lurgi High Pressure Gasification Process, which leaves as by-products such important fuels as brown coal tar, spent wash oil, crude benzole, and effluent liquor. Coke is not a by-product, as only ash remains when brown coal is used.[9]

As yet no metallurgical coke has been produced at Morwell on a commercial scale. The Gas and Fuel Corporation is now operating a pilot plant which has a daily production of twelve tons of hard coke from twenty-five tons of briquettes. The coke is produced by a specially controlled carbonizing process developed in the Engineering School at Melbourne University.[10] If this brown coal coke proves suitable for iron smelting (it has a 95 per cent carbon content and a relatively low ash content) then the way would be opened for even greater industrial expansion in the Latrobe Valley. A big steel industry in the Latrobe Valley would rely on rich deposits of high-grade iron ore at Nowa Nowa only 100 miles east of the coal fields. Coking coal and iron ore in close proximity is the geological 'accident' on which every great industrial nation of the modern era has been founded.

With the development of the Latrobe Valley brown coal resources, the increasing rate of production of electric power and fuel, and reticulation of town gas to centres in the Valley, the industrial future of the region seems assured. Indeed, the rate of the recent development has prompted many observers to liken the Valley to the great Ruhr Valley in Germany.

It is perhaps too early to speak of the analogy between the Latrobe Valley and the Ruhr. For one thing the Latrobe Valley lacks the steel industry. The existing industries, besides the SEC undertakings, are not as yet very numerous though the most important of these, the Australian Paper Mills factory at Maryvale, in 1959 produced 80,000 tons of paper pulp and 60,000 tons of kraft paper. The company recently built a chemical plant at Maryvale to supply its caustic soda, chlorine, and other chemicals. More than 1,300 men and women work for APM in the Valley and the firm has built 1,000 houses as well as hostels, boarding-houses, and other amenities.

Other secondary developments in the Valley are two factories erected at Morwell and Traralgon by La Mode to give work to 400 women. A third small factory which also produces women's clothing at Moe employs forty women. A recent development at Moe is the nucleus of a textile industry in the form of a spinning mill erected by the Yarragon Textile Mills. The factory employs forty women and thus provides a suitable outlet for family labour. The introduction of a spinning mill to Moe was recently followed by the beginning of a weaving industry. In June 1961 a British firm, Thomas Mason Pty Ltd, announced that it had purchased land next to the Yarragon spinning mills. The two textile factories in Moe can be said to form a nucleus of a textile industry in that they will be complementary to each other: one spins yarn from the raw cotton while the other weaves yarn into cloth.

The establishment of these secondary industries has received considerable encouragement from the state government. This and other secondary industry developments are essential, for they provide work for the sons and daughters of the employees of the SEC and the Gas and Fuel Corporation as well as for the families of the hundreds of farmers in what is one of the finest dairying regions in Australia.

In 1948 a committee was set up by the Victorian government to report on the future development of the town of Morwell, which has been built over rich deposits of coal. This committee (called the Morwell Project Co-ordinating Committee) pointed out that it was desirable to prepare a plan to cover the whole of the development of the Latrobe Valley. After much activity and reporting, the Victorian Parliament passed the Latrobe Valley Development Loan and Application Act now consolidated as the Latrobe Valley Act No. 6290, providing for:

(a) the establishment of a fund of one million pounds for expenditure on approved works designed to develop the Latrobe Valley, and

(b) the constitution of the Latrobe Valley Development Advisory Committee whose functions are—

  (i) to make recommendations for the provision of financial assistance to public and municipal authorities towards meeting the cost of approved works or land compensation; and

  (ii) to convene conferences with the object of securing co-ordination of developmental works in the area.

On an unofficial level there is the Advance Latrobe Valley Association (ALVA), which was formed in 1959 to press for further and more diversified development of the region. The association has been actively lobbying in the Victorian Parliament for the establishment of secondary industries in the Latrobe Valley. Its aims also include sponsorship of the tourist industry, and publicity is designed to encourage business firms to establish factories and shops in the region.[11] In a long submission to the Victorian Distribution of Population Committee in 1960 the association argued a strong case for bringing new industry to the region. The submission also argued the case for the establishment of a teachers' college in the area and urged the government of Victoria to provide the necessary finance for the improvement of road and rail transport linking the Latrobe Valley region with the metropolitan area of Melbourne.

The activities of the ALVA are interesting, for they foreshadow a move towards the unified control of the development of the Latrobe Valley. This is seen, for example, in a statement made by the then Leader of the Country Party in the Victorian Legislative Assembly, Sir Herbert Hyland, who recommended the appointment of a full-time co-ordinator for the Latrobe Valley to control and direct its development.[12]

Whatever the fluctuations in the economy of Victoria and Australia as a whole, there seems no doubt that the future of the Latrobe Valley is assured. The Latrobe Valley is clearly emerging into what might be described as the pulsating heart of Victoria's development. Without doubt the tremendous expansion of secondary industry in Victoria within recent years has been greatly influenced by the fact that industrialists have been aware that Victoria, through its power projects in the Latrobe Valley, offers a permanent and expanding source of the 'life blood' of industrial development.

The Latrobe Valley area is Victoria's basic source of power and fuel and an important supplier of town gas, so that it is attractive to those industries requiring large quantities of fuel because of the ease of obtaining supplies and the consequent substantial saving in costs. The establishment of these basic industries will naturally be followed by secondary industries and there is unlimited scope for the establishment of all types. With such opportunities offering, the Latrobe Valley area cannot fail to fulfil the prophecies already proclaimed for its great industrial future.

PLATE 1 *above*: The home in 1951 of a Ukrainian family for five years. *Centre*: The permanent dwelling the Ukrainian family built in Old Newborough. *Below*: A shack in Old Newborough previously occupied by a Polish family, now occupied by a Maltese family. Note the T.V. aerial.

PLATE 2 *above*: Cross Street, Newborough, 1961. *Centre*: A garage occupied by a family of six Maltese whose energies and savings are spent developing a bushland tract in Yallourn North into a market garden. *Below*: The Ukrainian Hall under construction at Newborough in 1961.

2

LIFE AND LABOUR

Small centres of population were first established in Gippsland in the 1850s but their growth was slow until the discovery of gold. After the discovery of gold at Stringer's Creek the rich mining field at Walhalla sprang into existence, by 1863 some three hundred diggers were working in the creek, and before the end of the decade the gold mines attracted 3,000 men.[1] Walhalla soon became a prospectors' mining town, and until the end of the century it was the largest centre of population in what is now known as the Latrobe Valley Sub-Region.

The foundation of other centres in the Latrobe Valley was associated with the construction of a road between Gippsland and Melbourne. In 1860 Moe, Morwell, and Traralgon were as yet small changing places along the road to Melbourne. Coaches stopped there and, while horses were being changed, passengers had a meal at a roadside inn.[2] Bush tracks were cut from these places to Walhalla and other mining centres north of the highway, but it was not until after the opening of a railway between Melbourne and Gippsland that these towns began to develop.

The growth of population in the Latrobe Valley Sub-Region compared with the population of Victoria is shown in Table 1.[3] This shows an impressive rate of growth between 1933 and 1954, more than three times that of Victoria as a whole. In the last intercensal period (1954-61), however, the rate of growth of the sub-region was reduced to less than half what it was in 1947-54. In spite of this the Latrobe Valley share of the state's population has continued to increase.

Who were the people who came to live in the Latrobe Valley and contributed to such a rapid rate of growth? The ethnic origin of these people is shown in Table 2. Of those who were born outside Australia, most came from the British Isles and until 1947 constituted around 80 per cent of the population in that category, and most of the remainder were from Germany, Scandinavia, and Italy, apparently engaged in gold mining, saw milling, quarrying, and various kinds of construction work.[4]

Increasing economic activity in the 1920s is reflected in the rising population enumerated in the 1933 census and an increase in the numbers of the overseas-born. The census of 1947 showed

C

an absolute decline in the numbers of overseas-born residents which, no doubt, was caused by the cessation of immigration during World War II. Only the Italian and the Maltese groups increased slightly in size.[5]

The results of the 1954 census show a dramatic departure from the previous pattern in the emergence of several new ethnic groups, some of which were not separately shown until that time.

TABLE 1

Population of the Latrobe Valley Sub-Region: Census Years 1891—1961*

	Males	Females	Total	Annual average rate of growth†	Population as % of Victoria	Rate of growth—Victoria†
1891	6,174	4,765	10,939		0·96	
				1·22 (10)‡		0·52
1901	6,701	5,643	12,344		1·03	
				0·61 (20)		1·21
1921	7,644	6,299	13,943		0·91	
				2·67 (12¼)		1·42
1933	10,732	8,510	19,242		1·06	
				2·47 (14)		0·87
1947	14,838	12,238	27,076		1·32	
				8·57 (7)		2·56
1954	25,560	22,575	48,135		1·96	
				3·18 (7)		2·58
1961	31,761	28,169	59,930		2·05	

* No figures available for Latrobe Valley in 1911 census.
† Intercensal.
‡ The figures in parentheses are the intercensal periods in years.

The pattern of the change with particular reference to 1947-61 is shown in Table 3. This table highlights such features as a decline in the proportion of Australian-born from just under 92 per cent in 1947 to 75 per cent in 1961, with a corresponding increase in the proportion of overseas-born; an appreciable rise in the numbers of the persons born in the British Isles and a fall in their proportion in the total population; and a very large increase in the numbers of people from several European countries, for example the Dutch, Italians, Germans, Maltese, and Poles.

An influx of such a magnitude of immigrants from many countries hitherto practically not represented in Australia did not upset the trend towards a more balanced distribution of the sexes in the population of the Latrobe Valley. Table 2 shows that this trend has continued from 1891, with a temporary upset in 1933 due to the immigration of the 1920s. The high index of masculinity in 1891 suggests that the immigrants of that period were mainly males, who as gold seekers, labourers in the timber industry, and members of construction gangs on the railway and roads were not necessarily permanent settlers. Their successors in 1961, on the other hand, included an appreciable proportion of families with children, and the masculinity rate for the latter census year was appreciably lower.

The more settled type of population in the Latrobe Valley can also be seen in its age structure when compared with that of Victoria. Table 4 shows that the Valley has a 'younger' population than the State of Victoria, with a higher proportion in the 0 to 14 age group and a significantly lower proportion in the 60 and over group. The proportion of males in the working population (those aged 15 and under 60) was also a little lower in the Latrobe Valley at the last two censuses.

In any study of immigrant adjustment it is important to examine the conjugal condition of the population, as this affects all sorts of activities, notably intermarriage. Table 4 shows that the proportion of males in the 'Never Married' category is higher than that in Victoria as a whole. This is partly the result of the unusual age structure and partly a reflection on the relatively higher masculinity of the Valley's population. It is interesting too that the Valley has a higher proportion of 'Never Married' females, a fact which must, however, be attributed to the much bigger proportion of females aged 0 to 14 in the population. A lower proportion of widowed females in the Valley can be attributed partly to a shortage of women in the marriageable age group.

Table 5 shows details of the period of residence in Australia of the overseas-born persons. Here again the impact of post-war immigration, and high rate of population growth during the intercensal years 1947-54, is shown in the proportion of the immigrants in the Latrobe Valley whose period of residence in 1954 was under seven years. The proportion of immigrants in

TABLE 2

Population of the Latrobe Valley Sub-Region, by Birthplace, Censuses 1891-1961

Birthplace	1891	1901	1921	1933	1947	1954	1961
Australia	7,924	10,109	12,403	16,638	24,830	36,633	44,973
New Zealand	63	70	96	148	126	137	146
British Isles	2,475	1,796	1,227	2,023	1,772	6,246	6,873
Netherlands	1	1	—	—	4	1,117	2,181
Scandinavia	75	51	30	43	22	†	62
Other N.W. Europe	39	24	9	20	*	†	81
Italy	58	72	35	122	128	483	1,076
Greece	—	1‡	—	2	11	56	220
Malta	—	—	—	22‡	27	716	962
Germany	84	82	42	49	37	997	1,367
Hungary	—	—	—	—	—	62‡	90
Latvia	—	—	—	—	—	107‡	100
Lithuania	—	—	—	1‡	—	66‡	70
Poland	—	—	—	—	6	419	439
Ukraine	—	—	—	—	—	209‡	164
U.S.S.R.	5	7	1	12	4	54	62
Yugoslavia	—	—	—	5‡	3	198	318
Other Europe	16	4	16	9	41	307	319
U.S.A.	47	24	8	15	13	22	26
Other parts of world	152	103	76	88	52	306	401
Total	10,939	12,344	13,943	19,242	27,076	48,135	59,930

TABLE 2—*continued*.

Birthplace	1891	1901	1921	1933	1947	1954	1961
Percentage ratio in total population							
Australian-born	72·4	81·9	89·0	86·7	91·7	76·1	75·0
British-born	22·6	14·5	8·8	10·5	6·5	13·0	11·5
British-born, overseas population	82·1	80·4	79·7	79·1	78·9	54·3	46·0
Percentage ratio males to females							
Australian-born	111·4	108·0	116·3	119·3	117·4	108·0	107·1
British-born	168·7	164·1	160·0	177·1	168·9	124·0	124·7
Other foreign-born	468·4	322·1	240·2	213·5	203·8	142·0	138·0
Total	129·6	118·7	121·4	126·1	121·2	113·2	112·8
Victoria	110·4	101·1	97·2	98·5	97·4	100·8	101·3
Boroughs and shires included in the sub-region	Narracan Walhalla Traralgon	Narracan Walhalla Morwell Traralgon	Narracan Morwell Traralgon	Narracan Morwell Traralgon	Narracan Morwell Traralgon	Narracan (excl. Trafalgar) Yallourn Works Area Morwell Traralgon	Narracan (excl. Trafalgar) Yallourn Works Area Moe Morwell Traralgon

Note: Slight changes in the overall boundaries of the area took place over the years but the main towns remained within the area included.
Figures for 1911 not available as census of that year gave counties only for Victoria.
* Not shown separately for 1947.   † Not shown separately for 1954.   ‡ Not shown separately for earlier censuses.

TABLE 3

Intercensal Comparisons of Overseas-born Persons in the Latrobe Valley, 1947–1961*

Birthplace	1947	1954	Increase 1947-1954	1961	Increase 1954-1961
Total number	2,246	11,502	9,256	14,957	3,455
Percentages					
British Isles	78·9	54·3	252·8	46·0	10·0
Netherlands	·2	9·7	†	14·6	95·3
Germany	1·6	8·7	†	9·1	37·1
Malta	1·2	6·2	†	6·4	34·4
Italy	5·7	4·2	277·8	7·2	122·8
Poland	·3	3·7	†	2·9	4·8
Ukraine‡	} 12·1	1·8 }	460·3	1·1	—21·5
Other countries		11·4 }		12·7	44·1
	100·0	100·0	412·1	100·0	30·0

* See Table 2 for the number of persons in individual birthplaces.
† Very large increase.
‡ Included with 'Other countries' for 1947.

that category was about 81 per cent compared with just under 60 per cent in the State of Victoria. This figure alone underlines the significance of post-war migration as a factor contributing to the development of the Latrobe Valley. The post-war arrivals were, with few exceptions, people who came to start a new life in the Valley without any links with pre-war settlement. As shown earlier most of them, like the Dutch, Poles, and Ukrainians, were practically not represented in the population until 1954; the others, like the Germans and Italians, had very few links with those of their compatriots who had lived in the area before World War II. The only exception was the Maltese, whose immigration was largely the result of the 'chain' processes that were started in the early 1920s with the arrival of the first pioneers (see p. 111).

The 1961 census reveals in a striking manner the extent to which the overseas-born population of the Latrobe Valley has changed its character. With the slowing down of the rate of increase (as shown in Table 1) the proportion of persons resident in Australia under seven years has more than halved in comparison with 1954. The extent of this shift in the distribution of the overseas-born in the Latrobe Valley has been more pronounced than in Victoria as a whole. Just over 50 per cent of the immigrants in the Latrobe

TABLE 4

Age Structure and Conjugal Condition, Latrobe Valley and Victoria, 1954 and 1961
(%)

	Males				Females				Persons			
	1954		1961		1954		1961		1954		1961	
	Latrobe Valley	Victoria	Latrobe Valley	Victoria	Latrobe Valley	Victoria	Latrobe Valley	Victoria	Latrobe Valley	Victoria	Latrobe Valley	Victoria
Total Number	25,560	1,231,099	31,761	1,474,395	22,575	1,221,242	28,169	1,455,718	48,135	2,452,341	59,930	2,930,113
Age Group												
0—14	36·2	28·2	37·3	30·4	38·5	27·1	39·2	29·3	37·3	27·6	38·2	29·8
15—19	5·7	6·4	7·5	7·6	6·0	6·1	7·4	7·3	5·8	6·3	7·5	7·5
20—29	15·1	15·0	12·5	13·4	15·5	14·0	12·6	12·6	15·3	14·5	12·5	13·0
30—49	29·8	28·9	28·4	27·8	27·6	27·7	27·4	26·6	28·8	28·3	28·0	27·2
50—59	7·5	10·1	8·5	10·0	6·4	10·5	6·9	9·8	7·0	10·3	7·7	9·9
60 and over	5·7	11·4	5·8	10·8	6·0	14·6	6·5	14·4	5·8	13·0	6·1	12·6
Total	100·0	100·0	100·0	100·0	100·0	100·0	100·0	100·0	100·0	100·0	100·0	100·0
Conjugal Condition												
Never married	53·9	49·1	55·9	51·0	47·4	43·3	49·1	44·6	50·8	46·2	52·7	47·8
Married	43·2	46·3	41·4	45·1	47·8	46·2	45·8	45·4	45·3	46·3	43·5	45·2
Separated and divorced	1·4	1·8	1·3	1·8	1·1	2·2	1·1	2·2	1·3	2·0	1·2	2·0
Widowed	1·4	2·5	1·4	2·1	3·7	8·1	4·0	7·8	2·5	5·3	2·6	5·0
Not stated	0·1	0·3	—	—	—	0·2	—	—	0·1	0·2	—	—
Total	100·0	100·0	100·0	100·0	100·0	100·0	100·0	100·0	100·0	100·0	100·0	100·0

TABLE 5

Period of Residence, in Latrobe Valley and Victoria, of Persons born outside Australia, 1954 and 1961

(%)

Period of residence in Australia	Latrobe Valley		Victoria	
	Censuses		Censuses	
	1954	1961	1954	1961
Total number	**11,502**	**14,957**	**368,962**	**569,690**
Under 7 years	81·1	36·5	59·2	41·6
7 years and under 15 years	1·2		3·4	
7 years and under 14 years		50·9		35·6
14 years and under 21 years		1·0		1·8
15 years and over	17·0		35·8	
21 years and over		10·6		19·1
Not stated	0·7	1·0	1·6	1·9
	100·0	100·0	100·0	100·0

Valley in 1961 (as compared with about 1 per cent in 1954) are persons with the residence standing of seven and under fourteen years in Australia.

The centre of the area under survey (see frontispiece map) is the town of Yallourn, which was visualized and planned as a model town in 1921 at the time work began on the power station, the open-cut, and briquette works. At present it contains about 1,100 houses, and had, in June 1961, a population of 5,010 persons.[6] Compared with other towns in the district it is unusually attractive, pleasantly laid out with ample parks and gardens, and has adequate provision for all forms of social life. It is built on SEC property, the houses are owned by the SEC, and the Commission also provides all community services such as hostels and boarding-houses, and many shops have also been erected. Buildings not owned by the Commission include such premises as the post office, police station, schools, banks, churches and their associated dwellings, and several shops. Public buildings and shops are arranged about the centrally-situated Monash Square, which contains the memorial to Sir John Monash. The town has now reached its maximum development.

In the post-war years, when the SEC began to expand its Yallourn works, it became necessary to provide more accommodation for its employees. To this end the SEC established two satellite townships, one at Yallourn North, and another at Newborough. Yallourn North had existed as a small township since the reopening of the site of the Great Morwell Coal Mining Company in 1917, and after the war the SEC enlarged it by building 275 houses for many of its skilled workers. These houses are for rental or purchase by instalments (which are slightly higher than the rentals). As well as the SEC houses there is also a private section of Yallourn North where many of the houses date back to 1920 and 1930, some of which are inhabited by Maltese and Italian immigrants who have been working with the SEC from that time. Many of the post-war immigrants and displaced persons have also built their own homes in the private section of Yallourn North.

The other satellite town is divided into three sections known as East, North, and Old Newborough. East and North Newborough consist entirely of prefabricated houses brought out in 1950 and 1951 from England, mainly to house the British tradesmen sponsored by the SEC for employment at Yallourn. There are nearly 700 houses in East and North Newborough for rental or purchase by SEC employees on the same conditions as the SEC homes in Yallourn North. There is a private part of Newborough, known to the local inhabitants as 'Old Newborough', which started in 1930 as a string of houses along Monash Road (formerly Old Yallourn Road). Since 1953 many SEC employees have built their own houses in Old Newborough.

The construction of the SEC Housing Estate in East and North Newborough and the private development of Old Newborough underline the division which exists between the two parts of the town. Each part seems to live a life of its own and there is as yet little communication between the two. Moreover East and North Newborough are separated from Old Newborough by a wide green belt on both sides of a busy road taking the main traffic from Moe to Yallourn.[7] East and North Newborough have sewerage, electricity, and water, not to speak of footpaths and sealed streets. Old Newborough has water and electricity but no sewerage and mostly unmade roads. It has, however, a fine shopping centre, something which is completely lacking in North Newborough, the inhabitants of which have to walk a distance of up to a mile to a small shopping centre in East Newborough or to the main centre in Old Newborough.[8]

The divisions between the main parts of Newborough seem

to lead to antagonisms between the two parted sections of the town. The vigorous Tenants' Association, which was formed in the early years of the town's existence, has lapsed in East and North Newborough and there seems little community spirit amongst the inhabitants.[9] Most of the community effort in Newborough has been centred in Old Newborough, which has a vigorous Progress Association, Pre-School Centre Committee, and a number of social and sporting bodies. The story of the Newborough Public Hall is a good example of a community effort. The construction of the hall was undertaken in 1956 by the Progress Association, later re-named Public Hall Committee, led by a former Scots migrant, who also represents Old Newborough on the local Council.[10] Some £1,500 was raised and this was supplemented by the state government on a £ for £ basis. Next a group of people put up guarantees in the form of securities, and the State Savings Bank advanced £2,000. The hall was built mostly by voluntary effort and took approximately seventeen months to complete. It was erected of brick, and has a spacious dance floor, a large supper room, and other facilities.

The other two towns whose inhabitants were included in the survey are Moe and Morwell. These towns, together with Traralgon, had earlier beginnings than Yallourn, Yallourn North, and Newborough. Moe and Morwell (as well as Traralgon) are situated on the main east and west rail and road routes. Furthermore, they are junctions for feeder routes which run to the north and south into the surrounding hill country. With the increased exploitation of the region's resources these towns have grown rapidly.

Until World War II Moe was a country town serving the population of the surrounding district. It also served as a rail junction for a narrow gauge line (since closed) running north to Walhalla, which by this time had lost its mining population and was now an historical relic and a small tourist resort. The population of Moe in 1947 was only 2,556, by 1954 it had risen to 12,442,[11] and by June 1961 to 15,454. This rise can be attributed mainly to the extension of the Yallourn undertaking of the SEC, for which Moe became another one of the three dormitory towns. The Housing Commission of Victoria built houses in the town which rapidly began to spread up the southern slopes of the Valley.

In 1955 Moe, with its boundaries extended to include Newborough, became a borough with a council of nine to represent its three wards. The first council drew up a town plan which envisaged an impressive city of the future. Steps were taken to provide sewerage and nearly all the town of Moe is now sewered, and a scheme for Newborough is being undertaken. To a visitor Moe presents a picture of considerable activity, though it still has no outstanding municipal buildings. Situated on the Princes Highway—6,000 cars pass through the town in an hour in peak times—Moe serves as an important shopping centre and stopping place for people travelling on the highway.

Some eight miles due east of Moe is the town of Morwell which, in spite of its size (14,352 in 1961) has not yet been created a borough. The town and the surrounding districts are dominated by the triumvirate of industrial giants: the SEC with the Morwell Power and Fuel Undertaking and the new Hazelwood power station under construction south of the town, the Gas and Fuel Corporation's undertaking, and the Australian Paper Manufacturers' mill at Maryvale some five miles to the north.

The town itself presents to the visitor a picture of great activity and has an air of prosperity, no doubt due to the enormous rate of recent expansion. Many of the immigrants and local Australians when interviewed spoke of it as the 'boom' town, recalling the years of 1955-7 when the construction on the SEC undertaking was in full swing. Unlike Newborough and Yallourn, practically all housing for the SEC employees in Morwell is provided by the Victorian Housing Commission. The standard of housing is as good as in Moe and the town's street lighting, roads, and drainage facilities seem very satisfactory. A great effort is being made by the Morwell Shire Council and the local business and community organizations to promote the various aspects of town life and improve its facilities and amenities. In the Victorian Premier Town Competition in 1958 Morwell was judged to be the town in the State of Victoria which had made the greatest effort in town promotion.[12]

Some seven miles east of Morwell on Princes Highway lies the town of Traralgon, which has developed from a small settlement to a modern town with a population of 12,298 at 30 June 1961. The town developed steadily with the growth of the Morwell district and the establishment of a railway servicing depot, and then the construction of the paper and pulp mills at Maryvale in 1937 stimulated a rapid development of the residential areas. Good recreation facilities, well-paved streets, and good sewerage make it one of the most advanced towns in the district. In addition to the Maryvale plant of the Australian Paper Manufacturers Limited the local industries include the Great Eastern Brick Company with an estimated workforce of fifty men, and the Gippsland Cement and Lime Company which has an estimated workforce of 120 men.

A substantial proportion of the working population of the Latrobe Valley is accommodated in hostels. In Yallourn itself there are hostels for single men or men without their families in the district. They are the Staff Mess for salaried employees, and West Camp and Eastern Road Hostel for wage employees. The Eastern Road Hostel, with accommodation for about 650 men, is claimed to be one of the most modern hostels of its type in Australia. West Camp, on the other hand, consists of temporary quarters. In Morwell there is the large Ridge Hostel which, in 1959, accommodated about 250 employees of the SEC and contracting firms.

The age structure of the population of the Latrobe Valley explains a certain emphasis which is placed on educational facilities. There are state and Roman Catholic primary schools in all towns as well as state secondary schools in Yallourn, Moe, Newborough and Morwell. A Roman Catholic secondary school in Moe caters for the Catholic children of the surrounding district. The needs of local industries for skilled and semi-professional labour are provided for by the Yallourn Technical College and the Junior Technical School in Newborough. An important feature of educational facilities in the Valley is adult education, which receives every encouragement from the local authorities and the SEC. The latter established the Public Library in Yallourn, which serves as the centre for adult education and provides facilities for holding art exhibitions, lectures, discussions, etc. Moe had, from 1885, a Mechanics' Institute, which served as a library centre where meetings and lectures could be held and where films could be screened. In 1960 the institute was taken over by the local council, which demolished the old building and sold the block of land on which it stood. From the proceeds of that sale the Moe Borough Council has erected a modern library building with facilities for adults and children.

As in all country centres there are several important voluntary organizations in the towns of the Latrobe Valley. First there are the business organizations like the chambers of commerce, which are in the forefront of the various schemes for the promotion of local industries and business activities and seem to be the driving force behind the Advance Latrobe Valley Association. Next there are the ex-servicemen's associations and such service clubs as Rotary and Apex. These organizations are notable for the part they play in rendering service to the community. Some typical examples are the erection of a scout hall in Moe by the local Rotary and the part played in the raising of funds for the National Heart Foundation by the Apexians in Morwell.

An important local institution in the Latrobe Valley is the press. Three newspapers circulate in the towns included in this study— the *Advocate*, the *Live Wire*, and the *Advertiser*.

The *Advocate* started in 1888 in Moe as a one-man newspaper for circulating in the Narracan Shire and it eventually grew into the large organization it is at present. In 1949 the *Advocate* was sold to the Latrobe Valley Newspapers Pty Ltd, which later sold some interest to the Victorian Broadcasting Network, proprietors of the local broadcasting station, 3TR, and other radio stations in the district. It is now a large organization, which also publishes the *Country Leader* and the *Live Wire*.

The *Live Wire* was first established in 1925 as a letter sheet by the SEC in Yallourn. It carried local news and a certain amount of advertising. In 1956 it was sold to the Latrobe Valley Newspapers.

The Morwell *Advertiser* was founded in 1884 as a small country newspaper. In 1906 its circulation was 200 but by 1961 it was 3,900. The paper aims—in the words of its editor—'to print the local news without fear or favour'.[13]

There is little in the layout and contents of the three newspapers to distinguish them from one another. Local news and comments seem obviously the greatest source of interest to the readers and together with advertising they occupy most of the space.[14] Reports of meetings, functions, and events are a large part of the local news. They vary considerably in length according to the importance attached to them; but usually pride of place is given to news items relating to the development of the Latrobe Valley, and in particular the places from which the papers are published. Thus the visits to the Valley of the Latrobe Valley Advisory Committee are reported on the front page, together with statements of the activities of the Advance Latrobe Valley Association, the decisions of the SEC affecting the inhabitants of the Valley, the meetings of local councils, etc. Considerable publicity is also given to local organizations, and clubs are reported at length with descriptions of the people who were present at any particular function, what they wore, who won the trophies, what the guest speaker said, and so on. Finally, the papers give considerable coverage to local sport.

An interesting sideline of the local newspapers is the extent to which they are used to foster town promotion. The readers are constantly reminded of civic pride in their towns and this is frequently coupled with references to the rivalry between towns. For example, the Moe readers are reminded in the *Advocate* (9 September 1960) that 'Morwell never fails to push the barrow', which is a reference to the fact that Morwell has succeeded in 'putting itself on the map' though in size it is smaller than Moe.

Throughout the Latrobe Valley the Melbourne metropolitan newspapers circulate daily and are widely read. Consequently the local press does not cover the general news to any considerable extent, as it is also conveyed to the local population through radio and television.

This picture of the amenities and the community institutions in the Latrobe Valley would not be complete without reference to an unpleasantness to the household and to the businessman in the form of smoke, dust, and smell. The SEC forces its boilers, and grime and soot settle over new paintwork, washing on lines, on goods displayed in shops, and on the green pastures that surround the industrial settlement in the Valley. The smell of noxious effluent which is released several times a day from APM's works at Maryvale can be smelt as far west as Trafalgar, and on a wet autumn day, or a hot day, is all-pervasive.[15] Pollution of air by local industry is a subject of constant complaint in the local press. Morwell alone seems to be free from pollution, and this is a point which the local council often emphasizes in its favour.[16]

Of all the towns described, the most 'Australian' in 1954 and 1961 was Traralgon, with about 84 per cent of its population Australian-born. This compares with the national proportion of 86 per cent Australian-born at the time of the 1954 census and 83 per cent in 1961 (the proportions for Victoria were 76 and 75 per cent at these dates). Next in order of Australian-born proportion follow Yallourn, Morwell, and Moe with proportions appreciably below the national averages. Newborough is the least 'Australian' town in the Latrobe Valley, and in fact it had the lowest proportion of Australian-born in the population (43 per cent) of all towns in Australia at the time of the 1954 census. The details of the distribution of immigrants are shown in Table 6, which also

TABLE 6

Distribution of the Overseas-born Population in the Latrobe Valley: Censuses 1954 and 1961
(%)

Locality		Country of Birth								Total Number			Ratio of overseas-born resident less than 7 years to all overseas-born
		British Isles	Nether-lands	Ger-many	Malta	Italy	Poland	Ukraine	Other	Males	Females	Persons	
Moe	1954	45·0	13·2	12·5	8·6	1·8	3·3	2·2	13·4	1,265	1,098	2,363	89·2
Newborough	1954	60·2	7·3	6·9	9·1	1·1	4·5	3·7	7·2	1,068	1,013	2,081	94·8
Total		52·1	10·4	9·9	8·8	1·5	3·9	2·9	10·5	2,333	2,111	4,444	91·8
Moe*	1961	45·1	17·5	10·3	9·2	2·4	3·1	2·0	10·4	2,930	2,544	5,474	36·6
Yallourn Works Area	1954	63·6	3·6	4·3	4·2	3·3	3·3	1·0	16·7	992	322	1,314	58·4
	1961	61·4	3·8	5·9	2·8	1·3	3·5	0·7	20·6	834	362	1,196	32·2
Yallourn North	1954	29·0	3·0	13·2	21·8	9·6	3·4	1·9	18·1	245	224	469	75·5
	1961	31·7	4·8	10·3	23·0	8·5	3·0	1·0	17·7	279	225	504	27·6
Morwell	1954	65·2	11·6	9·2	3·1	2·2	1·1	0·4	7·2	1,261	1,030	2,291	84·9
	1961	45·4	14·5	9·9	4·9	10·5	2·3	0·3	12·2	2,494	1,804	4,298	44·3
Traralgon	1954	59·7	14·8	4·0	1·9	5·6	2·9	0·4	10·7	780	606	1,386	77·6
	1961	48·1	17·2	7·5	1·6	9·4	3·5	0·2	12·5	1,136	953	2,089	31·7
Rural areas	1954	39·7	7·5	11·0	4·3	12·6	7·5	2·8	14·6	930	668	1,598	69·0
	1961	39·8	12·0	7·0	4·6	17·2	2·8	1·6	15·0	829	567	1,396	26·2
Total	1954	54·3	9·7	8·7	6·2	4·2	3·7	1·8	11·4	6,541	4,961	11,502	81·1
	1961	46·0	14·6	9·1	6·4	7·2	2·9	1·1	12·7	8,502	6,455	14,957	36·5

* The borough of Moe, created since 1954, includes Newborough.

includes some information on the length of residence in Australia. The contrast here is between Yallourn, with 41·6 per cent of its overseas-born who, in 1954, were residents with more than seven years of residence, and Moe and Newborough, where only 8 per cent belonged to that category. By 1961, however, the proportions in that category were nearly the same.

The towns that have become strongholds of certain national groups can be identified from Table 6. In 1954 Morwell had the highest proportion of British-born settlers (65·2 per cent) of all the towns in the Latrobe Valley; Yallourn works area (i.e. the town of Yallourn and the workers' hostels) followed closely with 63·6 per cent British-born in its immigrant population. Seven years later, as shown in the 1961 census, the proportion of British-born in Morwell's overseas-born population dropped to 45·4 per cent, while in Yallourn it was only slightly reduced, to 61·4 per cent.

Nearly 1,000 Dutch-born settlers out of the total of some 2,200 who were enumerated in the Latrobe Valley in 1961 live in Moe and constitute 17·5% of the town's immigrant population. Every tenth foreign-born person in Moe and Morwell is of German birth. The Italians also demonstrate a preference for Morwell, where their number increased ninefold between 1954 and 1960; today they constitute a tenth of the town's foreign-born population. Yallourn North seems to be the stronghold of the Maltese settlers, who in 1954 and 1961 represented between one-fifth and a quarter of its immigrant population.

One other characteristic of the distribution of immigrants in the area is worth noting, and this is masculinity. Table 7 shows that Newborough is the town with the most balanced immigrant population. As shown already, this town is mainly settled by families, and the existing type of housing is well suited to the needs of Australian and immigrant families. The town with the highest masculinity rate is Yallourn, a fact which most certainly reflects on the location of two large hostels for single men.

The masculinity rates in the different ethnic groups are important in any study of adjustment. These are shown in Table 7 for all the main towns in this survey. The high indices shown for some clearly reflect the smallness of certain ethnic groups, but for the larger groups the figures are of greater significance, though those for Yallourn are, of course, distorted by the location of workers' hostels. The British-born have a nearly balanced population in Newborough but an index of masculinity of just under

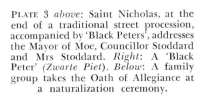

PLATE 3 *above*: Saint Nicholas, at the end of a traditional street procession, accompanied by 'Black Peters', addresses the Mayor of Moe, Councillor Stoddard and Mrs Stoddard. *Right*: A 'Black Peter' *(Zwarte Piet)*. *Below*: A family group takes the Oath of Allegiance at a naturalization ceremony.

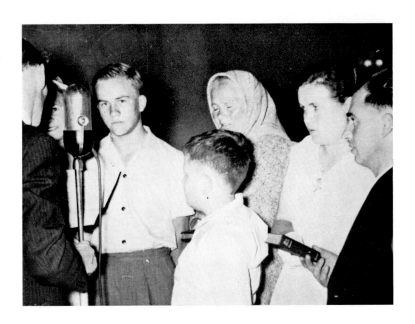

PLATE 4 *above*: The Ukrainian Community of Newborough welcomes a visiting Canadian Catholic Archbishop of the Greek Rite. *Below*: A ceremony of baptism performed by Archbishop Hermaniuk.

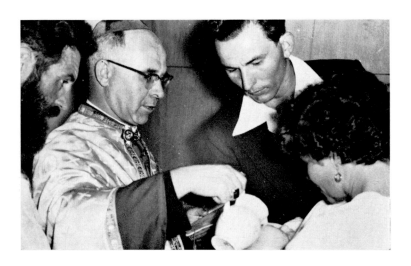

TABLE 7

Masculinity Rates* in the Latrobe Valley and Victoria, Census 1954

Birthplace		Place of Residence								
	Moe	New-borough	Yallourn Works Area	Yallourn North	Morwell	Traralgon	Rural areas	Total Latrobe Valley	Victoria
Overseas									
British Isles	111·8	101·9	248·3	119·4	109·4	117·1	136·1	124·0	117·9
Netherlands	129·4	130·3	220·0	133·3	134·5	108·1	130·8	129·4	135·4
Germany	89·1	90·7	366·7	93·8	144·2	139·1	109·5	113·0	102·7
Malta	116·0	100·0	1,733·3	96·2	105·7	116·7	126·7	123·1	167·9
Italy	115·0	100·0	975·0	73·1	525·0	310·5	192·8	207·6	188·2
Poland	172·4	116·3	388·9	166·7	550·0	141·2	140·0	165·2	149·4
Ukraine	147·6	113·9	160·0	80·0	28·6	66·7	131·6	117·7	137·7
Other	125·7	127·3	544·1	142·9	160·3	184·6	145·3	171·1	143·6
	115·2	105·4	308·1	109·4	122·4	128·7	139·2	131·8	132·5
Australia	100·8	94·8	130·6	108·9	102·7	101·0	116·1	108·0	96·1
Total Population	104·5	100·7	156·9	109·0	107·4	104·9	119·2	113·2	100·8

* Number of males per 100 females.

D

120 in Yallourn North. Again, the German-born people seem to have a surplus of females in at least three towns, which probably indicates that many of the east European migrants married German women whilst in the Displaced Persons' camps in Germany after the war. The Dutch people have a masculinity rate well in excess of 100—a fact which indicates the presence in the Latrobe Valley of a large contingent of Dutch single men brought from the Netherlands as assisted migrants.

The industries established in the Latrobe Valley, such as electricity generation, briquette manufacture, gasification, paper and cement manufacture, all use brown coal.

This fact determines not only the choice of the biggest industries that have come to the Latrobe Valley, but also job opportunities. In 1954 the workforce was estimated at 15,500, of whom 13,400 were males and 2,100 females. This represents less than one female to every six males, an abnormally low proportion, the reason for which is, of course, the nature of the industrial activities in the Latrobe Valley. The State Electricity Commission now has male workers mostly on operations and construction, and only a small minority are females employed on administration; the Gas and Fuel Corporation needs male workers in the operation of its Lurgi Gasification Plant; and, likewise, there is a considerable male workforce in domestic and industrial commercial building. Private industry in the Valley includes the Australian Paper Manufacturers Limited, and the cement works at Traralgon (both employing mainly men), and a few textile units.

The reasons for the predominance of males in the region's workforce are economic, but the effects are mainly social. Girls leaving school have little choice of occupation, and some are no doubt unemployed so that family incomes are reduced. According to submissions prepared by the Advance Latrobe Valley Association (ALVA) :

> . . . evidence from employers generally throughout the Latrobe Valley Area shows that there is no constant large surplus of unmarried female labour, but that this is attributable to the basic law of supply and demand. It has been found that when girls leave school and when the industry and commerce in the area has absorbed these to apparent capacity, the surplus, which does quite clearly exist temporarily, tend to move out of the area to the Metropolitan area.[17]

If young women have to seek jobs outside the region—perhaps at Warragul, Dandenong, or in the metropolitan area of Melbourne—further disadvantages follow. There is the cost of travel and board, the tendency to break up family life, and the constant pressure to draw the whole family away from the Latrobe Valley to the metropolitan area.

The situation with regard to the employment of women and the existence of a potential if not a real surplus points to a lack of balance in the industrial development of Latrobe Valley. The solution to this problem, according to a submission of the Advance Latrobe Valley Association to the Distribution of Population Committee of March 1960, lies in the provision of 'small secondary industries particularly those which could employ unmarried females and thus prevent the breaking-up of family units'.

Some steps taken in recent years have gone part of the way towards achieving this objective. Chapter 1 indicates the extent to which small textile firms have provided employment for women in Morwell, Traralgon, and more recently in Moe. In addition, more office employment has been created lately as a result of decentralization sponsored by the Victorian government. Thus, the Crown Law Department of Melbourne established the typing pool in Moe, which in December 1960 employed fifteen typists. The same government department established a branch of the Titles Office in Morwell. The Totalizator Agency Board, which is a government instrumentality in Victoria, also established its branch in Moe, and, according to a note in the local newspaper, employs forty-four part-time clerks.[18]

But the problem seems to be getting more acute each year. A study of the age structure of the population of the Valley (see Table 4) suggests that the supply of young adolescents entering the labour market will increase each year. An additional factor of some significance is the gap between the expected and existing jobs in the Valley. This was demonstrated in a survey by the A.N.Z. Bank in which some four hundred secondary school children in Yallourn, Moe, and Traralgon replied to a questionnaire distributed through their schools in 1954. The object of the questionnaire was to find what kind of work the scholar expected to do when he or she left school. The children were asked also to indicate what kind of work their parents expected them to do, and whether the type of work a child expected to do could be found in the Latrobe Valley or found locally. About a quarter of all replies received from the children revealed disappointed ambitions. Most of the jobs the children would like to do did not exist in the Latrobe Valley, and for that reason the children had to undertake other work or else leave the area and seek opportunities elsewhere.[19]

The expected rate of increase in the workforce from the younger age groups is bound to raise a serious problem for the future of the Latrobe Valley. Moreover, the prospect of a potential surplus of young women, and the disrupting effect on local community and family life, has encouraged further efforts to bring about more diversified industrial opportunities in the area. The Advance Latrobe Valley Association in its submission to the Committee on the Distribution of Population of March 1960 was asked to comment on the following terms of reference of the committee:

> What urban and rural districts of the State offer particular opportunities or present particular problems in respect to the distribution, reception or retention of population and what industries or other sources of employment could effectively be established or encouraged in each such district?

The ALVA replied:

> Particular opportunities present in the Latrobe Valley area can be obtained from adequate electric power, cheap brown coal and briquette fuel, gas supply and its increasing variety and quantity of by-products, adequate present, and future, water supply and waste disposal at decreasing costs, constant good average rainfall, availability of primary products and raw materials, including dairy products, wool, livestock, timber, ceramic clay, limestone, bauxite. [It is also expected that the] female labour force will grow with demand. [Next, there are] good educational facilities in all main towns; medical and hospital services are of a very high standard and exceed needs at present; shopping facilities and amenities compare more than favourably with other urban areas, including T.V. reception, excellent telephone service, swimming pools, theatres, sporting facilities. Internal transport system linking all towns may be deemed one of the State's best. Within the three main industries, there is assured continuity of employment, for continued production is a fundamental State necessity. Train services to Melbourne by electric locomotives include some of the State's best urban services.

The same submission of the ALVA indicated some of the main problems associated with the area. These were listed as: 'The cost of operating industry in comparison with similar Metropolitan industries and in particular rail freights, restriction on cheaper road transport, higher power costs.'

The last point with regard to power costs is worth special emphasis. It is a fact that at present, with a uniform industrial tariff operating throughout the area served by the interconnected State Generating System, electric power for industry is sold in the Latrobe Valley at the same prices as in Melbourne and provincial centres throughout most of Victoria. The real cost of supplying power within a few miles of the power station at Yallourn and Morwell would, however, appear to be less than supplying power to places distant one hundred miles and upwards from the sources of supply. This point was also argued in a report of the Local Government Board of Victoria in the document entitled 'Future Development of the Latrobe Valley':

> The Board is of the opinion that consideration should be given to the desirability of creating favourable tariffs for electric power in the sub-region as an added incentive to the establishment of approved industries in the zones provided for such purposes. This would be a practical step towards economic and effective decentralisation of industry.

More diversified economic opportunities must have their counterpart in various services and facilities such as education and transport. The ALVA presented a strong case on education to the State Development Committee Enquiry on the Economic Development of Gippsland in March 1961:

> A Teachers' Training College in Gippsland is a very practicable proposition now, not only because of the growth of Primary and Secondary Schools particularly in the Latrobe Valley, thus providing adequate practical training facilities, but because of the high proportion of girls from Gippsland who apply for entry to the Teachers' Training College, Melbourne. An officer of the Education Department has advised that over recent years the percentage of such applications represents 35 per cent of girls leaving school.

The submission also argued for the establishment in the Latrobe Valley of a university college taking the students for possibly two or three years after they have completed their secondary school training and supplying the needs of those who do not require a complete university course but do need those further two or three years to study in their chosen field. Such a college would probably be an extension of the present Yallourn Technical College. Other proposals include the establishment of a Latrobe Valley Business College to provide better training for girls who wish to receive intensive business and typing training after they leave school so that they can compete with older employees. These, then, are some of the steps that have been suggested to provide not only more diversified economic opportunities in the Valley but to remedy some of the social defects of the present position.

3

SOURCES AND METHODS OF GATHERING INFORMATION

The first two chapters described the setting of this study. The description of the brown coal industry, and an account of the growth of the population and its distribution in the Latrobe Valley, emphasized certain unique features of the region. For present purposes the crucial feature of the Latrobe Valley is an unusually high concentration of the overseas-born (or immigrants) in the population. Not only are they proportionately more numerous than in any other comparable area in Australia but, as shown in Chapter 2, the foreign-born have a much higher proportion of men of working age than the population of Victoria.

The Sample of Immigrants

The principal source of information in this study was a sample survey of the foreign-born male employees of the State Electricity Commission undertaking at Yallourn and the employees of the construction firms working on the SEC installation at Morwell (see Appendix B). The size of the sample was set at 550 men, of whom about a third were to be persons born in the British Isles and the remainder men born in continental Europe. Nine men of those selected refused to be interviewed, and the final survey was confined to 541 men. The number of persons who were interviewed was, however, much greater for, in the case of married men, both husband and wife were questioned.

The decision to confine the statistical universe for the main field survey to the male employees of the SEC at Yallourn and to the much smaller workforce in the employment of SEC contractors at Morwell was also dictated by an important practical consideration. At the time when the study was designed the SEC installation at Morwell was in the final stages of completion but the constructions of the Hazelwood undertaking had scarcely begun. The foreign-born employees of SEC contractors working on the construction of the Morwell SEC complex (the open-cut mine, the briquette factory, and the associated power-generation installations) were included in the study because as hostel dwellers, living away from their families, they presented an interesting group whose pattern of adjustment was somewhat different from the remainder of the sampled population. It was impracticable, however, to include the men on the SEC payroll in Morwell, for at that time they were still being recruited and assembled to start work later in 1959. Unlike the employees of the Yallourn undertaking, those at Morwell were only just settling in.

The findings of this study, in so far as they describe and analyse the position of the foreign-born component of the workforce of the SEC at Yallourn and that of the SEC contractors in Morwell, can nevertheless be said to apply to all immigrants employed in the brown coal industry in the Latrobe Valley. As shown in Chapter 1, that industry had its beginnings in Yallourn. It was the brown coal mine, the power station, and the briquette factory at Yallourn which for nearly forty years was the main industrial undertaking in the Valley, and its development has set the pattern for the new installations at Morwell and Hazelwood. 'Yallourn' has become a symbol that stands for more than technological achievement; it stands for a set of human relations over and above employment and embracing all aspects of life: family, standard of living, and social participation.

The Interview Schedule and the Training of Interviewers

The five objectives of this study, which were formulated in June 1958 after two short visits in the field, demanded the use of a fairly elaborate and comprehensive questionnaire. Each called for a specific type of information ranging from objective facts about the immigrant and his family to 'reasons' for specified behaviour (for example, non-participation in community life). The usual procedure at this stage is for the research worker to formulate his objective or problem in terms of working hypotheses, that is, statements regarding the relationships which one expects the study will yield. A collection of these statements constitutes a conceptual framework.

In this study the conceptual framework consisted of a list of characteristics or factors arranged in five sections according to the research objective they were meant to elucidate. The characteristics ranged from a simple statement of the immigrant's rural/urban background to a complex classification of his social relationships in Australia.

When the list of analytical concepts or characteristics had been compiled, the next stage was the construction of 'dummy tables' showing the various relationships of particular significance in this study. This procedure served to eliminate certain items and suggest others that had to be included in the conceptual framework. It also became clear that there were certain key factors and that they had to be used in the analysis of each of the five objectives. Such items as country of birth (sometimes referred to as 'birthplace' or 'ethnic group'), age group, and length of residence in Australia were to become major controls in the cross-classifications of the material the survey would yield.

It was now possible to 'translate' individual items in the conceptual framework into questions and to build up an interview schedule. This was to be used in personal interviews with individual respondents and not to be completed by the respondent himself. The first two drafts of the interview schedule were tested with selected informants in Canberra and then considerably revised in the light of experience gained during the pilot survey in August 1958. Seventeen names were chosen at random from the files of the staff officer at the Yallourn SEC. These included all the ethnic groups that were to be represented in the sample, scattered in the four towns and three hostels included in the study. Of these, thirteen interviews were completed. Two men (a Yugoslav and an Estonian) refused to co-operate; and a further two (a Lithuanian and another Yugoslav) could not be traced at the addresses given on the files. It appeared that, though still on the SEC payroll, they were now living some miles away on farms in the surrounding country, and, because of pressure of time, these two were not followed up.

The results of the pilot survey were particularly useful in that they suggested that different ethnic groups react differently to this type of inquiry. The southern Europeans were evidently the easiest, eager to answer questions on any subject. The British and the Dutch settlers seemed reluctant to give details of their income and spending; they also wanted to know more about the purpose of the survey and why they had been selected.

The interviews with the immigrants of east European origin were the most difficult; we soon sensed that they were extremely suspicious, mainly on political grounds, often suspecting that any stranger with a form to fill in was an agent of the communist government from their country of origin. This was something unforeseen for which we had to prepare ourselves before starting full-scale interviewing the following January.

Several important changes were introduced in the schedule as the result of testing, and its layout was considerably modified. The original intention of probing deeply into the respondent's pre-migration background was abandoned chiefly for the sake of the east European groups; we realized that questions about the places of residence before and during World War II, and about the immigrant's family and other personal details, would be completely unacceptable to the refugee groups. Another important modification was in the order in which questions regarding the respondent's income, expenditure, and savings were put. Experience has taught us that this type of personal information was forthcoming more easily if questions were first asked about the respondent's housing, possession of a motor vehicle, and consumer durables. Questions relating to sources of income and such confidential information would follow almost naturally and, as subsequent work in the field confirmed, there was no difficulty about tackling this difficult subject.

Several points of administrative procedure arose out of the pre-test. For example, there was difficulty in finding a time in which immigrants could and would talk. A large proportion of them were employed on a shift system and could not be found at home in the evenings. If they were home at night then their wives could not be interviewed since they were likely to be busy with children, putting them to bed, supervising homework, and doing other domestic duties. For those that worked the night shift (midnight till 8 a.m.) interview appointments during the day were not convenient as they mostly rested during the day. All in all, experience suggested that several attempts had to be made to arrange an interview, and much time was wasted in this way. Next was the time taken up by the interview itself which was to be a factor of some considerable significance, since at least an hour and a quarter was necessary to interview a married couple.

Another problem was to overcome the widespread suspicion about the sponsorship and aims of the survey. Several steps were taken. In the first place a publicity handout was prepared and sent to the *Advocate, Live Wire* and *Advertiser.* Each of these papers also published articles supplemented by interviews with members of the research team who were in the field. Next the *SEC Magazine* published a special article in the Christmas number which was issued about a month before the survey and distributed free of charge to all employees of the Commission. The article encouraged the immigrants to volunteer the information and concluded as follows:

All the interviewers will sign a pledge of secrecy, and the

completed questionnaires, which do not name the men interviewed, will be kept under lock and key by the University authorities. The report on the survey will not quote individuals.

This is a golden opportunity for newcomers to help themselves in the long run by providing the data necessary for a balanced judgment on the vital problem of migrant settlement. There are no 'strings' to the queries, and no compulsion to answer them, but the willing co-operation of the chosen five hundred will assure a Happy Future in the Valley as well as a Merry Christmas.

Thirdly, about eight weeks before the survey, a public meeting was held at Yallourn to which local councillors, members of the clergy of all denominations, prominent citizens in the district, representatives of the press, and leading members of migrant organizations were invited. The meeting was addressed by the author, who answered queries about the survey.

Finally, the actual beginning of the survey in January 1959 was heralded by articles in the local papers with photographs of the interviewers and by frequent announcements broadcast on the local radio stations.

Two final steps remained before the start of field survey operations. The first was the completion of the interview schedule. This involved the design of a coding system suitable for use with I.B.M. punch cards, and a last check on the various points of content and appearance of the questionnaires. Furthermore, procedures for using the schedule were spelt out in detail throughout the document (see Appendix C). Lastly, an interviewer's report sheet was added to the schedule in which the interviewer was invited to record his own observations and impressions of the respondent, his family, and the appearance of the house in which the interview took place. These additional reports proved very valuable in the assessment of the data collected in each interview as well as in providing a store of additional information which is used in the pages that follow.[1]

The second important step was the selection and training of a team of interviewers. Eight students (two men and six women) from the Department of Social Studies in the University of Melbourne were selected in August 1958 and briefed about the survey. The interviewers were selected on the basis of previous interviewing experience, general maturity, interest in the research, and performance in previous practical work placements. A few weeks before the commencement of interviewing operations in the field each one of them received a 25,000-word interviewers' handbook which described the objectives of the survey, the industrial setting of the district, and then dwelt at length on the background of each of the ethnic groups in the survey, with special reference to some of the problems that might be encountered by interviewers. The last section of the interviewers' handbook described the structure of the survey.[2]

Field Survey, January to March 1959: Formal Interviews and Informal Participant Observation

On arrival in the district the interviewers were divided into two groups of four, one stationed in Yallourn and the other in Moe. Each group spent approximately twelve hours in training sessions during which the specific purpose of each question was discussed, and care taken that each of the interviewers grasped the reasons for the inclusion of each question. Practice interviews were conducted in the presence of all members of the team and the method of recording the information was discussed. The interviewers were taken on a conducted tour of the SEC installations in Yallourn and Morwell, and later were shown around the places where they were to work.

During the following six weeks all the members of the research team, that is, the eight interviewers, the Research Assistant, and the author, met daily at Yallourn to discuss progress of operations. These briefing sessions were particularly useful, for they enabled members of the team to compare notes on their interviews and exchange information on local events and personalities. The leader of the team commented on the quality of reports received the previous day and generally saw to it that the interviewers maintained a uniformity of standards in reporting.[3] Any obvious gaps and omissions in the schedules were noted and the interviewer concerned was asked to follow up the respondent once again.

Each interviewer received basic information about the respondents included in his particular group of immigrants. The information included the name, address, age, country of birth, length of employment with the State Electricity Commission, and trade classification. These personal details were copied from the records of the Commission and proved of great value in planning interviews and in preparing the interviewer for his immediate task. He would be able to estimate the number of questions to be omitted (there was, for example, no point in asking the questions about housing if the respondent lived in a hostel). He would also be able to guide his conversation more specifically to the respondent's ethnic background, relying on the basic facts supplied in the interviewers' handbook and general knowledge about the country of origin or some significant events connected with migration to Australia learnt from previous interviews.

Each interviewer was assigned a specific locality and consequently carried out most of his interviews in a place that he got to know quite well. Towards the end of field operations interviewers were switched to other areas where there were many outstanding interviews to be completed.

After the first two weeks of the survey it became clear that there were two pockets of what we may call here 'initial refusals'. Upwards of a dozen men in the Eastern Road Hostel and West Camp belonged to one group of those whom we classified as initial refusals. There was no distinct ethnic pattern among the hostel dwellers in this category. They were men who belonged to half-a-dozen nationalities, all in their thirties and forties, mostly divorced or separated from their wives. For them to be interviewed represented an attempt to pry into their private lives; they wanted to be left alone, they were 'browned off'.

The other group of initial refusals was concentrated in East Newborough and Moe and included mostly men of east European background. The problem there was one of suspicion on political grounds. These men regarded the interviewers (not excluding the author) with extreme suspicion, and stories spread amongst immigrants that the material collected in interviews would be made accessible to the Soviet Embassy in Canberra. Others claimed that although they had confidence in the author and the student interviewers, some unauthorized persons would get hold of their completed questionnaire forms once they were taken to Canberra. One Lithuanian refused to be interviewed on the grounds that only a week ago he had sent in an application for naturalization to the Department of Immigration in Canberra; he argued that if he were interviewed this would prejudice his application. It was futile to try to persuade this man that there was no connection whatever between an independent inquiry conducted by a university and the business of a government department. All these cases were symptomatic of a suspicious frame of mind on the part of an appreciable proportion of immigrants from eastern Europe and particularly those who had been victims of communism, such as the Ukrainians, the Poles, and the people from the Baltic states, that is Estonia, Latvia, and Lithuania.[4]

No record has been kept of the numbers of initial refusals. The numbers fluctuated every day as news travelled fast over the 'bush telegraph' of a bad interview or some suspicious circumstances that prompted the immigrant to refuse to be interviewed. Suffice it to say that the problem of first refusals assumed frightening proportions in the third week of the survey when it seemed that the majority of the Ukrainian, Lithuanian, and Latvian men in the sample would not respond. This setback necessitated an all-out effort to win the co-operation of these people and convince them that the survey had nothing to do with politics and that the research workers were people whom they could trust. To achieve this objective an approach had to be made to the group leaders of the communities from eastern Europe, their visiting chaplains, and their state secretaries in Melbourne.

Another approach was tried with the initial refusals among the hostel dwellers. There we used the good offices of a manager of the Y.M.C.A. Club in Eastern Road Hostel, himself a migrant of Dutch origin, a man of considerable social skills and thoroughly acquainted with the immigrants of all kinds of background. With his co-operation and by means of the measures just described we managed to overcome opposition and reduce the number of definite refusals to a hard core of nine.

In addition to formal interviews with the sample, every opportunity was taken to meet the local people (Australians, and particularly the immigrants) on an informal basis. All members of the team received invitations to dinners, parties, dances sponsored by various national groups, religious services, soccer matches, meetings of various clubs and societies. Some interviewers participated in certain activities to which they gained introductions from personal contacts in the field. For example, one attended English language classes for migrants in two schools in the district, and another sat in the Health Sister's Office at the Yallourn Health Centre. A third interviewer made a special study of the Maltese community at Yallourn North and established a useful contact with the Maltese chaplain, a Catholic priest. Senior members of the team spoke at meetings of the local Apex clubs, the Moe Rotary Club, Moe Chamber of Commerce, and at a Naturalization Ceremony on Australia Day at Moe.

Such occasions provided background information and possibilities for more informal, intimate, and off-the-record interviewing. They consequently acted as a source of hunches and insights into the dynamics of community life and presented opportunities for rough validation of previous hunches.

Members of the team were encouraged to record their impressions made during the course of participant observation. At first these were reported at the daily briefing sessions, but later each interviewer was given a special assignment in the geographical areas or in the situation in which he had established good contacts or had gained special insights. The reports on these special assignments were presented by each interviewer at the conclusion of field operations in March 1959 and extracts from these are quoted in the following pages.[5]

At the conclusion of the field survey operations in March 1959, completed interview schedules were taken to Canberra where a team of research assistants started the work of editing and coding the data. This lasted approximately three months and towards the end of June 1959 the first of some three hundred tables was run by the I.B.M. Data Processing Centre in Sydney. The next stage was the tedious work of decoding and editing the tables. This got under way in August 1959 and continued well into 1960.

The Life History Material

An unexpected by-product of the interview survey was the life history material supplied by thirteen immigrants in the district. Friendly contacts with a group of Dutch people led to the discovery of a typescript of a play purporting to be based on the migration experience of its author—a Dutch woman. The reading of this play convinced the writer that its author had given some rare insights into the mechanism of adjustment. The woman then offered to write a short autobiographical sketch with particular reference to her migration experience.

This incident gave rise to an idea that similar autobiographical material might be obtained from other immigrants in the district, not necessarily persons included in the interview survey. To allow for a measure of uniformity in writing the autobiographical sketches, a 'Life History Schedule' was designed and distributed to about thirty persons selected at the discretion of the interviewers.[6] No monetary incentive was offered and no promise of publication given to those who were approached, beyond an assurance that the story, if published, would not give the name of the author.

Four of the thirteen life histories were selected for publication in full; extracts from others are used in the pages that follow.

The life histories used in this book, either in the form of excerpts or in full, are not meant to satisfy the strictly objective tests prescribed by John Dollard.[7] For one thing not one document stresses 'the continuous related character of experience from childhood through adulthood'; on the contrary, all the documents highlight the events connected with the experience of migration to the exclusion of other perhaps equally significant events. For this reason the personal documents used in this book have an illustrative, expositional value. They show how the writer has experienced the particular aspect of the process of migration and adjustment to new conditions in Australia and trace the sequence of events associated within this process. Some of them devote more space to the description of life before they were uprooted,[8] others concentrate on the story of the actual move and record their first impressions of Australia.[9]

However limited may be the scope of individual life histories collected here, their undoubted value lies in the fact that they are *personal* documents and as such reveal the 'participant's view of experiences in which he has been involved'.[10] Since they are written in the first person they give a subjective account of the processes analysed in this book. In this sense they supplement the objective accounts and observations of the members of the research team, and thus supply the necessary documentation to give an historical understanding of the immigrants in their present setting. The reader may find in these documents new conceptual 'hunches' and be able to formulate new hypotheses; but this is not the primary reason why the inclusion of this material has been thought worth while.

The Sociometric Survey, December 1960 to April 1961

A statistical analysis of the data collected during field work operations in 1959 revealed that one important area of the behaviour of the immigrants in the Latrobe Valley did not lend itself satisfactorily to precise quantitative treatment. It soon became apparent that by combining all members of an ethnic group the study concealed important differences in social participation within each group. Evidence collected in interviews and observations by members of the research team pointed to a link between the primary group affiliation, that is, membership of informal cliques, regional groups, and churches on the one hand, and the readiness to participate with the outside community on the other. To examine this relationship it was decided to make a special study of two ethnic groups—the Dutch population of Moe and the Ukrainian population of Newborough (see Chapter 9).

A study of primary group affiliation must, by definition, embrace all members of a given territorial unit. To make it manageable it was decided to carry out a complete enumeration of all adult persons of Dutch and Ukrainian origin in the towns which had relatively large concentrations of these people.[11] Special efforts were made to prepare a complete list of all Dutch adults in Moe and Ukrainian adults in Newborough. Names included in the original sampling frame from which the 1959 sample had been drawn were checked again, and that list was subsequently amended by the addition of the Dutch and Ukrainian-sounding names from the latest 1960 edition of the electoral roll for the Borough of Moe and also from the records of the Housing Commission. Finally, the interviewers systematically checked houses street by street inquiring about persons belonging to the two groups. Moe and Newborough are residential towns with a fairly static population confined almost exclusively to privately-owned or rented, small, one-family-type cottages. There are no industrial hostels or boarding-houses. In these circumstances it was possible to make a virtually complete enumeration of all adults of Dutch and Ukrainian origin.

The interviewing provided an opportunity for checking the preliminary enumeration. Invariably it was discovered that some persons were wrongly identified as persons belonging to the two ethnic groups selected for the purpose of study. Other names were added if the interviewer was satisfied as to the correctness of the ethnic classification. The final enumeration produced a population consisting of 420 persons of Dutch origin of whom one refused to be interviewed. The corresponding figures for the Ukrainian group were eighty-five and four.

The main technique used in the study was the sociometric method,[12] combined with a brief formal interview and supplemented by observation. By asking 'Name three of your closest friends' and, later on in the interview, 'What three people do you see the most of socially?' the author aimed at the identification of the persons concerned, leaving the interpretation of 'friendship' or 'seeing socially' to the respondents. In some instances the same three persons were named in both categories; in most cases, however, different people were named in each category.

In addition to the names of persons chosen in the sociometric test, other categories of information were obtained. These included address, country of birth, age, religion, and occupation.[13] Each of these items represented a characteristic used in the analysis of the pattern of sociometric choices. The same set of questions was asked at each interview and the information obtained was supplemented by the interviewer's assessment of the subject, his home, and social situation. Subsequent chance meetings with the subject and any observations relating to his position in the group were carefully recorded.

Other Sources

Throughout the four years it has taken to collect and analyse the data used in this study the writer and other members of the team read current copies of the three Latrobe Valley newspapers, the *Advocate*, the *Live Wire* and the *Advertiser*. These newspapers were systematically analysed, abstracted, and the contents filed according to the provisional schedule of chapter headings. The information so obtained proved to be of great value in checking some of our preliminary conclusions, noting reactions to our presence in the field, and giving us a reliable record of current events and personalities.

The files of the State Electricity Commission on the various recruiting schemes were of special value and so were the interviews with the senior officials of the SEC in Melbourne and Yallourn. Finally, the writer benefited from conversations and correspondence with a number of local residents, local government officials, members of voluntary organizations, and clergy of all denominations.

A Note on the Statistical Tests

Two methodological problems arise from the use of sample data derived from a sample survey. The first is to distinguish between chance or random variation and variation due to sampling error. The second is to evaluate any variation which arises from a significant relationship between two characteristics. The second problem is, of course, the converse of the first, in that it applies to a variation which is due neither to chance nor to sampling error.

The solution to these methodological problems is based on the theory of probability and is embodied in the statistical tests of significance. The test most frequently used in this work is the chi square test of significance. Chi square is a statistic similar to t and F in that its sampling distribution is known and that it is also used for testing hypotheses. It is particularly applicable to situations where we wish to compare the departure of *observed* frequencies in a given sample distribution with the frequencies we would *expect* on the basis of a given hypothesis. This type of hypothesis—known as the null hypothesis—postulates 'that there is no difference between the observed and expected frequencies that cannot be attributed to chance or [random] variation', or 'that the observed sample data have been drawn from a population distributed according to the observed frequencies'.

The null hypothesis has been applied to the sample distributions in the majority of tables in the chapters that follow. Its rejection was signified by the value of chi square with a given number of the degrees of freedom and at a corresponding level of significance. The rule observed in this study is that if a value of chi square (χ^2) obtained in a test is such that it would occur on the basis of sampling variation alone (i.e. by chance) 5 per cent or less of the time, then this may lead to the rejection of the null hypothesis at a defined level of significance. In this work the term *significantly different* will refer to the 5 per cent level of significance and the term *very significantly different* to the 1 per cent level. If, for example, a single test to compare the job satisfaction/dissatisfaction of several birthplace groups produces a chi square value which at a given number of degrees of freedom corresponds to the level of significance $p < \cdot 001$ then this means that the difference between the behaviour of these groups could have only occurred by chance less than one time in a thousand.

Once a significant difference in the distribution of a given characteristic has been established we will refer to this finding as a *statistical association* between any two variables—say, birthplace and English language standard. It is important to realize what a finding of statistical association and the test that leads to it do, and do not, tell us.

Three major points should be borne in mind in examining this type of quantitative material. First, the tests serve a most useful function in disciplining the quantitative aspects of the inquiry into some sort of order and then suggesting to the investigator the lines along which further inquiries may be made, whether these be statistical in nature or not. Experience shows that

guessing significant differences by eye from a frequency distribution or a table of proportions may sometimes lead, especially
when the sample is small, to emphasizing unduly differences that
are statistically insignificant even at a 10 per cent level, and to
overlooking differences that are statistically significant even at
the 1 per cent level.

Secondly, statistical significance cannot be identified with
sociological, economic, political, or historical significance. To
say that membership of an ethnic group is statistically associated
(at a defined level of significance), or statistically varies, with
the standard of spoken English does not necessarily mean that
there is a relationship of cause and effect between the two
characteristics. There may be other *sociologically* significant
factors that enter this relationship. Thus the final interpretation
of the statistical material must depend on non-statistical processes
such as common sense and the frequent use of qualitative
material in the form of descriptions and personal documents.

The third major point concerns the danger of identifying
statistical association with causal connection. Various possibilities
suggest themselves in this connection:

1. When tests show a significant association between two
factors or characteristics we can infer the following conclusions:

(a) The related factors are in direct causal relationship in
that A causes B, e.g. a given length of residence in Australia
causes greater language fluency;

(b) The related factors are in an *indirect* causal relationship,
in that an unstated C causes both A and B; here the inference
must endeavour to expose C or suggest possible Cs and show how
these could cause A and B to vary together. An example of such
an unstated factor in this study is the recruitment policy of the
SEC which causes a variation of birthplace together with length
of residence in Australia and occupational grade.

(c) There may be a purely fortuitous association. However
unlikely this may be in this study it is, nevertheless, always a
possibility.

2. When tests show no significant association we can draw the
following inference:

(a) The sample may be too small to show significant association—i.e. a larger sample might show an association which would
then have to be examined according to the three possibilities

under 1 above. For instance, the Maltese and Yugoslavs at Yallourn North appear to the investigator to display sociologically significant differences from other migrant groups in that they seem to congregate on the fringe of the town and set up peasant-like establishments, with cows, poultry, etc. The numbers of Maltese and Yugoslavs are too few for this behaviour to reveal itself as statistically significant at the 5 per cent level; yet the phenomenon has undeniable sociological significance, for the rural way of life sets this small group of settlers apart from the rest of the immigrant community.

(b) There is no statistical association but there is a causal connection—e.g. when the immigrant's rural/urban background accounts for differences in linguistic habits. This particular connection can be argued on the strength of interview material obtained from the immigrants of either origin, whilst no statistical association could possibly be detected even in a considerably larger sample.

In this study, then, the terms 'statistical association' or 'statistically varies with' will be used in a special sense and in purely statistical context. All other associations will be referred to in such terms as 'linked with' or 'related to'.

PART II
THE SETTLERS

4

THE SETTLERS' BACKGROUNDS

The men who were interviewed in the field survey in 1959, and whom we take to be representative of the immigrant workforce of the brown coal industry in the Latrobe Valley, were classified into ten groups according to the country of birth (see Appendix B). Table 8 shows the breakdown by birthplace in conjunction with the place of residence in the Latrobe Valley. The pattern emerging from this table confirms the census figures which were quoted in Chapter 2 (see p. 14), with certain important refinements: the 1954 census figures give one total for the whole of Newborough; for the purpose of this study the town has been split into two parts described as Old Newborough and East and North Newborough. The former has a large proportion of settlers born in eastern Europe, but the substantial majority of the immigrants in East and North Newborough have come from the British Isles. The survey figures also give an indication of the ethnic composition of the hostel dwellers in Yallourn and Morwell (Ridge Hostel), neither of which is shown separately in the census.

Analysis of the distribution of the immigrants by religion reveals several interesting points (see Table 9). First is the extent to which four ethnic groups (Greece, Italy, Malta, and Poland) are virtually homogeneous in their denominational composition. Of these, Greece has the highest proportion of the adherents of the Orthodox religion, and Italy, Malta, and Poland are the strongholds of the Roman Catholic religion. Second, the membership of the Lutheran Church seems to be restricted to two groups only, the German-born and the settlers from two of the Baltic countries (Latvia and Estonia). Third, the Orthodox religion has its adherents only in three of the sampled birthplaces—Greece, Yugoslavia, and the Ukraine. Finally, about a quarter of those interviewed among the Dutch-born have been listed as 'Other Protestant'. The men so classified are mainly members of the orthodox Calvinist group which is known as the Reformed Church of Australia and New Zealand and is based on the teachings of the *Gereformeerde Kerk* in the Netherlands (see pp. 173-4). The Dutch-born also have a substantial proportion of the immigrants who did not reply to the question on religion or who declared

51

TABLE 8
Residential Distribution of Immigrants in the Latrobe Valley

Place of Residence

Birthplace	Yallourn private homes		Yallourn hostels		Yallourn North		Old New-borough		E. & N. Newborough		Moe		Ridge Hostel (Morwell)		Total	
	No.	%	No.	%	No.	%	No.	%	No.	%	No.	%	No.	%	No.	%
British Isles	27	73	31	30	10	18	9	12	56	64	43	30	7	18	183	34
Netherlands	1	3	3	3	—	—	5	7	8	9	26	18	2	5	45	8
Greece & Italy	—	—	20	20	5	9	2	3	1	1	5	3	19	50	52	10
Malta	1	3	18	18	24	42	5	7	11	13	23	16	1	3	83	15
Germany	1	3	6	6	2	4	1	1	7	8	11	8	—	—	28	5
Poland	3	8	5	5	2	4	22	29	—	—	11	8	3	8	46	9
Yugoslavia	—	—	5	5	11	18	4	5	1	1	9	6	1	3	31	6
Baltic countries	—	—	8	8	2	4	4	5	2	2	6	4	—	—	22	4
Ukraine	1	3	—	—	1	2	20	27	—	—	6	4	1	3	29	5
Other central and eastern Europe	3	8	6	6	—	—	3	4	2	2	4	3	4	11	22	4
	37	101	102	101	57	101	75	100	88	100	144	100	38	101	541	100
Percentages with urban background	78		51		53		45		82		74		39		62	
Percentages with rural background	22		49		47		55		18		26		61		38	

Note: Figures in each birthplace may not add to 100 because of rounding.

TABLE 9

Religious Distribution of Immigrants within each Birthplace
(%)

Birthplace	Church of England	Presbyterian	Lutheran	Other Protestant	Roman Catholic	Orthodox	Other religions	No reply No religion	N =
British Isles	46	31	—	8	12	—	1	2	183
Netherlands	2	13	2	24	38	—	—	20	45
Germany	4	—	61	6	25	—	4	—	28
Italy	—	—	—	—	96	—	—	4	23
Greece	—	—	—	3	—	97	—	—	29
Malta	—	—	—	—	100	—	—	—	83
Poland	—	—	2	—	93	—	—	—	46
Yugoslavia	—	—	—	6	36	58	—	—	31
Baltic countries	—	—	54	—	36	9	—	—	22
Ukraine	—	—	—	—	62	38	—	—	29
Other central and eastern Europe	—	4	5	4	64	18	—	5	22
	16	12	6	5	45	12	1	3	541

TABLE 10

Pre-migration Socio-economic Status of the Immigrants
(%)

Indices of Socio-economic Status	Birthplace										Total
	British Isles	Nether-lands	Germany	Greece & Italy	Malta	Poland	Yugo-slavia	Baltic countries	Ukraine	Other C. & E. Europe	
(a) Father's occupation*											
N =	**183**	**45**	**27**	**52**	**83**	**46**	**31**	**22**	**29**	**22**	**540**
Rural	4	9	7	69	18	74	61	45	76	32	29
Professional, etc.; administrative, clerical and commercial	22	33	26	6	13	4	19	18	7	32	18
Craftsmen and operatives	46	38	56	13	24	11	16	18	10	32	31
Protective and unskilled labourers	28	20	11	12	45	11	3	18	7	5	22
(b) Educational attainment of the immigrants											
N =	**183**	**45**	**28**	**52**	**74**	**46**	**31**	**21**	**29**	**22**	**531**
Primary	45	47	25	81	86	70	45	10	86	27	56
Secondary and higher	55	53	75	19	14	30	55	90	14	73	44

(c) Pre-migration occupation*

N =	171	43	28	50	82	40	28	21	26	21	510†
Rural	7	2	—	46	2	43	39	19	58	19	17
Professional, etc.: administrative, clerical and commercial	12	12	4	12	9	8	18	29	8	10	11
Craftsmen and operatives	64	65	79	16	40	23	32	43	19	43	47
Protective and unskilled labourers	16	21	18	26	49	28	11	10	15	29	24

(d) Pre-migration residence

N =	181	45	27	52	83	46	31	22	29	22	538
Urban	83	80	93	33	46	41	48	73	21	64	62
Rural	17	20	7	67	54	59	52	27	79	36	38

Note: Percentages may not add to 100 because of rounding.

* See Appendix D: Classification of Occupations.

† Excludes 28 who were full-time students or pre-school children, distributed: British Isles 11, N.W. Europe 2, S. Europe 1, Malta 1, Poland 5, Yugoslavia 3, Baltic countries 1, Ukraine 3, Other C. & E. Europe 1.

that they had no religion. Unlike, perhaps, some other ethnic groups, the Dutch are well known for the frankness with which they admit that they do not wish to be identified with any particular religion.[1] In the study 20 per cent of the immigrants were classified in this category as compared with 25·2 per cent in Victoria in 1954.[2] The discrepancies in this respect are undoubtedly due to probing by interviewers—something which cannot be done in a population census.

Four characteristics were assessed during the field survey to yield information on the pre-migration socio-economic status (see Appendix C), namely, the occupational background of the immigrant's father, the immigrant's educational attainment, his occupation, and his urban/rural residential background before emigration from Europe to Australia.

The most striking feature of Table 10, which summarizes this information, is the distinct ethnic pattern revealed in the close link between birthplace and the four characteristics under review. Thus it seems clear that immigrants from central and eastern Europe (except Baltic countries), and to a lesser extent from southern Europe, have sizeable proportions of men with a rural family background and rural residence in their native country. In this they stand in direct contrast to the British, German, and Dutch, who are predominantly sons of urban workers ranging from craftsmen to unskilled labourers.[3] The British, Germans, and Dutch are, on the whole, better educated than the southern Europeans, and the Baltic countries have a higher proportion of men with secondary or higher education than any other group. A closer comparison of the level of educational attainment and background reveals, as one would perhaps expect, that educational opportunity is closely related to urban origin.

The settler's occupation before migration reveals that a significantly lower proportion of men have come from a rural background than was the case for their fathers.[4] Perhaps this finding might point to a degree of upward movement in the social and occupational ladder, combined with a measure of internal migration from the village to the town. The number of settlers who were still at school before emigration to Australia and who intended to pursue rural occupations is unknown, but even so, a comparison of the absolute numbers of fathers and their sons in the category 'rural' reveals a trend towards non-agricultural pursuits. This, of course, is a story familiar to students of European migration where rural over-population, combined with fragmentation of land, and a pull of employment opportunities resulting from steady industrialization, has contributed to a considerable outflow from rural areas to the cities. The following excerpt from an autobiographical sketch, written by a Maltese migrant who now lives at Yallourn North, illustrates this process. The writer's English and spelling are preserved:

Both father and mother were of peasant parents. My father's occupation was farming and run a few milk goats, for in my young days that was the main source of milk at Malta. 4 a.m. go with the milk round return home between 7 and 8 a.m. and then go and work on the farm till dark for six day per week. Holy days Christmas and Good Friday they had to do it because they finished up with fifteen children in the family. Religion strict R.C. . . . . Death nine of the children at different times the last was my father and brother during the Blitz on the island and my mother and oldest brother two years ago.

I started school at 5 year of age and I like it very much I made a lot of new friends. I took studying (went to private school) for apprenticeship in the dockyard but you had to be very lucky to get because there was as many as two hundred pupils sitting for the examination and they might only want 6 or 8 apprentices so that ended it and went to work on the farm. But for me there was no going back to the farm. There was too many of us in the family and I and six of my brothers went to factories and dockyards. I got a job at the Dockyard at 18 years and got the sack about 8 months after wages was 1/4 per day.

Back on the farm again for two years then I got a job again at H.M.S. Dockyard as a labour. 1914-18 war broke out and I was promoted to a driver's attendant then I volunteered for overseas with the Merchant Navy. That was an experience. Things went well for a while until 21st May 1918 we got torpedoed between Sardinia and Carlo Forte, anyhow I saved my skin, we got back home and a few weeks after the war was over, then I worked on merchant-ships as an A.B. [able seaman]. That was a great job the best I ever had although 4 hrs. on and 4 hrs. off at sea returned home for a spell then decided to come to Australia. The passage was round about £24 from Malta, we had an awful trip the ship (*Ville de Strasburg*) old, slow and hungry. It took over 40 days we landed in Melbourne everyone to himself not like today they come and meet you on the boat and take you to a hostel and find a job. I was in Melbourne for a week in search of work and then decided to go Bush. I landed at Yallourn and got a job lived in a tent for about a week then moved in a tin cubicle, and month after I boarded and lodged with a family.

The writer of this story retired from the SEC when he was 65. He now lives in a house he built himself, surrounded by two acres of fine orchard and a well-kept vegetable garden. As in Malta he has his own milk supply, though not from a goat but from a cow. He has, in fact, completed a full circle in the fifty years of his working life. Born and brought up on the land, he leads again, in the evening of his life, the peasant's existence.

Malta is an interesting case in its own right. Table 10 (c) shows that the proportion of the Maltese men who had a rural pre-migration occupation is only 2 per cent. Yet the proportion of Maltese men who, on the basis of their pre-migration residence in Malta, were classified as having rural background is 54 per cent (see Table 10 (d)). This striking discrepancy between occupation and residence is, of course, a commentary on the peculiar conditions obtaining in Malta. Ever since the middle of the nineteenth century the surplus rural population had to seek employment in the naval dockyards at Valetta and various public works that were initiated to improve the road system and sanitary services in the island.[5] This has necessitated commuting daily between the village and the town or the nearest public work depot. Often a paid job in the dockyard, in one of the small food industries, or in the Public Works Department is combined with the intensive cultivation of a tiny plot of land and the grazing of a few goats. This mode of life explains, then, the occupational distribution of the Maltese immigrants. It also throws some light on the continued practice of the Maltese settlers, particularly those in Yallourn North, of living a semi-rural existence.

Mode of Migration

The decision to emigrate from Europe could have come as a result of war-time displacement (here called 'uprooting' or 'forced' migration) or it could have been a purely voluntary choice prompted by any number of 'pull' and 'push' factors. These two possible kinds of decision are, understandably perhaps, related to ethnic origin (see Table 11 (a)). It appears that all save two respondents from a large group of countries including the British Isles, the Netherlands, Italy, Greece, Malta, and Germany were not uprooted or in any way forcibly displaced from their

Mode of Migration
(%)

Mode of migration and reasons	Birthplace										Total
	British Isles	Nether-lands	Germany	Greece & Italy	Malta	Poland	Yugo-slavia	Baltic countries	Ukraine	Other C. & E. Europe	
(a) Migration decision:											
N =	175	45	25	50	83	44	31	22	29	20	524
'Uprooted'	—	2	4	—	—	100	77	91	100	65	25
Voluntary	100	98	96	100	100	—	23	9	—	35	75
(b) Migration finance:											
N =	183	45	28	51	83	45	31	22	29	21	538
Assisted	83	78	86	45	82	98	100	95	97	95	83
Full fare	17	22	14	55	18	2	—	5	3	5	17
(c) Role of kin group:											
N =	183	45	28	50	83	46	31	21	29	21	537
Subjects with members of kin group in Australia before arrival	31	27	11	28	39	11	6	10	3	14	24
Subjects with no members of kin group in Australia before arrival	69	73	89	72	61	89	94	90	97	86	76
(d) Role of kin:											
N =	82	23	7	17	48	*	*	*	*	*	
Assisted by or assisting kin	41	43	100	65	67	*	*	*	*	*	
Not assisted by and not assisting kin	59	57	—	35	33	*	*	*	*	*	

* The information was not tabulated for the immigrants born in eastern Europe since most had no relatives in Australia.

countries.[6] A very large majority of the east European groups, on the other hand, left their countries as political refugees or were taken into captivity and forced to work in the factories and on farms in Germany.[7]

Ethnic origin is also linked with the method of financing the immigrant's passage to Australia (Table 11 (b)). The settlers born in Greece and Italy have a relatively high proportion of men who paid their own fares or were assisted by relatives; but the highest proportion of men who were assisted by the Australian government or international bodies like the International Refugee Organization (I.R.O.) is to be found in the central and east European group, who were mostly the former Displaced Persons (D.Ps.) uprooted from their homes during World War II.

For the men and their families who were helped by the I.R.O., the arrival in Australia marked an end of several years spent in the enforced idleness of refugee camps in Germany or Austria. Some had children born in captivity during the war; others married and started their families during the period of chaos that followed their liberation after the Third Reich had collapsed in 1945; all the Displaced Persons arrived in Australia with fresh memories of persecution only slightly dulled by that demoralizing experience of waiting and doing nothing. The following extract from a life history, written in English by a former Hungarian refugee who now lives at Moe, tells the story of what at least some of the refugees suffered through frustration and the entanglements of red tape in the artificial surroundings of refugee camps.

As soon as Australia announced its migration programme in 1948, I decided to apply for admission. However, at the first few months Australia banned the so-called 'ex-enemy' nations —we Hungarians belonged to this group.

After long months of waiting our patience was rewarded; we were called in to Schweinfurt Resettlement Center for Displaced Persons to undergo screening and medical examinations for Australia. At the time we had two children. We were accepted without any difficulty. After being accepted to Australia, we were transported back to our camp, and were told to make preparation for the trip. We hoped that the call will come soon, because my wife was expecting our third child, and the transportation depended on her condition. Expecting mothers over six months were not allowed on ship. So we lived in a state of nerves very hard to describe. Finally we received our call back to Schweinfurt for final shipment.

We disposed or sold things we thought unworthy to bring with us—what we had regretted after arriving at Australia. On the 22nd August 1949 our train has left Plattling Lager for Schweinfurt—after the next stop Melbourne. At least that what we thought will happen. Instead we had to face a 12 month period full of disappointments and suffering. Today I am glad that men cannot see into the future. I am sure I would cancel my migration for good. I try to give an objective account of the happenings that made me feel years older than I really was.

On 23rd August we arrived at Schweinfurt, happy and hopeful. We were told that in 6-7 days we will be sailing all ready. We were put into a room already occupied by two families, each with one child. The size of the room was about 17′ x 18′ and there were still two beds unoccupied. Late at night our last tenant arrived. A young family with two children. One of their children however cried all night so much that his mother called the doctor at 4 o'clock a.m. This is where our troubles started. The poor child had measles, and as it was customary in camps, all the children in the same room were sent to hospital. We were told that it only will be 6-7 days and if our children will not get measles they will be allowed to leave. So we missed the first transport. The days seemed to stop to move. Bitter, disappointed, disheartened we finally arrived at Wurzburg on the 7th day to pick up our children from the hospital. There was a transport to go in 3 days, so we hoped to catch that, what seemed to us the last chance to go before our third baby arrived.

At this point the family were held up for six weeks because one of the children had chicken-pox. When finally the family were ready to leave the writer called at the I.R.O. Office for his passage tickets.

The Clerk at the window advised me that my name had been removed from the list, due to my wife's advanced pregnancy. I went blank, speechless, could not move for long long minutes. After all these disappointment and torture we had to go through, our last hope was shattered to bits. I did not have to tell my wife of what has happened. She could read it from my expression.

The same day we were issued train tickets to go back to the camp we originally came from. Fortunately enough, my wife's parents were still in the Camp and they shared their shack with us. Slowly we settled down again to the Camp life again, getting used to the idea to wait another 10 months, and to start all over again. But evidently our time of probation was not over yet, for in November I received a telegram from

Schweinfurt to come at once because plane tickets were issued for us and our plane was due to leave in 7 days. We were also advised to take light parcels with us and, that it might take 3 months until our heavy baggage will follow us by ship. We hurriedly went through our very small possessions, selling or discarding anything we thought we could do without them. The next day we departed our camp again, and the same night we arrived at Schweinfurt. The next morning I reported in the office of the Australian Mission and stated our case. Much to my disgust, nobody knew about the telegram or about an air transport. I have never seen so many silly faces in my life before—not excluding my own. So all this fuss, expense and hope for nothing again. My intensive enquiries and investigation failed to reveal the true story behind the telegram. Finally we were staying in the Schweinfurt Resettlement Center till our baby was born—the 11th April 1950. After my wife was discharged from the hospital, we were transferred to Amberg, a Camp for pending cases. When our baby was 3 months old we were called to office where an officer of the I.R.O. advised us that we can no longer go to Australia because Australia is not taking families with more than 2 children for the time being. He advised us to try to go somewhere else. He issued me a return ticket to Schweinfurt and told me to see the U.S.A. consul. I duly arrived at Schweinfurt. The first men I met was the secretary of the Australian Consul. He greeted me with a big smile and told me to come back to Schweinfurt soon as our baby will be 5 months old and that we will be accepted without any further trouble. I do not know what I said or thought at that moment. To hear the opposite from one official what I was yesterday by another seemed to stalemate my brain.

He denied that there was any truth in what I was told yesterday anyhow since I had been accepted once already automatically qualifies me for transportation as soon as my child will be old enough to travel. So it happened. After a few months trying and re-enlisting, endless medical examinations, transfer from one camp to another on the 22nd December 1950 we were among the 200 migrants on the s.s. Fairsea to take us to our Land of Promise, to a new country where we decided to settle and live happily. . . . On 23rd January 1951 we arrived at Melbourne. We were impressed by the number of motorcars. I was surprised to see so many smiling, happy people, free of the impression of six years of war, free of seeing their towns destroyed to the ground. They seemed to be free of care and worries—God keep them so forever.

In the process of migration an important part is played by
family ties. Sometimes those who have already come to Australia
help to persuade a relative to emigrate with promises of accommodation, employment, and often financial aid. Some writers describe
this as chain migration: a process in which members of a family,
or often a village or a town, migrate to join the earlier migrants
and form a new group in Australia.[8] This process has been the
main *modus operandi* of migration from southern Europe; one
estimate suggests that, over the period 1890-1940, more than 80
per cent of southern European settlers came to Australia in this
way.[9]

The role of the kin group in the process of migration in aiding
the migrant and stimulating successive waves of migration from the
same family is not equally pronounced in all the birthplace
groups in this study. A comparison of immigrants who had no
relative in Australia before arrival in Australia with those who
followed their relatives to Australia shows that this characteristic
is linked with ethnic origin (see Table 11 (c)). The opportunity
to help one's kin is largely confined to those who migrate voluntarily, that is the west and south Europeans. In this group there
is a significant difference between those who received help from
members of the family already established in Australia or who
helped after arrival to bring others of their family here and
those who came without assistance from family and played no
part in the subsequent migration of their kin (see Table 11 (d)).

Amongst the settlers included in this study the various forms
of assistance by the kin group of the immigrant are noticeable
among southern Europeans and particularly men born in Malta.
Here the pattern of chain migration seems to have been in operation for at least forty years. Today the Maltese settlement in
Yallourn North includes a group of men in their late sixties who
came to Australia in 1921-3 and found well-paid work on the
Yallourn Open-cut.[10] By the end of the twenties they had paid
the fares of wives and children left behind in Malta; some paid
for the passage of their fiancées. Then in the late thirties, when
economic conditions had improved, a new wave of relatives was
assisted: the brothers and brothers-in-law of the first settlers, and
their wives and families. Fifteen years later, in the fifties, there
followed the third wave of immigration from Malta, financially
assisted by the earlier arrivals, as shown in the following extract
from a life history:

Soon after the war, we heard and read about the Immigration scheme to Canada, South Africa and Australia. Reading about the standard of living both in Canada and Australia, I had a desire to look for better opportunity. One of my work mates went to the Emigration Office in Valletta and brought few pamphlets about Canada and Australia. After few discussions about the opportunities both in Canada and Australia we agreed that he goes to Canada and I come to Australia with one condition that if the conditions in Canada suits him he nominate me and I go there—if the conditions in Australia are better, I will nominate him and bring him out here.

We finished up in Australia for I like the conditions and climate in this country so much that I nominated him and after that I nominated seventeen relatives and friends and another eight are on the way from Malta to Australia. They are all living happily in Australia and they are hundred per cent better off than they were in Malta.

Sometimes the period separating the arrival of the various links in the chain is very long. Depressions and wars delay the plans of bringing out one's family. Often the pattern is complicated by a temporary migration to other parts of the world, as in this life history written by a Greek immigrant, a café proprietor in West Camp at Yallourn:

I was born in 1894 in a small village in the mountains some 300 kilometres North from Athens. My father was a small farmer. There were six children in the family: three boys and three girls. I am the eldest.

When I finished 6th grade in 1908 my mother died and I went to work in Athens, and left home. I worked there for three years and then in 1911 went to America. I was there $8\frac{1}{2}$ years working under bad conditions and for long hours at poor wages, and I was not well. I had to give up in 1919 and go home. (I worked in North Carolina.)

I wanted to stay at home for 6 months for health reasons and return to the U.S.A. However, I was conscripted for military service for three years in the Greek expeditionary forces in Asia Minor. In the course of this campaign the Greek Army conquered Turkey. In August 1922 I lost one brother and one was taken prisoner. I was demobbed.

I married in 1922 in Greece and stayed until 1924. I could no longer return to the U.S.A. [because of the immigration quotas] so I came to Australia in 1924. I arrived in Melbourne in October of 1924 ill with malaria. I was out of work for 3 months.

At long last I got a job in tearooms as a counter hand: 9 a.m. to midnight at 35/- per week. I saved money to send to my family and to start a business. I worked there for 12 months. Saved £40-£50 and bought a little business in Elizabeth St. (City) and stayed there for 12 months selling it for £300. I then bought another business in King St. and stayed there for 2 years.

I went home in 1929 for 12 months for a holiday with the intention to bring out my family. But while I was away the business lost money in the hands of my cousin, so I came out again in 1930. I worked for 6 months in the business and lost it in the depression. I went out to look for work (bankrupt). I went to West Australia and was 3 months out of work. During this time my cousin kept me. I found a job in a milk bar and saved a little on £2 a week. I went to Willooma (gold town) for 6 months working at £5 wk. I paid off my debts in Perth and was then out of work for 2-3 months. I then worked for 2 years in a milk bar and in 1938 I left Kalgoorlie and returned to Melbourne with some money.

I started a business in Russell St and stayed 2 years. Then opened a butcher shop in Centre Way Arcade in Collins St. successful and stayed for 4 years [both places are in the city of Melbourne] 1940-44.

Towards the end of 1944 I decided to bring my family out of danger for I realized that the Civil War was going to break out shortly. I applied for naturalization papers and got them and sent permits for my family.

But by the time my family got all the necessary documents war broke out on my village and my wife took the children and went to live in a small provincial town which was in no immediate danger of attacks by the EOKA terrorists. They lived there in shocking conditions.

In the next three years I got only one letter from my wife. But all the time I was supporting them.

Eventually in 1947 I was able to arrange for their journey to Australia by air. I had not enough money to pay for my wife and children so John, my eldest son came first and I found him a job with the Dunlop Rubber Coy. A year later he and I saved up £800 sufficient to pay the air fares of my wife, daughter and the younger son, Con.

They left Athens by plane in November 1948 and a fortnight later landed in Melbourne. But my family was not complete because—what a tragedy—my daughter aged 18 died on the way and was buried at Singapore. I saw her last when she was a tiny baby a few weeks old before I sailed for Australia for the second time in 1930.

This man's and his family's Odyssey, extending over a period of some forty years, is by no means unusual of a large number of southern European immigrants in Australia. Born in the poverty of a mountain village he had to seek his livelihood away from home first in a large metropolis in his own country and subsequently in the U.S.A. and, when immigration restrictions were imposed by that country in the early 1920s, in Australia. There was the long interval separating his first arrival in Australia and that of his wife and his children, the agony of waiting through the years of World War II and the civil war in northern Greece, the frustrations, fears, and grief connected with his family's flight to Australia. Throughout this epic he worked ceaselessly to support his wife and children back in Europe and to establish himself economically in Australia. But the epic has a happy ending for today our hero lives with his wife, his two sons, and their wives and four grandchildren, in a spacious and well-furnished house which he built in Old Newborough, while the two sons look after the family milk bars in Moe and Yallourn. The old man still goes to work and helps his sons and can be seen, for six days a week, at work behind the counter in one or the other milk bar. His savings in the past ten years have been invested in paying the fares of his relatives, and at the time of interview (February 1959) thirty of his relatives had had all their expenses paid and received accommodation and jobs on arrival in Australia.

The epic story of the Greek café proprietor (and acknowledged leader of the Greek community in the Latrobe Valley), as much as the examples cited earlier in this chapter, convey something of a dream and what must be a traumatic experience associated with the process of migration. The examples serve to emphasize that the sociologist must regard migration not as a single act accomplished in a week or a month but as a social process extending continuously over a much longer period of time. It begins with conditions operating on the individual long before his actual upheaval. Agricultural over-population, depressed economic conditions, wars and deportations, the demoralizing idleness of refugee camps—all contribute to the decision to migrate and affect the mode of migration. But the process of migration does not end upon the arrival in a new country. It goes on for a long time until the immigrant becomes a completely adjusted member of the new community.

Duration of Residence in Australia and the Demographic Characteristics

Before we can look at the process of adjustment we must briefly examine some statistical material relating to the duration of residence in Australia, and also the demographic characteristics of the immigrants included in this study. The examination of the ethnic pattern revealed by this material will throw light on some matters discussed in later chapters.

The composition of the immigrants in terms of duration of residence is shown in Table 5. This confirms certain features of the background of these people already revealed in connection with their mode of migration. For example the great majority of 'forced' immigrants, the former Displaced Persons, had lived in Australia between six and fifteen years at the time of the field survey (1959); practically none arrived here before 1945.[11] By contrast, four-fifths of all British-born settlers had lived in Australia for six years or more, and at least a quarter of them have been in the country since before World War II. Several members of that group who had arrived in Australia in the twenties or thirties expressed amazement, and in a few isolated instances indignation, at being included in a survey of *immigrants*. They obviously did not consider themselves as immigrants any longer.

The differences in the length of residence in Australia and in the circumstances in which the settlers left their countries of birth explain the ethnic pattern of the demographic characteristics summarized in Table 13. This is seen, for example, in the differences in average age of the immigrants (and the wives). Thus, the British-born men and women are older than the immigrants from all other countries except the Baltic states; this is because the average period of residence in Australia of the British-born persons is substantially longer than in the case of all other groups (see Table 12). The Baltic people, on the other hand, consist mainly of persons older than the average for all immigrants because, unlike the Poles and the Ukrainians, they did not leave their countries as forced labour drafted to work in Nazi Germany but as evacuees migrating to Germany under the terms of an international treaty. The forced labour draft in the German-occupied territories applied mainly to the 15-24 age group for both sexes, but the evacuation from the Baltic countries affected whole family groups including many aged people.[12]

TABLE 12

Period of Residence

(%)

Birthplace	Under 6 years	6 years and under 15	15 years and over	N =	Average residence in Australia (years)
British Isles	21	55	24	**183**	13·6
Netherlands	56	40	4	**45**	6·5
Germany	93	4	4	**28**	5·1
Greece and Italy	75	17	8	**52**	6·3
Malta	45	48	7	**83**	8·3
Poland	2	98	—	**46**	8·4
Yugoslavia	16	84	—	**31**	7·9
Baltic countries	5	95	—	**22**	10·0
Ukraine	—	100	—	**29**	9·2
Other central and eastern Europe	36	59	5	**22**	8·4
	33	56	11	**541**	9·7

TABLE 13

Selected Demographic Characteristics of the Immigrants

(Averages)

Birthplace	Age of		Duration of Marriage (Years)	Children (Number)	Size of Household (Number)
	Immigrant	Wife			
British Isles	44·7	44·5	19·1	2·3	3·9
Netherlands	40·2	38·0	14·8	3·3	5·2
Germany	38·7	37·6	14·7	2·1	3·6
Italy and Greece	34·0	41·0	15·9	2·0	3·8
Malta	38·5	37·3	15·0	4·1	5·9
Poland	40·4	37·1	12·1	2·6	4·6
Yugoslavia	39·8	36·5	13·2	2·7	4·8
Baltic countries	45·1	41·6	19·2	2·1	4·0
Ukraine	39·6	36·8	13·6	2·9	4·7
Other central and eastern Europe	39·3	40·8	15·3	2·5	4·4
	40·9	40·0	16·1	2·8	4·5

The set of circumstances that explains the differences in the average age of the immigrants can also be taken to apply to the duration of marriage. The British-born have a higher duration of marriage than all the remaining ethnic groups except the Baltic people because of their longer period of residence in Australia. The Baltic people, on the other hand, have a relatively high average duration of marriage for reasons connected with the circumstances of their migration. For the same reason the Polish settlers have a low duration of marriage. Of the thirty-six couples interviewed, twenty-nine were married in the quinquennium 1945-9, that is during the period following their liberation from the slave labour camps in Germany and before emigration to Australia. The majority of these people were deported to Germany in their late teens or early twenties, before they had a chance to marry. Marriage was possible only when they were set free and started to re-create some semblance of normal family life in the squalor of D.P. camps (see Appendix A).

Size of Family

Are the differences in duration of marriage reflected in the size of the family, that is the average number of children per married couple? An inspection of the statistics summarized in Table 13 reveals that this is not the case. Indeed the birthplaces with the longest duration of marriage have comparatively small families (Baltic: 2·1; British Isles: 2·3). The birthplaces with large families (Malta: 4·1; Netherlands: 3·3) are not at all groups with the longest durations of marriage, a fact which points to a statistical association between ethnic origin and size of the family.

There is only one pointer in the statistical evidence collected during field work which can partly explain the existence of differences in the family size, namely religion (see Table 14).[13] Whether the association between the Roman Catholic religion and the above-average size of family can be taken as more than just a pointer remains a debatable problem. There are several examples in the statistics in Table 14 which would suggest that the relationship is not very clear cut. On the one hand there is the all-Catholic Maltese group with an average of 4·1 children per family;[14] on the other hand there is the Polish group, also almost exclusively Catholic, with the average of 2·6. This comparison makes no allowance for the differences in the age structure and the duration of marriage, nevertheless it suggests that the ethnic factor is more important than religion in explaining the

TABLE 14

Children in Family by Immigrant's Country of Birth (All Durations of Marriage):
Catholics and Non-Catholics

Country of Birth	Children in Family							Total No. of Families
	0	1	2	3	4	5	6 and over	
British Isles:								
Catholic	2	2	5	2	1	1	1	14
Non-Catholic	16	20	41	27	12	3	5	124
Total	18	22	46	29	13	4	6	138
Netherlands:								
Catholic	—	—	6	3	3	1	2	15
Non-Catholic	1	5	4	6	1	3	4	24
Total	1	5	10	9	4	4	6	39
Greece and Italy:								
Catholic	1	—	6	2	—	—	—	9
Non-Catholic	—	1	2	1	—	—	—	4
Total	1	1	8	3	—	—	—	13
Malta:								
Catholic	3	5	11	9	10	8	14	60
Non-Catholic	—	—	—	—	—	—	—	—
Total	3	5	11	9	10	8	14	60
Germany:								
Catholic	1	3	—	2	—	—	—	6
Non-Catholic	1	3	4	5	2	1	—	16
Total	2	6	4	7	2	1	—	22
Poland:								
Catholic	—	9	9	9	5	4	—	36
Non-Catholic	—	1	—	—	—	—	—	1
Total	—	10	9	9	5	4	—	37
Yugoslavia:								
Catholic	1	2	1	1	2	—	—	7
Non-Catholic	1	1	6	6	1	1	2	18
Total	2	3	7	7	3	1	2	25
Baltic:								
Catholic	—	2	1	—	—	—	—	3
Non-Catholic	—	1	5	4	—	—	—	10
Total	—	3	6	4	—	—	—	13
Ukraine:								
Catholic	1	2	7	3	1	3	—	17
Non-Catholic	—	—	3	2	2	2	—	9
Total	1	2	10	5	3	5	—	26

TABLE 14—*continued*.

Country of Birth	Children in Family							Total No. of Families
	0	1	2	3	4	5	6 and over	
Other C. & E. Europe:								
Catholic	—	1	4	—	2	1	—	8
Non-Catholic	—	1	1	1	1	—	—	4
Total	—	2	5	1	3	1	—	12
Totals:								
Catholic	9	26	50	31	24	18	17	175
Non-Catholic	19	33	66	52	19	10	11	210
Grand Totals	28	59	116	83	43	28	28	385

Number of mixed marriages (i.e. between Catholics and Non-Catholics) = 27.

differences in family size. It is probable, too, that the differences are simply a continuation of the patterns and trends in fertility that have been in force in the countries of origin.[15] With the exception of the 1950-4 quinquennium, the birth-rates in Malta have been higher than in Poland since 1930 as shown in Table 15.

The example of the Netherlands can be used to support these arguments. On the statistics quoted in Table 13 the Dutch families have the next highest fertility after the Maltese. Yet this cannot be wholly attributed to religious composition, for only about 40 per cent are Roman Catholics. In fact, a further comparison of the average sizes of Roman Catholic $(3 \cdot 33)$ and non-Catholic families $(3 \cdot 36)$ reveals that they are almost equal. It appears therefore that the relatively high fertility of the Dutch families can only be explained in terms of Holland's anomalous demographic trend, that is, the maintenance of the relatively high rates of natural increase in the face of simultaneous decline in the remaining northwest European countries ever since the middle of the nineteenth century.[16]

Finally, the preceding discussion has been based on observed differences in groups of unequal duration of residence in Australia, and therefore the statistical findings must be treated with caution.[17] Short of separating the families whose first child was born in Australia and the families with children born in Europe, it would be impossible to estimate the influence of Australian conditions on their fertility pattern. It is probable, however, that the ethnic and religious influences on patterns of fertility persist for a long time after arrival, and only a cohort analysis extending over at least two or three generations of immigrants, starting with the original settlers, would give an answer to some of the questions raised by this study.

TABLE 15

Malta and Poland: Crude Birth-rates, 1930–1954

	Malta	Poland
1930-4	33·2	28·9*
1935-9	33·6	25·4†
1930-9	33·4	27·3‡
1945-9	37·3	28·4§
1950-4	29·8	30·1
1954-9	33·6	29·5‖

* Provisional.
† Period 1935-8 only; data for the 1923-37 territory; provisional.
‡ Period 1930-8 only; data for the 1923-37 territory; provisional.
§ Period 1947-9 only; provisional.
‖ Period 1947-54.
Source: *Demographic Year Book of the United Nations*, 1959.

5
OCCUPATIONAL ADJUSTMENT

Among the various aspects of the adjustment of immigrants in the receiving society, occupational wellbeing is perhaps the most significant. It is both an important aspect of physical survival and one of the most important elements of social and cultural adjustment in new surroundings. The migrant's feelings of satisfaction about his working conditions, and consciousness of doing a job which takes full advantage of his skills and capacities, are fundamental to successful adjustment.

Eleven questions in the interview schedule were concerned with several aspects of occupational adjustment (see Appendices C, D), including a comparison of pre-migration and present occupation, present occupation and its relationship to ethnic origin and urban/rural background, and stability of employment, job satisfaction, and assessment of the overall change in occupational status.

Migration and Change of Occupation

A sizeable proportion of the immigrants of southern and east European origin were employed on the land (see Chapter 4) ; few immigrants from most of these countries had possessed a skilled occupation.

The position at the time of the field survey as compared with the immigrants' pre-migration occupation is shown in Table 16 separately for each birthplace or group of birthplaces. Several striking points emerge from this comparison.

First is the fact that no rural occupation is represented in the group studied. This is, of course, due to the nature of the brown coal industry. But beyond this statistical finding there is hidden a story of occupational and cultural readjustment that must have occurred in the lives of the Italians, Greeks, Poles, Yugoslavs, and Ukrainians, to whom migration meant not only a change of country, but a radical transformation of the way of life and the values associated with it. This transformation, as shown in Chapter 4, was, no doubt, cushioned for the Poles, Yugoslavs, and Ukrainians by their displacement during World War II and the years spent in Germany, where they mostly worked in industry and experienced an urban way of life. But what a far cry for

73

TABLE 16

*Comparison of Pre-migration and Present Occupations**

(%)

Birthplace	Occupations														No reply	N =
	Rural		Professional and Administrative		Clerical and Commercial		Craftsmen and Operatives		Service and Protective		Unskilled Labourers		Students			
	P.M.	P.O.	P.M.	P.O.	P.M.	P.O.	P.M.	P.O.	P.M.	P.O.	P.M.	P.O.	P.M.	P.O.		
British Isles	6·5	—	2·1	3·2	9·3	2·7	60·1	73·2	3·3	1·6	12·0	19·1	6·0	—	·5	183
Netherlands	2·2	—	—	2·2	11·1	6·7	62·2	60·0	—	—	20·0	31·1	4·4	—	—	45
Germany	44·2	—	—	—	3·6	3·6	78·6	78·6	10·7	—	7·1	17·9	—	—	—	28
Italy and Greece	2·4	—	—	—	11·5	3·6	15·4	23·1	3·8	2·4	21·1	76·9	1·9	—	1·9	52
Malta	37·0	—	—	—	8·4	—	39·8	47·0	10·8	2·2	37·3	47·0	1·2	—	—	83
Poland	35·5	—	3·2	—	6·5	—	19·6	37·0	4·3	—	19·6	60·9	10·9	—	2·2	46
Yugoslavia	18·2	—	9·0	—	12·9	—	29·0	61·3	6·4	—	3·2	38·7	9·7	—	—	31
Baltic countries	51·7	—	—	—	18·2	—	40·9	86·4	—	4·5	9·1	9·1	4·5	—	—	22
Ukraine	—	—	—	—	6·9	—	17·2	48·3	—	3·4	13·8	48·3	10·3	—	—	29
Other central and eastern Europe	18·2	—	4·5	—	4·5	—	40·9	72·7	9·1	—	18·2	27·3	4·5	—	—	22
	16·5	—	1·4	1·3	9·2	2·2	44·7	59·0	4·8	1·5	17·6	36·0	5·2	—	·5	541

P.M. = pre-migration occupation.
P.O. = present occupation.
Note: Figures may not add to 100 because of rounding.
* See Appendix D: Classification of Occupations.

Italian *paesani* or Greek *chorikos* to come and live in a Yallourn hostel or one of the other places described earlier! Few of these men had had any experience of industry before coming to Australia. No wonder then that, lacking special skills, three-quarters of that group are unskilled labourers. No other group has such a high proportion of men in this category.

This aspect of the change of occupations from rural pursuits to unskilled labour is the second feature of interest in Table 16. A glance at the percentages in each birthplace shows that, whereas a little more than a third of all the immigrants included in this study are unskilled labourers, some ethnic groups contribute much more than this share of their numbers, for example, Poland with 60 per cent, Ukraine and Malta just under 50 per cent. The Baltic states, Germany, and the British Isles, on the other hand, contribute proportionately few.

The disproportions in the occupational distributions point to the existence of marked differences in the occupational status and ranking of different ethnic groups. The tabulation of birthplaces in terms of the highest proportion of unskilled labourers and of skilled and semi-skilled (craftsmen and operatives) shows that the order is almost identical whilst the rank numbers increase in opposite directions (see Table 17).[1] Assessed in these terms it is clear that the immigrants from the Baltic states have the highest occupational status, followed by Germany and the British Isles.[2]

The special position of those from the Baltic states justifies a further comment on the composition of this small but intensely interesting group. Early in 1941 about half of them left their countries, then under Soviet occupation, under a German-Soviet treaty which provided for the evacuation of ethnic Germans (*Volksdeutsche*). The terms of this treaty were such that many people who simply declared themselves to be of German descent were recognized as *Volksdeutsche* and were eligible for evacuation to Germany. This applied especially to Estonians and Latvians who preferred German citizenship to the prospect of life under Soviet rule. This group included members of the professions, public servants, regular soldiers, and generally people of middle-class status.[3]

The other half of the Baltic group studied belongs to the second great movement of the nationals of the Baltic states who fled in the summer of 1944 under the threatening prospect of a second Soviet occupation. Some fifteen thousand Estonians and nearly five thousand Lithuanians and Latvians fled to Sweden, while an

G

unknown number—probably tens of thousands—sought refuge in Germany and joined the retreating armies of the Third Reich.[4] At the end of the war some 179,000 nationals of the Baltic states (excluding ethnic Germans) were found in Western Europe; of these 36,000 were registered in Sweden and the remainder in the American, British, and French zones of Germany.[5]

TABLE 17

Proportions of Unskilled, Skilled, and Semi-skilled Occupations Ranked by Birthplaces
(%)

Unskilled		Skilled and semi-skilled	
Rank order	Birthplace	Rank order	Birthplace
1 (highest)	Greece and Italy	9 (lowest)	Greece and Italy
2	Poland	8	Poland
3	Ukraine	7	Malta
4	Malta	6	Ukraine
5	Yugoslavia	5	Netherlands
6	Netherlands	4	Yugoslavia
7	British Isles	3	British Isles
8	Germany	2	Germany
9 (lowest)	Baltic states	1 (highest)	Baltic states

Unlike the Poles and Ukrainians, a very great majority of the Baltic people arrived in Germany voluntarily and were, on the whole, well treated by the Germans. Many retained their former occupational status and received responsible positions in industry and administration; others received special training in skilled trades and subsequently worked in the German armaments industry.[6]

The superior occupational training, and above all the fact that such a high proportion of them were skilled tradesmen, favoured the refugees from the Baltic states (or 'the Balts' as they came to be known) for early emigration overseas under the assistance of the International Refugee Organization. Australia received its full quota of Balts in the first I.R.O. transports. All of them served their two-year contract in the industries that demanded skilled tradesmen, including the Yallourn undertaking of the SEC; of the twenty-two men in our sample fourteen went straight to Yallourn and at the time of the survey had been on the payroll for ten to eleven years.

In examining the differences in occupational status, attention has been given so far to two related factors: birthplace, and urban/rural background. Other evidence suggests that ethnic group membership and the values associated with a particular culture appear to play a significant part in the choice of occupation. This is how the Maltese residents of Yallourn North have been described by one of the interviewers:

> Occupations of the male Maltese are predominantly of the unskilled and semi-skilled variety. Many were on construction jobs when they first arrived but when these finished they preferred to stay in the SEC with steady work and housing, even though doing labouring work, rather than to have to move elsewhere to keep up their trade (if any). The great majority of the men do not seem to be interested in bettering their positions by night study or moving elsewhere, and several have been in the same labouring job many years. One who arrived in 1932 has had the same job all the time—pick and shovel work in the open-cut—and has been very happy with it.
>
> Those who had higher education in Malta and obtained their Oxford Entrance Certificate have clerical jobs and are classed as salaried staff. They feel there are more opportunities for them here than in Malta. One of these, a young man of 25, is doing accountancy by correspondence, and his uncle with whom he lives has a fine collection of books, including the *Encyclopaedia Britannica*.
>
> Some of the children of these Maltese families have had good school careers and are in good jobs, but the majority of the parents seem to have little ambition for their children. Many children expect labouring jobs like their fathers and some of the girls from larger families stay at home to help their mothers.

Stability of Employment and Job Satisfaction

One of the questions included in the interview schedule concerned the employment history of the immigrant (see Appendix C, Part III). All those interviewed were asked to list their employers between the time of arrival in Australia and the time they started work with the Yallourn undertaking of the SEC.

A crude measure—the Index of Employment Stability—was designed to assess the frequency with which immigrants had changed employment. Those that had fewer than one change of employer in a year were separated from the men who scored one and over, which meant that before joining the SEC at Yallourn they had at least one change of employer per annum.[7]

The analysis of the Index of Employment Stability shows some interesting results. Contrary to popular conceptions current in Australia about some ethnic groups,[8] the statistical evidence shown in Table 18 gives no ground for arguing that, in the Latrobe Valley at any rate, there is an overall statistical association between employment stability and birthplace.[9] There is no statistical association between stability of employment and the length of residence in Australia.[10]

TABLE 18

Employment Stability by Birthplace
(% Distribution)

Birthplace	Employment Stability Score		
	Less than 1	1 and over	N =
British Isles	88	12	**182**
Netherlands	78	22	**45**
Germany	96	4	**25**
Greece and Italy	75	25	**52**
Malta	94	6	**81**
Poland	91	9	**46**
Yugoslavia	73	27	**30**
Baltic countries	86	14	**22**
Ukraine	93	7	**29**
Other central and eastern Europe	64	36	**22**
	86	14	**534**

Note: Score 1 = one change of employer per annum, before joining the SEC at Yallourn. The immigrants who went straight to Yallourn on landing in Australia were given index value 'less than 1'.

The interview material yielded two more measures of occupational adjustment. The first of these was a series of responses relating to questions on how the subject felt about the physical conditions of his present job, whether he was satisfied with the rates of pay and whether—if free to choose—he would change. An overall assessment of these responses was classified under 'Satisfied' or 'Dissatisfied' and tabulated with birthplace, urban/rural background, occupation, and length of residence (see Table 19).

An analysis of these findings suggests that there is an association between birthplace and Satisfaction/Dissatisfaction, and that the British, Maltese, Poles, and Yugoslavs seem more satisfied than the

TABLE 19

Satisfaction with Present Employment
(%)

	Satisfied	Dissatisfied	N =
(a) *Birthplace*			
British Isles	74	26	**183**
Netherlands	60	40	**45**
Germany	61	39	**28**
Greece and Italy	46	54	**52**
Malta	75	25	**83**
Poland	76	24	**46**
Yugoslavia	74	26	**31**
Baltic countries	68	32	**22**
Ukraine	66	34	**29**
Other central and eastern Europe	73	27	**22**
Total	69	31	**541**
χ^2	20·4		
Level of significance	·05		
(b) *Background*			
Urban	67	33	**336**
Rural	72	28	**202**
Total	69	31	**538**
χ^2	1·4		
Level of significance	*		
(c) *Present Occupation*			
Professional, semi-professional, administrative, clerical and commercial	74	26	**19**
Craftsmen and operatives	74	26	**319**
Unskilled (including Service and Protective)	61	39	**203**
Total	69	31	**541**
χ^2	10·6		
Level of significance	·01		
(d) *Residence in Australia*			
Under 5 years	56	44	**163**
5 years and under 10	73	27	**279**
10 years and under 15	61	39	**41**
15 years and over	93	7	**58**
Total	69	31	**541**
χ^2	32·0		
Level of significance	·001		

* Not significant at the 5 per cent level.

Dutch, Italians, and Greeks. The existence of such an association was assumed in this study and the statistical findings have validated it. As one might have expected, too, present job satisfaction is related to the immigrant's position in the occupational hierarchy. The proportion of the respondents in the 'Dissatisfied' category is considerably higher among the unskilled workers than in the remaining two composite groups. An even greater degree of association is to be found between length of residence in Australia and job satisfaction. Although the pattern is not very neat, it seems, nevertheless, that at longer duration of residence the proportion of immigrants who are dissatisfied with their present job is on the decrease (see Table 19 (d)).[11]

The final measure of occupational adjustment used in the survey was a reply to a straightforward question: 'Do you feel that as a result of your migration your occupational and economic position in the world has risen, remained unchanged or fallen?' (Question 32). Analysis of replies to this question has revealed that there is no apparent variation between the birthplace groups with respect to a feeling of being upgraded or downgraded as a result of migration (see Table 20 (a)).[12]

On the matter of rural/urban origin there is a clear cut statistical association between the immigrant's assessment of change in occupational status and his pre-migration background. The figures in Table 20 (b) clearly show that the proportion of respondents who declared themselves as 'Upgraded' is considerably higher among those whose pre-migration background is rural. This conclusion is in line with the findings reported in Chapter 4— the trend away from rural to urban occupations, observed in a comparison of the occupational distribution of the settlers in this survey with those of their fathers. To an average immigrant, a change from the rural way of life and a rural occupation to a job in industry represents a distinct improvement in status.

Finally, as in the case of job satisfaction, the immigrant's assessment of change in occupational status statistically varies with length of residence.[13]

The fact that ethnic origin is not statistically associated with two of the three measures of occupational adjustment used in this chapter—stability of employment, and overall assessment of change in occupational status—means that we must look elsewhere for a causal explanation of these differences among individual immigrants. It is suggested that the factor of crucial importance in this regard is the personal experience and individual pre-dispositions of the immigrants. The following documents show at least three ways in which personal experience affects the issue.

The first consists of extracts from an autobiographical sketch written by a British immigrant. This man had a very unhappy childhood. His father died when he was only two. His mother subsequently married a regular soldier—an N.C.O. in the Guards Brigade in London. He was a harsh man and a great disciplinarian who treated his stepchildren like army recruits.

TABLE 20

Subjects' Assessment of Change in Occupational Status
(%)

		Downgraded and Unchanged	Upgraded	N =
(a)	*Birthplace*			
	British Isles	20	80	174
	Netherlands	20	80	44
	Germany	29	71	28
	Greece and Italy	23	77	52
	Malta	16	84	82
	Poland	22	78	46
	Yugoslavia	21	79	29
	Baltic countries	43	57	21
	Ukraine	14	86	28
	Other central and eastern Europe	29	71	21
	Total	21	79	525
	χ^2		10·3	
	Level of significance		*	
(b)	*Background*			
	Urban	25	75	321
	Rural	15	85	201
	Total	21	79	522
	χ^2		7·8	
	Level of significance		·01	
(c)	*Residence in Australia*			
	Under 5 years	27	73	162
	5 years and under 10	20	80	268
	10 years and under 15	26	74	39
	15 years and over	7	93	56
	Total	21	79	525
	χ^2		10·0	
	Level of significance		·05	

* Not significant at the 5 per cent level.

His idea of bringing up two young boys (my four older sisters had since married) was—rise at 6 o'clock, sniff salt water through the nasal passages, clean teeth, and shoes in freezing weather in the back yard of the dingy slum house where we lived. After this we would then be brought to the breakfast table, and whether we wanted it or not, had to eat two pieces of bread and butter (not margarine as was the custom in the London of my youth), one large cup of good tea and then out by quarter to seven for a walk along the Albert Embankment across the Lambeth Bridge, turn right along the Victoria Gardens, thence down by St. James' Park, en route to the changing or mounting of the Guard in front of Wellington Barracks. My stepfather had told us how to differentiate between the various Guards who performed the mounting duties, and woe betide us if we lied (which we often did) and he checked up to see if we hadn't done what he wanted. . . . To give some idea of just what this man was like, I will illustrate the point by telling, that anything my mother bought, had to be British, and woe betide her or the article if it wasn't. I have seen him smash 2 dozen eggs and the receptacle they were in just because they were stamped 'Holland'. Argument followed argument and I and my family were relieved when he eventually passed away, some 12 months after I returned home, from cancer of the colon.

Meanwhile the writer completed his training in a Technical School and had several jobs as a mechanic in London and Blackpool. When the war broke out he volunteered for the Forces and was eventually trained as an air gunner in the R.A.F. He served in England, the Middle East, and Burma. In 1946 he returned to England and was demobilized but could not settle in civilian employment. He continues his story:

During the years from 1946 to 1950 I squandered money on horses, drink, etc., which I had saved so hard during my service years. I decided on the spur of the moment to emigrate to Australia without giving it much thought. Things moved very quickly and in no time I was en route to 'Down Under' on board M.V. *Georgic*.

Conditions on board weren't anything to enthuse over. We were used to rationing and the like, so the austere conditions on board didn't upset me unduly. I arrived in Australia on February 10, 1950, and was at once impressed with the size of Melbourne and the very obviously high standard of living as compared with Britain. I started work 3 days after my arrival in an agricultural machinery engineering shop, my wages being

£9.3.0 for a 40 hour week, compared with the £6.5.0. for a 44 hour week in England. My workmates were good to me and though one or two took exception to my being a 'Pommy' I really got on very well with them. So much so that ten years after, I am still friendly with some of them. Some 12 months after my arrival I married an Australian and during a period of two years we made 3 moves. First to Swan Hill then back to Kerang and then to Geelong.

I was during this time nursing a desire to return to the United Kingdom, and suddenly homesickness got so much for me that on an impulse I sold up and went home, only to find on arrival that no longer could I live that narrow life that I once enjoyed.

It had been a costly venture for me for I decided after just four months to return, and on January 2, 1956, with my wife seven months pregnant, we arrived back in Australia. My elder daughter was born at Tallangatta on February 21 to our great joy, and nine weeks after we came here to live in Moe where I rent a Housing Commission home for £3.12.0. I work for a firm of Construction Engineers now and am well paid drawing £24.10.0. for 40 hours. Our second daughter Miriam Ann was born on Anzac Day, and our family was complete.

. . . I am absorbed in my garden and home and am certain of one thing, that with two young girls growing up, I would not change my domicile here for England whilst living conditions remain as they are.

The writer of this story is obviously well settled in his job and has found peace and stability after years of living under most trying and unsettled conditions. His successful adjustment is firmly rooted in happy family life. Perhaps this factor alone—a contrast with the man's youth and lack of security right up to the point of his marriage—explains why he has apparently struck deep roots in Moe.

The second document is an extract from an autobiography written by a Hungarian tailor,[14] whose first experience in Australia was full of disappointments. He had hoped to work in his trade on arrival in Australia but was told before he landed in Melbourne that under the terms of contract he would probably be required to work for two years as an agricultural labourer.

From the ship we were taken to Bonegilla Camp for registration to work, and since it was January, the fruit-picking season, our first offer was grape-picking in Barmera, S.A. Myself and two friends registered for this work and were duly despatched to Barmera on 7th February, 1949. Our geographical knowledge of Australia was nil, so we had no idea of the direction or distance we travelled. After travelling practically non-stop for 24 hours we arrived at our destination, Barmera. I could already speak some English, so it was relatively easy to overcome the first day's difficulties in entirely new surroundings. The weather was very hot and the district looked dry, almost explosive. Our first employer was a very fair-minded chap. Being a bachelor, he did the cooking himself—unfortunately he was not very good at it. For a few days we lived on bread, tea and grapes. We did not enjoy any other food. The grapes were not yet ready to pick and we had to wait two weeks before beginning our work. We experienced great difficulties because of this delay and it gave us a very bad start in our new country.

From the day we left the camp we had to pay for the food our families received in Bonegilla, as well as our own board at the farm. Having then 3 children I was charged £4/15/- for a fortnight in Bonegilla and my own board was £3 a week. So when I received my first payment of £2/16/-, after my board for two weeks was taken off, I owed £4/15/- in Bonegilla. The situation grew worse every week. I always owed more than I actually received. This is a point I want to emphasise because it is the cause of many disappointments and bitterness amongst newcomers. We did agree to work away from our family as a term of our contract, but none of us knew about the great distances in Australia. My family was over 500 miles away from me and there was no hope of a quick reunion. There were family camps nearer to us, but because they were fully occupied we had to wait for our turn, which could mean long months. Under the financial conditions mentioned above, I had no hope of saving enough money to be able to visit my family even once a month. Many of our group realised this and left work and returned to Bonegilla, risking deportation or some other punishment. It was also impossible to leave my wife and children without a penny to spend. So we realised that the sooner we found our own accommodation the better. [After four weeks of fruitless search the writer found a disused Nissen hut which had to be fitted with the furniture, bedding, etc.]

How did I manage? Well, I learned for the first time the meaning of H.P. I was able to obtain a table, chairs and three beds on time payment and the farmer gave us two disused mattresses. Only the blankets still had to be obtained. Like an angel from Heaven one day a lady called on us—a representative of a church organisation—and gave us four blankets, some plates and cutlery and a number of other useful things.

I was very happy indeed to receive these goods—not because of their actual value, but because of the intention and the spirit with which they were given to one. They never asked whether I belonged to the same church—as I did not—the only thing they were interested in was to render assistance and help where they were most needed.

My family arrived from Bonegilla in good shape and spirit. The room was not big, but the fact that we were together again was worth more than the number of rooms or the value of the furnishings. Later we were able to add one kitchen-like construction to the hut, and life was much easier from then on.

And so slowly we settled down in our new home and country. We needed a lot of things but we were happy just the same. We knew that with hard work and patience we would be able to improve our condition. I could hardly settle in any work at the beginning. The pick and shovel were too heavy for me, but after three months I was as good at it as any of us, and what was more, I could enjoy my work. I have learned a lot of useful things. When, two years later I left the job to join my brother-in-law and his family in Gippsland, I was a qualified construction worker. We built channels, pipelines, special boxes for water wheels and meters for measuring the quantity of water used up by the lands at irrigation time. I came in personal contact with the pioneers of the district, who had faced and conquered flood, fire and famine for year after year to break up the virgin land, cleared bushland to grow wheat and breed cattle and sheep. It was an unforgettable experience to see the new blocks growing out of rabbit infested areas into a prosperous land of grapes and orchards of citrus. It is gratifying to know that I too have contributed to what it is today in a small way. However, being a tailor for twenty years, I always wished to work at my trade again. This was the main reason for my leaving my job there and moving to Gippsland where a job awaited me. After working one year for a firm here, I decided to start on my own. I worked at it for four years and this period proved to me that my trade was not as good here as it had been in my native country or in Europe for that matter. I could make a living out of it but I could see no advancement nor could I see security in the future. So I gave up my shop and took a position with Gippsland's biggest firm as manager of their footwear department.

This is a story with a happy ending as well as a moral. The writer has been reunited with his family, has a home in Yallourn, and has made friends with many Australians: he has also achieved satisfactory occupational adjustment in spite of a realization that he cannot pursue his old trade.

The third example is that of an unmarried Maltese who decided to emigrate when he was in his late twenties. He, too, was born in poverty—the youngest child in a family of eight. His father eked out the family's living as a stonemason while the four sons worked in the Valetta Dockyard. Carmel (the author of this biography) became an Air Raid Warden during World War II and witnessed many tragedies resulting from the sustained bombing of Malta by the enemy.

> 16th November 1940 we received Air Raid warning—I switched on the siren then we took our positions in the post. Two enemy airplanes were flying low (about 5 o'clock a.m.) —one of them dropped two delayed action bombs—the first one went off in about five minutes and the second ten minutes later. When the first bomb exploded no one was hurt (this tragedy happened near St Mary's Church in Zebbug) and very little damage was done. Soon after the first explosion people rushed out from the underground Air Raid Shelter and went to their nearby houses to see what damage their houses suffered; and this happened when everyone was outside the shelter. This is the most horrible picture I have ever seen in my life—sixteen people were killed instantly, three died on the way to hospital, four later on and twenty-three injured, some of them seriously. A family of seven were completely wiped out, except a small baby who was living with his grandmother. . . .
>
> I left Malta on S.S. *Asturias*—November 28, 1950. Conditions and food aboard the ship were satisfactory except that it was crowded.
>
> When I came ashore at Fremantle I thought that I was dreaming. I was so seasick on board that I thought I was never going to reach Australia alive—three people died on the voyage. In Melbourne I was delighted when I saw the beautiful tall buildings. I never realised that Melbourne was so advanced. I always had the impression that Sydney was the only big city in Australia—Melbourne was less publicized in Malta—so I was wrong.
>
> Through Radio and newspapers I heard about the major projects of Yallourn and Morwell, Victoria. Incidentally, a friend of mine was working in Yallourn with the State Electricity Commission of Victoria . . . The following morning we travelled by train from Flinders Street Station to Moe Station, then by bus to Yallourn. I had a quick round of Yallourn then to the Industrial Officer—he gave me a job as Storeman

with the State Electricity Commission of Victoria. The first few days I lived at the Western Camp then I moved to Eastern Road Hostel—more expensive than the Western Camp but better conditions and good meals. . . .

I spent three months in the Main Store. During this period I was doing a Radio Course by correspondence with the Marconi School of Wireless (Melbourne). At this time I needed some practical experience which was impossible to get in the Main Store. I asked to see the Superintendent of Stores and explained why I wished to be transferred to the Communications Section. He was very kind and ten days later I was transferred to the Radio and Telephones where I am still working up to date. I am very happy to be in Australia and do the job I like. I feel safe here away from the conflicts that rock the Old World.

It is clear from this story that the writer's satisfaction with his job and living conditions, his stability of employment and generally successful occupational adjustment are associated with contrasting conditions between Malta and Australia. The poverty, insecurity of employment, and the horrors of war have been left behind. He feels secure and satisfied in his present situation.

There are, of course, other immigrants whose bad adjustment and feeling of dissatisfaction with the job, and their present status, can also be explained in terms of personal experiences. Often such bad adjustment is connected with separation from family and the uprooting caused by the war. The following example is a case in point—a 49-year-old Latvian labourer as described by the interviewer:

Subject is a sorry, pathetic sight. His only hope was in wife and two children. In 1944 he was a partisan in the forests. He returned to find that the Russians had taken his family. Here, in Australia, he still thinks about them, and it is on these occasions that he drinks. He boasts of spending all his money on gambling and drink. He has lost all hope of returning to Europe to find his family. Here he reads cheap literature and leads a degenerate life.[15]

Sometimes bad occupational adjustment is caused by loss of status resulting from migration; an example is another Latvian who before he fled his country was manager of a large electrical workshop which employed many skilled tradesmen. Today, at the age of 64, he works as an electrical fitter, and his Australian-born foreman is at least twenty years his junior. During the interview he said that the present SEC job seemed a 'great come down';[16] at his age he cannot aspire to a supervisory grade and he is greatly worried about the fact that on account of residential qualifications he will not be able to receive an old age pension.[17]

Yet another example in this category is that of a 32-year-old Russian whose lack of satisfaction with job and general living conditions is aggravated by a feeling of loneliness and homesickness. He was only 16 when, in 1943, his mother and four brothers and sisters were forced by the German invaders to leave their native village in Russia. For the next two years he worked in a German dynamite factory and after the end of the war he was employed by the American Occupation authorities as a truck driver. Then in 1948 he got a job which to him seemed a zenith of his ambitions: a movie camera operator in a Y.M.C.A. film unit in Germany. He had hopes of emigrating to Argentina to work in the film industry but his mother and elder brothers decided to emigrate to Australia. He went with them in 1950 and worked for the first two years with the N.S.W. railways. Subsequently he got a job in the boiler house at Yallourn as conveyor attendant. When interviewed in 1959 he presented a sorry picture of a terribly lonely and homesick man. Much of the trouble with him, as he admitted in the interview, was that he was unable to meet a girl who would want to marry him. There were no Russian girls in Yallourn and few in Melbourne, where he spends the weekends. His sisters and brothers were all married and he had little in common with them. He spends all his earnings on drink and gambling. When he first left his country he did hope to return after a few years. Today, some sixteen years later, he is still determined to return 'as soon as Cold War stops'.

This is how the interviewer describes this man:

> Subject says he cannot speak against Communism. He is a Russian and as he does not really know what happens in Russia he can't very well be a traitor. Is very firm in his condemnation of certain Australian practices. He says that Australian families are selfish. They stick to themselves and are unneighbourly. He thinks agrarian people from Europe should be encouraged by the Government to settle here in their large families. Land leases should be provided. He is unhappy with the Australian government's propaganda to migrants. His promised job was not given to him and he disliked being in a tent when he first came (and unemployed) especially as

he was persuaded to come here instead of Argentina. In this man's room there is evidence of much drinking and card games.[18]

The cases examined in this chapter all point to factors other than ethnic origin in determining the immigrant's occupational adjustment. An immigrant can be considered to be successfully adjusted when he is employed at work in which full advantage is taken of his skill and the social reward, in income, recognition, and status, stands in proportion to his capacities. The Latrobe Valley material suggests that the immigrant's national origin plays little or no part in this nexus.

6

STANDARD OF LIVING

An inquiry into the living standard of the immigrants included in the field survey was one of the central features of the research project. A whole section of the interview schedule (Part IV) contained questions designed to ascertain the basic facts relating to the wages earned by the immigrant: additional sources of income in the family; main heads of expenditure; and the amount of savings. Next, the housing position was recorded, especially with a view to discovering who lived in rented accommodation as opposed to owner-occupied houses; how much the house cost and how the finance was obtained; and the size of the house together with the building material used in construction. Finally, questions were asked with regard to possession of a motor vehicle and some six selected consumer durables (see Appendix C).

This discussion of the findings is primarily concerned with the relationship between the country of origin and the level of income and consumption. The working hypothesis used throughout postulates a statistically significant association between birthplace and wage, family income, spending on consumer durables —to name only a few characteristics. In other words, it is assumed that, depending on the immigrant's birthplace, he can be placed at a given point of income and consumption scales. This, in turn, implies that it might be possible to predict any immigrant's consumption patterns once his origin is known. The following discussion will test some of these assumptions.

Income, Expenditure, and Savings

A summary of the statistical information relating to income, expenditure, and savings is given in Tables 21 and 22. The first of these tables shows striking differences of income and consumption levels in the ten birthplaces.

The distribution of the wage data demonstrates the apparently dominating position of the British-born settlers, whose average weekly wage is the highest and exceeds that of the lowest-paid group (Italy and Greece) by £3 10s. This figure, in fact, is a measure of the spread of the wage levels. Ranking of average wage from the highest to the lowest further reveals the privileged status of the immigrants born in the Baltic states, who come second, followed by Yugoslavia, Germany, and the Netherlands. This picture is in line with the distribution of such pre-migration characteristics of the immigrants as the standard of education and the proportion of skilled workers to unskilled.

Quite apart from differences in the standards of education and levels of skill, there is yet another factor which contributes to the spread of average wage levels amongst the countries of origin. This is the duration of length of residence in Australia. Table 22 (a) shows that, taking all settlers irrespective of birthplace, the level of wages is very significantly different at the specified durations of residence; the average wage goes up by more than £1 at each duration into which the numbers have been grouped. To this effect of time on the earning power of the immigrant must also be added differences in the age structure which were examined in Chapter 4.

It would appear, therefore, that although the level of wages is statistically associated with the immigrant's origin it is not necessarily determined by it. What appears to determine the level of wages is a variety of factors connected with the decision to emigrate, the skill acquired before and after migration, the level of education, and the length of residence in Australia. Thus the Italians and Greeks in the Latrobe Valley do not earn less because they are natives of Italy and Greece but because they tend to be mainly of relatively inferior occupational skills and low educational standards, and with a short period of residence in Australia. Similarly, the British immigrants do not command the high level of wages because of their British birth but by virtue of the length of residence combined with relatively high occupational skills. This last seems to be the decisive factor in determining the level of wages as shown in the case of the Baltic group.

Family income, as defined in this study, bears only indirect relation to occupational skills. Besides the wages of the immigrant wage-earner himself, family income includes any additional earnings that go to make up total receipts of the family over a week. These include overtime, wife's earnings, and board paid by children and lodgers.

In spite of this limitation, however, certain features of the statistical material on family income may be worth comment. First—as noted previously of wages—is the disparity between the highest, Netherlands £23, and the lowest, Italy and Greece £16 8s. The difference is £6 12s., which is greater than the difference in the level of wages. It is clear from an analysis of the main

H

TABLE 21

Selected Economic Characteristics of the Immigrants by Birthplace*

Item	Birthplace										Total	χ^2†	d.f.	Level of significance
	British Isles	Netherlands	Germany	Greece and Italy	Malta	Poland	Yugoslavia	Baltic	Ukraine	Other C. & E. Europe				
(a) Wage‡														
N =	183	45	28	52	83	46	31	22	28	22	540			
A.M.	19·3	17·9	18·3	15·8	17·3	17·3	18·4	18·5	18·1	17·8	18·1	68·7	27	·001
S.D.	4·1	2·7	3·4	2·8	2·6	2·2	3·3	2·8	2·9	2·8	3·4			
(b) Family income‡														
N =	183	45	28	52	83	46	31	22	28	21	539			
A.M.	22·4	23·0	21·8	16·4	19·1	19·8	21·5	20·7	20·7	19·7	21·0	73·4	18	·001
S.D.	6·1	6·9	4·9	3·7	4·3	4·5	6·0	4·4	5·1	4·9	5·5			
(c) Family expenditure‡														
N =	182	45	28	52	83	46	31	22	28	21	538			
A.M.	19·0	20·2	17·7	12·6	17·3	17·5	18·5	17·0	19·4	16·6	19·2	52·9	18	·001
S.D.	5·9	6·8	4·9	3·9	4·9	4·9	3·8	4·4	4·2	5·4	4·5			

(d) Family savings‡

N =	106	24	21	34	35	19	13	15	8	10	285			
A.M.	3·1	2·5	4·0	3·7	1·8	2·2	2·7	3·7	1·3	2·7	2·8	9·0	9	§
S.D.	3·3	3·1	3·2	3·4	2·6	3·1	4·0	3·5	2·7	3·8	3·3			
Proportion of savers (%)	58·9	54·5	75·0	65·4	42·2	41·3	41·9	68·2	27·6	45·5	53·1	28·9	9	·001

d.f. = degrees of freedom.
A.M. = Arithmetic mean.
S.D. = Standard deviation from the mean.
* All those interviewed, married and single, were asked for full details of their receipts and spending.

The following definitions were used:

Wage: the amount received weekly under the appropriate award.
Family income: Wage, plus extra earnings (e.g. overtime, wife's earnings, board from children and boarders).
Family expenditure: All kinds of expenditure including consumer goods, services and durables, repayments of mortgage and interest.
Family savings: Residual—the amount left each week after expenditure as defined above.

The terms 'Family income', etc. applied to both married and single men.

† The computation of chi square is based on grouped data in which the numbers of those interviewed in the specified birthplaces were compared in the various categories of Wage, Family income, Family expenditure and Family savings.
‡ £ per week.
§ Not significant at the 5 per cent level.

TABLE 22

Selected Economic Characteristics of the Immigrants by Period of Residence in Australia

Period of Residence in Australia

Item	Under 6 years	6 years and under 15 years	15 years and over	Total	χ †	d.f.	Level of significance
(a) Wage†					35·4	8	·001
N =	**180**	**302**	**58**	**540**			
A.M.	17·1	18·4	19·5	18·1			
S.D.	2·9	3·3	4·5	3·4			
(b) Family income†					44·3	12	·001
N =	**180**	**302**	**58**	**540**			
A.M.	19·8	21·2	21·6	21·0			
S.D.	6·1	5·3	5·7	5·5			
(c) Family expenditure†					22·9	10	·05
N =	**180**	**302**	**57**	**539**			
A.M.	16·6	18·5	18·6	19·2			
S.D.	6·1	5·2	5·3	4·5			
(d) Family savings†					·616	2	§
N =	**76**	**154**	**22**	**252**			
A.M.	3·1	2·5	3·0				
S.D.	3·3	3·2	3·4	53·1	4·8	2	§
Proportion of savers (%)	57·3	49·0	61·4				

For definitions and notes see Table 21.

components of family income in the two extreme groups that the high ranking of the Dutch settlers is because a relatively high proportion of the men have grown-up children who live with the family and pay board.[1]

By contrast, Italians and Greeks in the Latrobe Valley are mostly single or have left their wives behind in Europe; many more of them live in hostels than do members of other birthplace groups,[2] and consequently they are unable to receive additional income from lodgers.

Secondly, the period of residence in Australia is a factor of some significance (see Table 22) . It appears that the longer the duration of residence in Australia the higher is the family income. This, however, is almost wholly accounted for by the rise in the immigrant's wage.

In the case of family expenditure (Table 21 (c)) , the disparity between the highest average weekly expenditure (Netherlands, £20 2s.) and the lowest (Italy and Greece, £12 6s.) is £7 6s., which is greater again than those of wages and family income.

These differences cannot be attributed solely to the size of family, as family income can. This can be shown by comparing the immigrants from the Netherlands with the Maltese. Both these groups have larger families than average,[3] and both consist mostly of fairly recent arrivals. Yet the Dutch settlers spend nearly £3 a week more than the Maltese people. It would seem that, because the Dutch and other immigrants from northwest Europe are used to a higher standard of living, they spend more. This points to the cultural standards imported from Europe as one of the determinants of economic behaviour. The other determinant, the size of family, is shown to explain the differences between some east European groups, for example, the Ukrainians and the Baltic people. The Ukrainians, whose family rank is as high as that of the Baltic people, spend £2 4s. per week more than the latter group. They do this not because they consume more as Ukrainian-born but because they have more children per family than the Baltic settlers, and a greater proportion of them are building their houses or are still repaying the interest and capital borrowed to do this.[4]

The relatively low expenditure on the part of Italians and Greeks is connected with the fact that they are mostly single men and hostel dwellers. In that group one specific item of expenditure is worth noting—remittances to the old country. This item is quite substantial: it averages 30s. a week for Italians and Greeks as compared, for example, with the Polish-born, whose spending under this heading amounts to 10s. per week. An average weekly outlay of 30s. per head in a group whose average expenditure amounts to about £12 10s. represents a not inconsiderable burden, and indicates the extent to which the immigrants from southern Europe support their kin who have been left behind. These regular remittances home, added to the relatively high savings,[5] no doubt reflect on the level of consumption amongst the Italians and the Greeks. Whether or not this is a permanent feature of their behaviour could only be ascertained by comparing the income, expenditure, and saving levels of several southern European groups of different durations of residence. The group in this study, however, consists mostly of recent arrivals whose behaviour seems typical of southern Europeans studied by other authors.[6] These Italians and Greeks maintain a very low level of consumption while saving up (through remittances to Europe and savings in Australia) in order to bring out their fiancées, wives, and other members of their families.

The statistical findings relating to family savings are a little more confusing. The point of interest here is the distribution of savers and non-savers by birthplace and the relationship between the average weekly savings and the proportion of savers in each birthplace.[7] The fact that there is a close statistical association between these two characteristics (savers/non-savers and birthplace) throws some light on the considerable range of average savings shown in Table 21 (d). Thus, the relatively high average weekly savings among the Germans, Italians, Greeks, and natives of the Baltic states reflect the high proportions of those who do save for reasons discussed in the preceding paragraph. Conversely, the relatively low average amount of savings amongst the Ukrainians is accounted for by the low proportion of savers in that group. A relatively high proportion (just under 60 per cent) of the Ukrainians included in this study are either still building their own houses or paying back the capital borrowed for the purpose of buying material and equipment; another, not inconsiderable burden, is the regular remittances to the immigrants' families behind the Iron Curtain. The average sum is about £1 2s. 6d. per week, which is considerably in excess of the 10s. a week amongst the Poles, and nearer to the 30s. per week of the Italians and Greeks.[8]

The period of residence in Australia statistically varies with the level of expenditure but not with the level of savings.[9] It seems that a rise from mean weekly expenditure of £16 12s., for those with length of residence of less than six years, by nearly £2 to £18 10s. for those resident six years and under fifteen years, represents a transition from the initial period of settling in to the second phase associated with such circumstances as increase in the size of the family, purchase or construction of one's own dwelling place, and all the consumer durables for the needs of the family. The transition is also seen in the drop in the proportion of savers in the critical period from six to fourteen years of residence. Beyond the fifteenth year of residence the proportion of savers rises again and so does the amount of savings, but expenditure stays almost constant; this is possible because at this duration of residence there is a slight rise in wage and family income.

Housing

The majority of all those interviewed in the field survey (401 in a group of 541) live in private houses.[10] A tabulation of the type of accommodation in conjunction with the duration of residence in Australia[11] (grouped in three periods: under 6 years, 6 years and under 15 years, 15 years and over) reveals the inverse relationship between the period of residence and the proportion of the immigrants housed in hostels;[12] the proportion of hostel dwellers decreases after six years of residence. This shows that, as expected, for a majority of hostel dwellers this is a temporary form of accommodation.

Among the immigrants who live in private houses there is a noteworthy distinction between two regional groupings of birthplaces (see Table 23 (a)). The majority, consisting mainly of the British, Dutch, and German immigrants, live in rented dwellings. On the other hand, in the east European group the proportion of owner-occupied houses varies from 84 per cent for Yugoslavs to 96 per cent amongst the Ukrainians.

The existence of such striking differences coincides with what has been earlier described as mode of migration, namely, the distribution between 'voluntary' and 'forced' migrants. It will be clear that most of the immigrants who live in owner-occupied houses are also mostly 'forced' migrants, that is, the Displaced Persons of World War II. That they tend to live in their own houses could, of course, be attributed to the policy of the SEC, which gives high priority in the allocation of houses at Yallourn and East and North Newborough to the settlers it sponsors, chiefly the assisted British immigrants.

TABLE 23
Privately–housed Immigrants: Statistical Summary

	Birthplace										Pre-migration Residence*		
	British Isles	Nether-lands	Ger-many	Greece and Italy	Malta	Poland	Yugo-slavia	Baltic coun-tries	Ukraine	Other C. & E. Europe	Total	Urban	Rural
(a) Method of acquisition:							(%)						
N =	**143**	**39**	**22**	**13**	**63**	**37**	**25**	**14**	**28**	**11**	**395**	**268**	**126**
Owner-occupied	13	23	23	62	35	86	84	86	96	45	41	31	61
Rented	87	77	77	38	65	14	16	14	4	55	59	69	39
(b) Purchase price:							(£)						
N =	**8**	**5**	**4**	**6**	**6**	**10**	**7**	**4**	**1**	—	**51**	**33**	**18**
Average price	2,188	2,550	2,125	1,500	2,000	950	1,036	2,250	2,250	—	1,721	1,917	1,361
S.D.†	1,148	758	1,251	689	1,215	889	567	409			1,027	1,109	758
(c) Cost of erection:							(£)						
N =	**10**	**3**	**1**	**2**	**15**	**22**	**13**	**8**	**26**	**5**	**105**	**47**	**58**
Average cost	1,850	2,083	250	3,250	2,117	2,659	2,865	2,688	2,683	3,000	2,526	2,447	2,591
S.D.	1,049	764	—	—	895	750	1,153	1,050	1,174	1,250	1,057	1,131	999

						(%)						
(d) Finance:												
N =	**18**	**9**	**5**	**7**	**19**	**31**	**17**	**9**	**26**	**5**	**146**	**79**	**67**
Loans	56	67	60	43	32	81	53	78	81	60	64	62	66
Own savings	44	33	40	57	68	19	47	22	19	40	36	38	34
							(%)						
(e) Structure:												
N =	**145**	**39**	**22**	**13**	**64**	**38**	**25**	**14**	**28**	**10**	**398**	**269**	**128**
Brick, stone, con- crete	12	5	—	15	2	24	12	21	29	9	12	10	14
Wood or fibro	88	95	100	85	98	76	88	79	71	91	88	90	86
							(%)						
(f) Rooms in dwellings:												
N =	**143**	**39**	**22**	**13**	**62**	**38**	**25**	**12**	**28**	**11**	**393**	**267**	**125**
Five or more	72	69	50	54	65	53	76	67	68	55	66	66	67
Less than five	28	31	50	46	35	47	24	33	32	45	34	34	33

* Totals for urban and rural sometimes differ slightly from those for birthplaces because a few are excluded in the 'not stated' category.
† S.D. = standard deviation from the arithmetic mean (average).

This argument, however, is scarcely defensible because several other ethnic groups, the Maltese, the Dutch, and the Germans, for instance, are also mainly housed by the SEC or the Housing Commission of Victoria. An answer to this puzzle probably lies in the circumstances connected with the mode of migration of the east European group as compared with that of the voluntary immigrants from western and southern Europe. To the 'forced' migrant home-ownership is an index of security, a triumph over the cruelty, disappointment, and privation of the long years of the war and its aftermath. Most of these migrants come, moreover, from countries where home-ownership is rare; where to own one's home is a sign of success and prosperity—a class symbol. Against their remembered background there seems little doubt that immigrants regard the purchase of a home in Australia as a substantial step up the social ladder. Again, a home of one's own, insulated against neighbours by a plot of ground, must often be regarded by immigrants as an effective refuge in a new and strange environment.

Of the 160 privately-housed persons interviewed only about one-third (53) did not build the houses they occupy. A few of these bought dwellings which they had been renting from the Victorian Housing Commission or the SEC, but the majority bought them through a local estate agent or directly from the owner. The figures given in Table 23 (b) indicate a large range of average prices from £950 (Poland) to £2,550 (the Netherlands), but the numbers are too small to permit statistical tests that would demonstrate any differences among the various birthplaces.[13] The only comparison that can be safely undertaken is the breakdown into 'urban' and 'rural'. This shows that respondents with rural background tend to pay less than those with urban background.[14]

Much the same difficulty has been experienced in the analysis of the differences in the cost of erection. The lowest average cost of erection has been recorded in the case of the ten British-born respondents (£1,850), and the respondents of east European origin seem to have built themselves more costly dwellings (for example Yugoslavia £2,865, Baltic states £2,688, Poland £2,659). These marked differences would perhaps point to the different periods when the houses were built. On examination of the data, however, it appears that only two out of ten British-born migrants who built their own houses did so before World War II; the majority—of whom some arrived in Australia as young children in the twenties—waited till the fifties. In this regard the British group do not differ markedly from, say, the Polish immigrants who also built their houses in the fifties. It seems that most eastern Europeans built in the latter part of the fifties and paid higher prices for building materials, but this need not wholly account for the differences noted in Table 23. The fact, however, that there is no statistically significant difference in the cost of erection between the 'rural' and 'urban' categories[15] suggests that there is a certain uniformity in the type and standard of dwellings erected by the immigrants, irrespective of their country of origin.[16] But this evidence is inconclusive.

From Table 23 (d) it is clear that the majority of the 146 immigrants who have paid for their own dwellings have raised a loan from one of the credit institutions such as banks or building societies, less frequently from relatives or friends. The only group which seems to finance housing from their own savings are the southern Europeans, who stand out in this respect from the rest of birthplace groupings.

Some interesting points arise out of the analysis of the type of structure. Only about one-tenth of the immigrants live in brick dwellings, but this proportion is not uniform for all birthplaces. Three of these stand out—Poland, Ukraine, and the Baltic countries—each with about one-quarter of dwellings built of brick. The only apparent explanation is that a brick dwelling seems to give the owner the impression of greater security, which is in line with the characteristic tendency towards house-ownership already observed amongst the former Displaced Persons. Some of the impressive residences built of brick or brick and timber are not necessarily those to which the immigrants have moved immediately upon arrival in the Latrobe Valley. Most families who now occupy houses they built themselves first lived in some kind of temporary accommodation. Often these were little more than shacks or garages which were gradually replaced by permanent dwellings (see Plates 1-2). In some instances a kind of ethnic succession can be observed: a Polish family, for example, vacated a shack they had built well to the back of their block of land in Old Newborough and moved to a spacious brick veneer residence on the same block, then they promptly rented the shack to a Maltese family of seven.

The final feature of the housing position is the size of the dwelling measured in terms of the number of rooms. This proved to be a rather unsatisfactory measure for observation, and visits to different types of houses suggested enormous differences in the size of rooms. For example, East and North Newborough with its large British-born population consists entirely of relatively small prefabricated SEC houses, some 80 per cent of which have five rooms or more; by contrast, the Ukrainian and the Polish people in Old Newborough live in much larger dwellings subdivided into fewer rooms. The size of certain rooms is a reflection of their importance in these homes. Observation suggests that the kitchen, in particular, has a very important function in east European families; often it is the largest single room in the house, and there the family eat, spend their leisure, and receive visitors (interviews were invariably conducted in the kitchen). A central feature of each kitchen is a large fuel cooking stove; electricity is rarely used for cooking, for wood can still be collected in the bush.

The immigrant's concern with the security of housing looms large in his process of adjustment, particularly when he is unable or unwilling to claim his share of the housing provided by his employer or a government instrumentality. This concern is not just a brief passing phase of the process of settlement but may take long years of saving, discomfort, and the sheer hard work of construction. As this study has shown, sometimes the immigrant's first home will be a shack or a garage erected on his block of land. This may have to suffice for several years while he saves up money to purchase building materials and eventually starts the slow process of building a house, usually with the help of his compatriots and neighbours. Even when the house is built it often consists of one or two bedrooms and a large kitchen which serves as living-room and parlour. More rooms are eventually added and the final product is invariably a large, spacious, and solidly-built residence.

Some immigrants are more fortunate, as for example a Dutchman who managed to crate up his prefabricated house and re-erect it in Moe. But, as shown in the story that he wrote himself (in English), the whole experiment was not without disappointments, and his Dutch home physically transported to Australia did not seem like a home at first.

> We had contacted a former friend—living in Yallourn and he could find accommodation for us for the first weeks in Moe. We had decided to go by plane, while house and furniture would travel by boat. It would arrive about six weeks later in Melbourne.
>
> Wednesday 18th April 1951 at 7 p.m. our plane leaves

Amsterdam after being farewelled by family and many friends. The K.L.M. brings us via Damascus—Karachi—Calcutta and Singapore within five days to Australia a touch down in Darwin a two hour stop in Sydney—with next stop Melbourne. But nobody there to welcome us. We had travelled faster than the telegram from Sydney. Dogtired we couldn't find any accommodation because we arrived the day before Anzac-day and all hotels were booked out. The next day we arrived safely in Moe. The house—we could use—was not yet finished but we had somewhere to stay. We had a look around in our new surrounding—heard the song of the magpies and noticed the smell of gumleaves. It was not hard to get a job as a labourer and I started working straight away. We bought a block of land on the outside of the town. After many weeks the boxes with house and furniture arrived and we started building.

We built our house in 22 days of which 21 days of pouring rain! What a difference with the movie we had seen before of 'sunny Australia'! We chopped bush and teetrees and dug trenches to get rid of all the water. There was no possibility of drying our clothes overnight so next morning we started again and again in our still wet clothes. And were we proud when the roof was on! But that's not the end yet. To get water except from the rain—the next main pipeline was over 600 feet away. We dug and laid a private line. The SEC didn't allow us to use the electrical installation. Instead of an installation—well covered and protected in pipes—an electrician had to 'wire' our house. Well it certainly *is* wired! Over the ceiling it is just a mass of unprotected rubber cable. I think I am very old-fashioned but I still prefer the European way of electricity-supply by far! And a lot more things had to be done. It's the finishing touch what makes the difference in a lot of things. We had a 'house' but not a 'home'. And we wanted to do so many more things like fences—the garden— the bathroom—painting the house and so on, but the financial circumstances stopped us in our efforts.

Ownership of Motor Vehicles and Consumer Durables

Two points of interest emerge from the statistical analysis of ownership of motor vehicles. First is the fact that, as compared with all Australian males aged 20 and over, the proportion of all those interviewed who own motor vehicles is considerably lower: 43 per cent of the immigrants, compared with about 60 per cent of Australian-born males.[17] Second, as Table 24 shows, there are very significant differences in the proportion of vehicle owners from each birthplace. The fact that there is a definite ethnic pattern is indicated in the varying proportion of owners of motor vehicles, ranging from 60 per cent of the British immigrants to 22 per cent of the Poles, and 20 per cent of the Italians and Greeks.

The relatively high proportion of British-born respondents who own a motor vehicle is almost precisely equal to the estimated proportion of vehicle owners among all males aged 20 and over in Victoria; the immigrants born in the Netherlands and those born in Germany have nearly as great a percentage. In comparison with these two birthplace groups (virtually all of whom arrived in Australia after World War II) the British proportion does not seem very high in a group nearly a quarter of whose members arrived in Australia before World War II, and presumably had better chances of establishing themselves.[18] The Italians and Greeks, on the other hand, are mostly recent arrivals: more than two-thirds had been in Australia less than four years at the time of the survey. Moreover, they have the lowest proportion of skilled and semi-skilled men (see Table 17), and have lower incomes than any other ethnic group (see Table 21). A combination of these three factors is clearly responsible for the low proportion of motor vehicle owners in that group.

The very low proportions of vehicle owners in the east European groups cannot be explained in terms of duration of residence, for the great majority of these men had lived in Australia for eight years and more. Nor is there a clear relationship between the level of income (Table 21), and possession of a motor vehicle. The explanation for this interesting characteristic of the east European groups must be rather sought in their inclination to own a house and the resulting very considerable financial burden. The impression gained in interviews strongly suggests that the Poles, the Ukrainians, and the people from the Baltic states are as keen to own a vehicle as any other respondent in the survey.[19]

Little need be said about the breakdown of vehicle owners into those who possess a new or second-hand vehicle (see Table 24). It would seem that, on the whole, the immigrants prefer to purchase a second-hand vehicle. There are differences in this regard between the birthplaces but there is no clear-cut pattern such as has been observed in the matter of ownership of motor vehicles.

TABLE 24

Statistical Association between Birthplace and Possession of a Motor Vehicle
(%)

Birthplace	Ownership of Vehicle N =			Kind of Vehicle N =		
	Nil	Own		New	Used	
British Isles	41	60	180	34	66	106
Netherlands	44	56	45	12	88	25
Germany	46	54	28	27	73	15
Greece and Italy	80	20	51	10	90	10
Malta	63	37	83	32	68	31
Poland	78	22	46	30	70	10
Yugoslavia	65	35	31	27	73	11
Baltic countries	77	23	22	20	80	5
Ukraine	69	31	29	67	33	9
Other central and eastern Europe	55	45	22	40	60	10
Total	57	43	537	31	69	232
x^2	49·7			*		
Level of significance	·001			*		
Urban†	49	51	333	29	71	170
Rural†	70	30	201	34	66	61
x^2	21·9			·530		
Level of significance	·001			‡		

* Test of significance not possible because of smallness of numbers.
† Totals may differ slightly from those for birthplaces because a few are excluded in the 'not stated' category.
‡ Not significant at the 5 per cent level.

One of the questions included in the interview schedule concerned the possession of certain consumer durables. The following household goods considered as the most important items were listed: vacuum cleaner, refrigerator, washing machine, television set, radiogram, and floor polisher. Score values were assigned to each of these so that the person who had, for example, three of the most expensive items (a television set, a refrigerator, and a radiogram) scored 15, someone who owned only two such expensive items scored 10, and so on.

The tabulation of the proportions of immigrants of each birthplace who scored different values reveals no consistent pattern, as was the case in the possession of a motor vehicle. Table 25 shows that the proportions in each birthplace who scored 10 or more points range from 23 to 68 per cent. There are puzzling differences within broad regional groupings which may be seen

TABLE 25

*Statistical Association between Birthplace and Possession of Selected Consumer Durables**
(%)

	Score Value†			
Birthplace	Under 7	7 and under 10	10 and over	N =
British Isles	21	24	55	145
Netherlands	40	20	40	40
Germany	27	23	50	22
Greece & Italy	62	15	23	13
Malta	25	23	52	64
Poland	53	16	32	38
Yugoslavia	16	16	68	25
Baltic countries	43	29	29	14
Ukraine	29	14	57	28
Other central and eastern Europe	50	—	50	12
Total	30	21	49	401
χ^2†		18·6		
Level of significance		0·5		
Urban	29	23	49	270
Rural	32	17	51	130
χ^2		1·8		
Level of significance		‡		

Note: Percentages may not add up to 100 because of rounding. Total number for urban and rural differs slightly from that for birthplaces because one has been excluded from the 'not stated' category.

* See also p. 105.

† Score values under 10 have been grouped in the chi square test.

‡ Not significant at the 5 per cent level.

in the following pairs of birthplaces: British Isles: 55, and north-west Europe: 40; Greece and Italy: 23, and Malta: 52; Poland: 32, and Ukraine: 57.

Another interesting feature of Table 25 is a similarity of standards between immigrants of rural and urban backgrounds. This suggests that all immigrants, irrespective of their pre-migration background, adopt a uniform pattern of behaviour in regard to material possessions. Perhaps time is the decisive and equalizing factor in the long run. Observations have shown that all the immigrants follow a definite system of priorities in furnishing and equipping their homes. First the immigrant buys his bedroom furniture, often the most expensive, which he proudly shows to visitors.[20] Next the kitchen is equipped with a refrigera-

tor and furnished with a dining table and chairs. Finally the
television set and a three-piece suite is purchased for the living-
room. The last two items, however, are often separated in time,
for the survey has shown that many living-rooms were found
completely empty save for a T.V. set.[21]

The style of furnishings and the interior decoration of the house
are also remarkably uniform in most of the houses that were
visited. It seems that the immigrants adopt the standards imposed
by the commercialized type of culture in which they live: the
quality and the style of their furnishings and decorations are
those which are common to most people in the district; the only
differences observed are based on the length of residence and size
of family income. An occasional embroidery hung up in the
bedrooms of Ukrainian homes, or a piece of lace proudly displayed
by a Maltese family, are about all that is left of the distinctly
ethnic character of the old homestead in Europe.

The only group that seems to have retained such ethnic characteristics as can be seen in furnishings and interior decorations
are the Dutch people. The following extract from a report by
one of the interviewers, whose work was mainly concerned with
the Dutch families, describes how several typically Dutch features
have been retained in the style of living:

> Dutch homes are mostly neat and trim in appearance, and
> inside are extremely neat and tidy. Many homes are furnished
> in the traditional Dutch style with dark-coloured furniture
> and a dark reddish-coloured thick tapestry pinned in a
> triangular fashion over the mantelpiece. Easy chairs are spread
> around the room, and there is usually a sideboard on which
> coffee cups are stacked ready for use; a distinctive Dutch
> habit is to place teaspoons in a cup on the sideboard. The
> heavier tones in furnishings are usually in the homes of older
> Dutch families, younger couples prefer light-coloured furniture
> with a small coffee-table in place of the sideboard. There are
> usually many small souvenirs and national symbols spread
> around the room—these mostly are plates or objects with the
> name of the town in Holland engraved on it. In the better
> class homes there are very small brass or copper objects placed
> around the room. Other popular objects include pieces of
> 'Delft blue' chinaware, wooden cuckoo clocks, on the tapestry
> a number of objects are tacked on, e.g., clogs, windmills and
> other reminders of Holland. Another distinctive Dutch feature
> is the number of wall lamps which give a soft glow. As further
> decoration many people hang a thick tapestry on the walls

I

of the lounge or entrance hall. Two or three families visited had furniture which they had shipped out from Holland, in this case the furniture was made of a very strong oak-wood.

There are differences in the style of decorations according to religion—in Roman Catholic families there are large crucifixes placed prominently in the room, and some families have made a special shelf on which to place statues of the Saints. In the Reformed Church families some have an organ and there is usually an engraved biblical text on the wall. There does not seem to be much relation between continuing the Dutch style of furnishing and personal and social adjustment in Australia—most women said that they furnished the house in a Dutch manner because they thought that it was more tasteful, and brighter than the Australian way of furnishing. They feel that Australian homes are too bare and that the only way to make the place look cosy and homely is to place large tapestries around the room. . . . Dutch houses are mostly distinctive from outside because of the open, spotlessly white curtains, and at night-time the families often sit together in a lighted room with the curtains wide open.

Dutch kitchens are different from other kitchens because of the habit of hanging large cooking utensils around the room. Often there is a tea-towel with a Dutch motto pinned up on the kitchen door. Nearly every housewife uses a primus-stove to cook with, as this saves electricity, and Dutch housewives prefer to cook this way rather than to roast food. The brightly painted solid earthenware saucepans and dishes also give a brighter appearance to the room. Many housewives have canisters which they bought in Holland.

Dutch families say they are able to eat more and better foods out here—they can give their children meat once a day, and also fruit, they eat butter instead of margarine, but still eat a lot of potatoes, with other vegetables. The table is usually set in a rather bare manner, with a large bowl of meat and vegetables placed in the centre, from which everybody helps themselves. A popular meat is continental smoked sausages. Those who are really homesick for Holland have Dutch foods for every meal—quite a few of the local stores stock imported Dutch foods at a little more than local prices.

The discussion of the living standards of immigrants in the Latrobe Valley has revealed several interesting features. First is the seemingly important part played by ethnic origin in determining the level of wages, family income, and expenditure, as well as the proportion of those who save. This assumption has not been fully proved. It has been found that the point on the income and expenditure scales at which an immigrant comes is only partly connected with his ethnic origin. The decisive factors appear to be the period of residence in Australia, the immigrant's occupational background in Europe, and his family situation.

Second is an overriding impression gained by the observer of a similarity in the standards of living among all immigrants, irrespective of their ethnic origin. In some parts of the world migrant groups have continued their own particular way of life and have resisted assimilation to the consumption habits, wage levels, etc. of those about them, for example, the Doukhobors and Old Order Amish. Though there was no reason to assume that there were any such groups in the Latrobe Valley it seemed worth while to test the hypothesis that people of different ethnic origins would behave differently. In fact, it is apparent that they do not do so, and that the migrant groups of the Valley are not dissimilar from the majority of those studied elsewhere.

We have found, for example, that the eastern Europeans prefer to build their own houses rather than live in rented accommodation, and the southern Europeans are conspicuous for their reluctance to borrow money for house-building, and yet that there is, nevertheless, broad uniformity in the style of living. Not only is it observable in the housing estates of East and North Newborough, Morwell, parts of Moe and of course in Yallourn, but also in such private housing areas as Old Newborough, Moe, and sections of Yallourn North. Everywhere the style of living is the same. Once the immigrant has graduated from some form of temporary accommodation in a shack or garage to a permanent dwelling he becomes indistinguishable from his neighbours. The impressive brick residences of Old Newborough house the Polish, Ukrainian, German, and Australian families alike, and, similarly, the rows of weatherboard cottages in the southern part of Moe, with their television antennae and trim little front gardens, look remarkably uniform, and their inhabitants cannot be readily identified as belonging to this or that birthplace.

Finally there is the feeling of pride and satisfaction shown by the immigrants when they describe their material possessions and invite the researcher to inspect their houses. This is how one of the interviewers recorded her impression of a Ukrainian couple:

I noticed that the subject had strong feelings of pride and satisfaction because he had come to Australia with nothing and by working hard had built a fine house in which he still continues to invest his money. It seems that he saves all money remaining after £10 has been spent on living. When the required amount has been saved he buys articles of furniture and other equipment for house. He always pays cash (*Interview No. 302*).

To this man the possession of a house and everything in it symbolizes the wellbeing and security gained in Australia. His roots have been struck deep in more than a physical sense.

7
THE IMMIGRANT FAMILY

The study of the immigrant family was one of the central features in the research reported in this book. Chapter 4 gave the broad features of the immigrant family in terms of its demographic characteristics, such as duration of marriage and number of children. This chapter is concerned with some of the functions of the family, and the way it meets the problems facing it in a new environment.

Kinship Ties

Mention has already been made, also in Chapter 4, of the part played by kinship in the process of migration and settlement. In the actual field survey an attempt was made to enumerate all persons other than the members of the nuclear family (husband, wife, and their children) resident in the respondent's home.[1] The data relating to the size and composition of the households, however, only partly reflect the influence of kinship on these processes.

Out of 385 households 344 are nuclear families, and only 41 households include other persons who were classified as 'boarders'. In a few instances these included persons of birthplace other than that of the head of the household, but in most cases were adult relatives, such as his parents, siblings, and cousins.[2] Only one instance of a three-generation household was recorded: a Maltese immigrant in Yallourn North who lived with his wife, one married son, and the grandchildren. He was one of the early pioneers in the district.

It seems clear, therefore, that, as residential units at any rate, the immigrant households do not absorb other members of the family who follow the head of the household and his wife. The extended family living in large households as in Malta, Italy, or Yugoslavia is rarely reproduced in Australia. The original immigrant's brothers, sisters, cousins, and their spouses may occasionally be accommodated in his house; but this is a temporary arrangement, and sooner or later lack of space compels them to move out and seek new accommodation. If they have a good job they will establish themselves in the same district and will

naturally maintain close relations with their relatives, as shown
in the following examples of Maltese families:

> Respondent arrived in Australia in 1950 and his wife one year
> later. He was preceded by his two brothers (1948, 1949) both
> of whom are married and live in Newborough. His unmarried
> sister arrived in 1955 and lives with the subject. Wife's kin
> include two nieces and a nephew who arrived in 1952-4 and
> now live in Morwell and a sister who lives in Moe (*Interview
> No. 250 (Yallourn North)*).
>
> Respondent has no relatives in Australia but his wife (year of
> arrival 1954) has one aunt (1950) who lives with them and
> another (1951) who lives in Geelong; her aunt's mother
> (1953) lives a few houses away in Yallourn North with two
> cousins (1950) one of whom is married to an Australian; a
> third cousin (1958) lives in Melbourne. The latest arrival is
> a brother, his wife and son (1959) who temporarily live in the
> respondent's house (*Interview No. 236 (Yallourn North)*).

These examples point to the importance of the extended family
(and the part played by kinship ties) among the Maltese settlers;
these are units not necessarily all under one roof but very often
they live in fairly close proximity to one another and therefore
perpetuate strong family ties that existed before migration.[3]

It would be difficult to find exact counterparts of the Maltese
extended family in other birthplace groups. Perhaps the nearest
example is that of a group of Dutch families in Moe who belong
to the *Gereformeerde Kerk* and who assisted one another by providing finance and housing in the process of migration (see pp.
176-7), but in no single instance does the ramification of kinship
ties extend in this group beyond the first cousins and the in-laws.

Amongst the east Europeans kinship ties as a rule are confined
to the nuclear family. This is, of course, understandable if one
remembers that for political reasons the immigrants from these
countries are unable to bring out members of their families. The
weakening of family ties as a result of emigration has been docu-
mented in several studies and there is no need to dwell on this
obvious point.[4] What is of interest, however, is the discovery of
a substitute relationship in the east European group and particularly the Ukrainians. The relationship that substitutes for kinship
ties is the *kum* relationship. It is well known in the Slav countries
and stands for a close tie uniting one family with another family
whose members have acted as godparents to one or more children
of the other family. Often these obligations are reciprocated and

the ties therefore become even stronger. To be a godparent implies a duty to provide for the godchild if the parents die or in other emergencies. The godparent should also remember his godchild at Christmas, feasts of the child's patron saint, religious ceremonies connected with the First Communion and Confirmation, and special family occasions. Under these conditions the *kum* relationship assumes a very important role in an ethnic community, particularly where there is no extended kinship.[5]

Family under Stress

Of the 384 family units in this study, a total of 187, or just under half, said that they had experienced difficulties and problems of one sort or another. No attempt was made to tabulate the incidence of these statements in conjunction with such characteristics as country of birth or period of residence in Australia. Such a procedure would be dubious, for it would ignore important differences in the personality and mood of the interviewee and the quality of *rapport* established between him and the interviewer.

What was found particularly when analysing different types of 'problems' reported by the interviewers was that about two-thirds of them affected the very integrity of the family as a social unit. Financial difficulties, illness, problems of finding employment for adolescent children, marital difficulties, child behaviour problems, excessive drinking, inexpert household management— these were some of the problems revealed in interviewers' report sheets. It soon became obvious that the very frequency with which these problems were reported revealed the extent to which the immigrant families in this study were suffering under stress. A further analysis revealed that the stresses were mainly rooted in the process of migration and the difficulties faced during the period of adjustment.

Immigration and consequent adjustment to a new society necessarily transform the internal structure of the family, the members of which react differently because of their different roles in the new society: the husband is influenced by his work situation, the wife by the home environment, and the children by the school. Such influences can cause members of the family to pull in different directions.[6]

A Scottish family in Moe has lived in the district for 35 years. In spite of the length of residence in Australia Mrs A. is still homesick and misses her relatives in Edinburgh. She has never

felt a member of the community unlike her husband who likes
Australia and is active in community affairs. The resultant
tension between Mr and Mrs. A. is aggravated by the illness
of their only son, a lad of 18. According to the interviewer
'The son is now receiving psychiatric treatment following
regression after an accident five years ago. He is not working,
just living in the house all day. His behaviour is equal to that
of an average 10 year old and he is a constant trial to his
parents who because he is an only son have been trying to do
everything possible for him. What struck me most during the
interview was the mental state of the mother. She is, I would
say, almost on the point of collapse herself. It seems an effort
for her to talk or think. She has no energy and cannot sleep.
The husband also is showing signs of strain' (*Interview
No. 630*).

Sometimes the stresses are due to marital difficulties, as in the
following case of a 43-year-old Englishman:

Mr B. came to Australia in 1948 under the Royal Australian
Navy Scheme having previously volunteered for service in the
R.A.N. He left behind his wife with a child born in 1941.
In Melbourne he met another woman and went to live with
her. He stopped writing letters to his wife who became
suspicious and applied for an Assisted Passage for herself and
her son. When Mrs B. arrived in Melbourne in 1950 her
husband at first refused to take leave of the other woman.
Eventually, however, Mr B. returned to his wife and they
went to live in North Newborough. But Mr B. became moody,
abusive to his wife and finally took to drink. Mrs B. thinks
that her husband is on the way to alcoholism. 'He has no
friends and all he does is to drink and does not know when
to stop; he is going peculiar and will not see the doctor.' This
condition probably explains a certain ambivalence in Mr B's.
attitude to his son. In the words of the interviewer: 'Before
I saw the son I had heard about how wonderful he was, how
he had recovered from a disability. He is good at sport, plays
the guitar, has many friends in every night at his home. Failed
in his Intermediate because he did not work hard enough.
He is popular with his friends. Yet he appeared to me surly
to his mother and father. His mother told me how her
husband picks on him when drunk and is nasty. His mother
also commented that underneath father was really fond of
him' (*Interview No. 455*).

Once the family breaks up the effects may be far-reaching, as
in the case of a 58-year-old Ukrainian labourer who lives with his

12-year-old son in Newborough. Before he was forced to work in Germany during the war Mr C. was manager of a service station and repair workshop in a country town in Poland. He and his Ukrainian-born wife arrived in Australia in 1949 and after two years in a tent in a SEC camp at Yallourn built themselves a house which Mr C. now occupies. All was well until suddenly in 1958 the wife eloped with a German migrant. From that point onwards Mr C. began to break all his social contacts. When interviewed in 1959 he still had a group of Polish and Dutch friends whom he used to meet, and he continued to attend English classes. Interviewed two years later Mr C. admitted that he no longer had any friends, he had ceased to attend the English classes, had hardly improved his standard of spoken English, and he was no longer interested in applying for naturalization. No longer did he care about his house which, in the words of the interviewer, had been completely neglected:

> The room in which the interview was conducted seemed to be a general living room combined with junk and store room. Apart from a dirty table littered with old newspapers, food, money, torch, tools, etc., there was a radio, an old sofa and a clothes line suspended from the ceiling with clothes hanging from it. On the other side of the room building materials were stacked. A pile of newspapers placed on a box acted as a chair.[7]

This example shows how the crisis situation in this family has brought about a complete withdrawal of the immigrant from his social contacts with friends and the wider Australian society and a lowering of personal standards. Mr C.'s own story may, of course, be one extreme in the series of many possible reactions to a crisis. The materials in this study illustrate a variety of reactions to a similar situation, because the external realities of a situation as seen by other people and the conception of the same situation by the person who is participating in it may be two very different things. Thomas and Znaniecki, in *The Polish Peasant in Europe and America*,[8] have pointed out the importance of the subjective definition of the situation in determining its effect on the person who is experiencing it. Time and again we interviewed families faced with circumstances that would be termed hardships by any observer and yet, in fact, served as a stimulus to better adjustment. Unfortunately the material brought together did not lend itself to the sort of analysis that would give insights into the subjective factors which, in the words of Thomas and Znaniecki, help to define the situation. All that we are able to do is isolate certain objective factors which seem responsible for the way the immigrant families face the stresses and occasional crises of the period of adjustment.

Among these objective factors is the conflict between Australian and immigrant behaviour patterns which manifests itself in the relations between parents and children. One of the principal orientations in the immigrant family, as indeed in any family, is the establishment of uniformity as well as conformity of behaviour. This is a tremendously difficult task in any circumstances, and even more so in those immigrant families where standards of behaviour and discipline differ most from the receiving society.

When children are still young this type of conflict concerns largely the problem of maintaining discipline, as shown in the following report by one of the interviewers:

> I noticed that the children spoke German to their parents which is the language of the mother. They do not speak the language of the father who is Yugoslav. There seems to be a good deal of tension between the respondent and his wife. He has a frightened look in his eye, his wife is big and harsh. I asked the respondent about his leisure pursuits and he said 'arguments'. His wife gave him a quick look. She also answered one question and she told him not to look at me 'like that'. There is obvious friction between this couple who are unable to discipline their children aged 9, 7 and 4. My visit to this family happened to coincide with the birthday party of their 7-year-old daughter. The children were riotous. The elder boy's behaviour particularly bad. He hit his sister several times. He hung around the lounge room where we were and demanded to put on the wireless to listen to Tarzan. His parents yelled at him to no avail (*Interview No. 729*).

Though there is clearly an underlying conflict between husband and wife in this family, the behaviour of their children is definitely out of keeping with the norms that the parents would like to impose. The boy who insists on listening to Tarzan is an example of the attitude of immigrant children in a rebellious mood.

Amongst older children a frequent instance of such differing standards of behaviour and discipline is the conflict about the freedom enjoyed by most Australian teenage girls who are allowed to go to local dances and pictures unaccompanied. Several immigrant families admitted that they faced such a problem and that their children rebelled against what they considered an unreasonable attitude on the part of the parents. Some Dutch families belonging to the orthodox Calvinist *Gereformeerde Kerk* and a number of Maltese families with teenage children exhibited an open, or at best latent, conflict of attitudes regarding what the children thought to be their right. In the words of an interviewer who reported on the Maltese community in Yallourn North:

> As the children grow older, conflicts tend to develop in some families between the Maltese and Australian ways; for example, single girls and men are not allowed out together until they are engaged. Some of the young working girls chafe at this attitude when they see their schoolfriends going out unaccompanied. Other families don't seem to worry about these things at all. They say they are completely Australian and, in some instances, the discipline may be too lax.

The conflict regarding the freedom to go out is perhaps symptomatic of many cultural differences between the immigrants and their children who are being reared in the traditions of the old world. Some of the older children interviewed felt tied to a value system which, for them, was stifling in their present surroundings. The majority were too young to express their dissatisfaction, but one sensed, nevertheless, that here was an important area of behaviour which one day would assume serious proportions. What now appears in only a few instances as rebellious behaviour is one way in which many immigrant children (or children born to immigrants) try to establish a meaningful life of their own. A serious situation may arise when such children break from these traditions before they have acquired Australian standards and behaviour patterns. Immigrant parents who have grown to maturity abroad are likely to have had their native cultural standards of behaviour so thoroughly ingrained that the more stable personalities at least are not prone to be confused to the point of a serious breakdown; but their children, brought up in a foreign country, become familiar with two sets of frequently conflicting behaviour standards, simultaneously and from competing authoritative sources. It is to be expected that some of these second-generation children will fail to build resistances to delinquency strong enough to stand the strains of the confusion of adolescence and the hardship of a possible economic depression.

Instances of such extreme rebellious behaviour are, fortunately, rare in the Latrobe Valley. Only one case of conviction by a Juvenile Court was recorded in the sample of 384 families; another half-dozen were found while examining the files of the Moe *Advocate* and the Morwell *Advertiser* for the years 1958-61. The reason for this must largely lie in the small size of the age group from which potential 'rebels' and delinquents could be drawn. As more children enter the period of adolescence the number of those exposed to the disruptive influence of what has been described as 'a conflict of conduct norms'[9] will increase. The potential instability of these situations suggests that the adjustment of immigrant youth will remain an important problem for future research.

The Integrating Forces

How does the immigrant family cope with the problems arising from the inter-generation conflict? In answering this question three areas of behaviour will be discussed: the language spoken at home, the reaction to external factors pulling the family apart, and the relationship between the family and the outside community.

Amongst the forces that pull the two generations apart is the increasing difficulty of communicating. This, of course, is true of any family, for the differences in age and outlook often make it difficult to bridge the gap separating parents from their children. But how much more difficult must it be for an immigrant family where the children, particularly when they are still of school age, learn to speak their new language more quickly than their parents, and thus begin to absorb the values and ideas of the receiving society at a faster rate.

This study has revealed widespread understanding of this problem by the immigrant families. The immigrant parents are mostly aware that to facilitate easy intercourse between themselves and their children any language barriers must be removed. The statistical picture of this behaviour pattern will be considered in Chapter 8 but the following examples show the connection between the ease of intercourse and good adjustment within the family. What matters here is not whether all members of a family make a conscious attempt to speak English, or whether the children have been taught to speak the native language of their parents, but whether the two generations can converse easily in one language. Obviously some of the better educated parents can and do learn to speak fluent English; others, however, find it too difficult during the critical years following arrival in the new country.

An Italian labourer who has lived in Australia since 1924. One of the pioneers of the Yallourn Open-cut. Has two grown-up sons, one of whom has five children. All live together in Yallourn North in a large house surrounded by three acres of garden, 'jam-packed with vegetables, fruit trees and grapes . . . Parents and sons evidently get on very well. The elder son was helping to paint his parents' house when I first met him despite his five children. Both sons have picked up Italian from their parents and can speak it fluently. The whole family speak mainly English and get on well with Australians although the majority of their friends are New Australians. A close-knit fine type of family who have apparently spent their time building or improving their homes and gardens' (*Interview No. 217*).

A German migrant who arrived in Australia in 1955. Has three children aged 4, 2 and 6 months. 'Parents love the children and keep them well disciplined. All speak German at home as parents think it a great help for children to have two languages. The parents both speak very good English' (*Interview No. 222*).

A Maltese labourer who has lived in Australia since 1949. Has seven children aged 6 to 17. 'The family appeared happy and united. The elder children spoke Maltese to their parents but the younger spoke more English. The parents told me how the children spoke English among themselves. But conversation between parent and child is mostly held in Maltese' (*Interview No. 229*).

In some cases bilingual children assist their parents as interpreters and assume partial responsibility for the family's financial matters, as in the following example of a Ukrainian labourer who has worked in the Yallourn Power Station ever since he arrived in Australia in 1948:

The elder boy (12) was the dominant member of the family without being the slightest bit domineering. The younger son (8) was following his brother's footsteps. They obviously got on well with their parents, e.g. young son sat on his mother's and then on his father's knee. He kept telling me he was an Aussie much to the family's amusement. The elder son acted as a wonderful interpreter and was never impatient with his parents even when they were slow to catch on to something. He spoke English and Ukrainian fluently. The younger boy does not want to speak Ukrainian. He prefers English.

I was very impressed with the intelligence of the two boys. . . . Apart from their ability to interpret, the comments they made in fun and in all seriousness were amazingly bright. The older boy had an open friendly smile as well as a serious expression on his face. He asked me about educational opportunities at the University and about the Survey. I was struck by the knowledge the two boys had on their father's financial matters and occupational position (*Interview No. 228*).

A Polish truck driver, who has lived in Australia since 1951, is married to a Russian woman, and has a 9-year-old son, has put up an interesting argument in favour of the bilingual approach to the children of immigrants:

I was impressed with the interviewee's conversation. Although his English was not outstanding he had the capacity to express his ideas and theories most graphically. He justified his child's attending classes in the Polish language by saying that if he and his wife died the child would have the means of remaining in contact with his relatives in Poland. If, however, he could not communicate with them due to ignorance of Polish he would lose contact with them which would be most undesirable (*Interview No. 310*).

In addition to conscious efforts to remove the language barrier inside the family, the reaction to external forces that pull the family apart takes yet another form. This consists of concern about the future of adolescent children, particularly girls, for whom no suitable training facilities at a tertiary level or employment opportunities may exist in the Latrobe Valley (see Chapter 2). This is a very real problem which will become more pressing as the children of the immigrants become older and wish to study for a university degree, or, as in the case of many girls, find that there are no vacancies for clerical positions or jobs in light industry in the Valley. The example of a Maltese painter (in Australia since 1955), his wife and twelve children (aged 1-18) shows how this man resists any thought of separation from his older children and is determined to carry the burden of maintaining them:

The children all speak Maltese. During interview all the children except the eldest stayed quietly in the lounge with the T.V. The eldest girl joined in discussions of the questionnaire with the father and seemed to know more about household management than the mother. The father was very much the head of the family and the children appeared somewhat in awe of him.

Subject is now having a struggle to make ends meet because two children cannot obtain employment. But he will not accept offers of jobs for them because it would mean their leaving home. 'As long as the family is all together everything will work out' is his attitude. As well as managing a large family, this man is very active in the Scouting Movement and is accepted by Australians. Also he spends much time making plaques and ornaments from any scrap metal he can lay his hands on (*Interview No. 640*).

Occasionally the desire to keep the family together is carried to extremes, as in the case of a Maltese fitter who has lived in Australia for four years, has six children aged 8-19, and has a good job in the briquette factory.

The parents have decided to go back to Malta because they came out here to improve their situation for the children, and now find that they are just making enough money to exist. There is no employment in the Valley for their four elder children, so that three of them are working in Melbourne and Mary (16) is staying at home doing nothing. They would be content to stay here if the whole family could live together, but this is impossible now. Cultural conflict is evident with the third eldest girl who wants to go out but is not allowed to because her father wishes her to do as she would have done in Malta (*Interview No. 655*).

One of the main obstacles to good adjustment seems to be overcome when the problem of separation is solved. This is shown in the following example of a Latvian family who have lived in Australia since 1949 and have two children, a girl aged 17 and a boy aged 10.

From what the father told me I would say that he had a very healthy attitude to their upbringing. He likes the children to join clubs and become Australian and hence become accepted in Australia. He likes Newborough because it is small enough for him to know the children with whom his children mix. He believes this district is safer for his son and daughter than Melbourne and he is pleased that his daughter has found a job here. What impressed me most during the interview was the way the respondent implied how he was looking toward the future of his children and not looking back at the past. I was struck by his friendly open manner (*Interview No. 452*).

It seems that most immigrants want a well-integrated family life and to maintain their own cultural values while they adapt

to the new. Friends, neighbours, and ethnic religious congregations all play an important part during this period of adjustment.
The following two examples illustrate how the immigrant
communities can ostracize a family with a bad reputation:

> A Polish labourer, married to a German woman. Has lived in
> Australia since 1952. One child—a girl of 14. 'The family are
> reported to be the worst in Newborough. It is stated quite
> definitely that they drink—husband and wife. . . . The parents
> seem to be completely ostracized and isolated from the
> community although their neighbours—and nearly all the
> people in the street—are Poles and Ukrainians whom I've
> found to be very sociable and have quite a communal life
> amongst themselves' (*Interview No. 367*).
>
> A Yugoslav labourer and his wife who arrived in Australia in
> 1953. Respondent's son aged 22 has left home and gone away
> with a married woman. His father has not heard from him for
> 2 years. Both parents say that they would not have him at
> home again. The parents feel they cannot make friends
> because of the shame brought upon the family by their son.
> An Australian friend appears to be making a genuine effort
> to help this couple become friendly and to participate in the
> social life of the community. The couple are not on visiting
> terms with other Yugoslav immigrant families (*Interview No.
> 216*).

The role played by the religious congregation is particularly
important in some of the smaller churches, where contacts seem
to be of a face-to-face type and where membership is restricted
to one ethnic group. This is revealed in the following extract from
a report by the interviewer who worked mostly with the Dutch
people in Moe:

> The Reformed Church (*Gereformeerde Kerk*) in Moe
> exercises a profound influence on the life of its members, and
> it is correct to regard the Calvinist family as a particular type
> of family, which has its basic roots and values in the teachings
> of the church. Members keep within their own tight circle
> and within the church the family is regarded as the all-
> important and basic unit. These Reformed Church families
> observe many of the customs that are carried out in Holland,
> although they have been somewhat relaxed since coming to
> Australia, e.g., they travel on Sundays if necessary. The home
> is regarded as a very important aspect of Christian life. Parents
> are expected to teach their children the Bible in several ways
> —reading from the Bible at every meal, by taking them to

church at an early age, and sending them to Sunday school. The elders of the church are responsible for seeing that the family carries out these duties. Calvinist teenagers seem to move in a very tight circle, and although the church is only a small one, the members seem to find friends from the same and opposite sex through gatherings of church members.

Much emphasis has been placed in this chapter on the differences between the generations in the process of integration or culture contact in a migrant family. These disruptive forces can encourage tension within the home—the children tend to pull strongly towards the culture of the host society, and the parents to pull towards the retention of some of the ways and customs of the country of origin. For obvious reasons the scope for culture contact is also unequal as between the husband and wife. For the breadwinner the work situation is a powerful force against segregation. By contrast the forces making for the integration of the mother are relatively weak, and it is there that contact with the culture of the country of origin can mean so much.

The research design of this study was focused on the male breadwinner and, although many questions were asked of the wife as well, the picture of the immigrant family that emerges is one in which the father occupies a central place. In future studies perhaps more attention should be given to the mother in the home and the forces that facilitate or hamper her transition between what she left and the situation to which she had to adapt.

The evidence presented in this chapter has not disclosed widespread disorganization within the family of the kind that other studies of immigrant behaviour have shown.[10] It seems that the few cases of delinquency, tensions in the family, and rebellious behaviour are but symptoms of the latent conflicts that may come into the open later. External forces, such as the employment situation and the extent, in the future, of wider employment opportunities, will determine whether the immigrant families will be able to remain together; but it seems likely that, in terms of occupational structure, the rising generation of immigrant children will be a very different group.

During the field survey questions were asked regarding the occupation of the eldest child of each respondent. Of the 336 children whose particulars were obtained only 108 were already in employment, and the remainder were below school age or full-time students. It is of some significance, however, that of the

K

108 persons who were employed only eight were unskilled labourers, forty-nine were in skilled trades, and the rest in commercial, clerical, and professional jobs. If this trend away from the labouring and semi-skilled occupations continues then the shortage of jobs outside the existing heavy industries will force many children of the immigrants to seek employment away from the Latrobe Valley.

Even for those who remain, the tendency will be to aspire to more skilled occupations than those of their fathers. There is ample evidence of this in the ever-increasing enrolments of immigrant children in the Yallourn Technical College, in inquiries addressed to the research team, and in the number of young residents of the Latrobe Valley who seek entrance to Melbourne and Monash universities. The overwhelming impression from interviews and informal conversations with the immigrants, teachers, clergy, and group leaders, is that most settlers have developed broader horizons for their children. It was noticeable, particularly among the immigrants of east European origin, how greatly the parents were concerned to give their children a better education and therefore a better occupation than they themselves had been able to get. The full meaning of occupational downgrading which was discussed in Chapter 5, particularly amongst the Poles and Ukrainians, can now be understood in the desire of these people to give their children a better start in life.

In the light of this discussion it seems likely that family solidarity amongst the immigrants in the Latrobe Valley will be threatened by the twin forces of a movement away from home in search of employment and the increasing difference between the occupational grading of the immigrant breadwinner and of his children. This last is bound to pose problems perhaps even more serious to the family unity than geographical separation: in addition to the problem of the language barrier, the differences in outlook due to age, and differences in the rate of integration, a new element, difference in social status, will be introduced. This, in turn, may lead to difficulties and tension resulting from the differences in the level of aspirations. To meet the challenge of this sort of situation immigrant families must show more flexibility than is normally expected of a family, and without it they will not be able to reorganize their old world values. This is the very essence of the process of adjustment, during which old values are gradually discarded or adapted to the norms of the host society.

Several studies of industrial communities with a similar occupational structure have emphasized family disorganization. For example H. R. Lantz, writing about a coalmining community in Illinois, observed that in the families he studied parents were preoccupied with 'monetary pursuits in various forms and were immersed in a way of life not conducive to the growth of close familial relationships'. He noticed that warm, meaningful associations between husband and wife and parents and children appeared only in a few instances. 'What might have been a positive influence counteracting the harshness of the external milieu failed for the most part to develop.'[11]

The generalizations made by Lantz do not seem to apply to the Latrobe Valley. With the exception of the few isolated cases cited in this chapter there is no suggestion that there is widespread disorganization. Why are the immigrants of Yallourn, Moe, and Newborough different from the people of 'Coal Town', Illinois? Perhaps the reason lies in the environment in which they live. Instead of heaps of coal slag and rows of dilapidated and unkempt tenement houses, the people of the Latrobe Valley enjoy the open spaces, the vistas opening up towards the foothills of the Alps and the Strzelecki Ranges, and the freedom of their neat one-family houses. Above all, there is in the Latrobe Valley no tradition of violence, no prolonged periods of industrial unrest, no bitterness resulting from the experience of unemployment and depression. The air of prosperity which has accompanied the progress of the Valley ever since Monash turned the first sod on the site of the present Yallourn 'A' Power Station has had a mellowing influence on family life. Perhaps this description of a Dutch family expatriated from Indonesia in 1951, temporarily housed in a makeshift dwelling, and only just able to make ends meet shows how the true spirit of family unity can overcome the exigencies of the process of adjustment.

> This is one of the most closely knit family groups I have ever met. There is obviously a strong bond between husband and wife and the children were receiving all the love and affection they could want. The parents had good control over the children even though they were being more boisterous than usual in front of a visitor. English was spoken at all times.

What is most striking is the unity of the family in spite of unfavourable surroundings. It was a perfect example of the happy family in a makeshift house so often written about but rarely experienced. Also the complete isolation of the wife from other adults because of her devotion to her family. In this family there was no suspicion. They answered questions openly and without hesitation. Even though they did not like their neighbours and did not agree with their ideals, they did not condemn them.

Even though they would not say their position and living conditions were worse here than what they had experienced, in later discussions with them I have found that they both come from well-to-do families and in Indonesia they were used to living very lavishly.

Unlike other migrants, they have no desire to move from the Valley. They want a better house but intend to wait and build it themselves *(Interview No. 601)*.

PART III
SOCIAL PARTICIPATION

8

COMMUNITY PARTICIPATION

When studying the immigrants' participation in the community at large it is important to examine differences in character and extent of participation in order to test an hypothesis which attributes such differences to ethnic origin. The main emphasis in this chapter will be on ethnic differences, but supporting evidence will be sought whenever possible to reveal any relationship between social participation and three other characteristics: rural/urban background, age, and length of residence in Australia.

Factors Responsible for Participation

Five principal factors were assumed to have a bearing on the character and extent of social participation of immigrants in the Latrobe Valley: the mastery of the English language; the extent to which the immigrant is exposed to such media of mass communication as the English language press, radio, and television; the reading of foreign language press and books; the language spoken in the immediate family circle; and the immigrant's intentions, or actual practice, with regard to the teaching of his native language to his children. The distribution of the various ethnic groups in conjunction with the frequencies listed under each factor is shown in Table 26.

The English language standard was assessed by the interviewer into one of the four check categories separately for spoken English and the reading knowledge of the language.[1] Combined scores of these two tests were then coded and tabulated, and the distribution of these on a percentage basis shows a distinct ethnic pattern: the Italians, Greeks, and Poles have three-quarters of their men listed as speaking and/or reading little English or none at all; and, by contrast, 50 per cent or more of the immigrants born in the Netherlands, Germany, and the Baltic states speak colloquial English and read with ease.[2]

The question we should ask now is whether this ethnic pattern implies a causal relationship. In other words does the fact that a given individual is, say, a native of Italy, predispose him to be a poor English speaker?

TABLE 26
Statistical Association between Birthplace and Factors bearing on Social Participation
(%)

Item	Nether-lands	Ger-many	Greece and Italy	Malta	Poland	Yugo-slavia	Baltic coun-tries	Ukraine	Other C. & E. Europe	Total	χ^2	d.f.*	Level of signi-ficance
(a) English language standard—scores:													
N =	45	28	52	83	46	31	22	29	21	357			
under 2	2	7	29	20	20	3	9	10	5	14			
2 and under 4 }†	16	29	52	36	57	58	36	59	43	42	55·7	8	·001
4 and over	82	64	19	43	24	39	55	31	52	44			
(b) Exposure to mass communication media—scores:													
N =	45	28	52	83	46	31	22	29	21	357			
under 5	9	4	31	27	28	3	5	28	19	20			
5 and under 8	40	36	29	30	39	42	36	45	19	35	34·1	16	·01
8 and under 11 }†	42	43	31	25	26	39	14	28	57	32			
11 and over	9	18	10	18	7	16	45	—	5	13			
(c) Native language reading:													
N =	45	28	52	83	46	31	22	29	21	357			
Never	31	11	19	49	24	45	18	24	33	31			

										χ^2	d.f.*	p
Less than once a month ⎫ †	24	4	4	25	9	3	4	7	33	14			
Once a month ⎭	16	18	8	11	9	16	18	14	14	13	30·1	8	·001
Once a week	25	57	44	6	58	26	32	48	20	32			
Every day	2	11	17	2	—	6	18	3	—	6			
No reply	2	—	8	6	—	3	9	4	—	4			
(d) Language spoken at home:													
N =	**44**	**28**	**52**	**83**	**45**	**31**	**21**	**29**	**21**	**354**			
Native	16	50	17	20	56	13	52	72	24	32			
Native and English ⎫ †	59	36	71	71	40	74	33	28	52	56	‡	8	·001
Mainly English ⎭	25	14	12	8	4	13	14	—	24	12			
(e) Teaching of native language to children:													
N =	**35**	**18**	**10**	**55**	**33**	**22**	**11**	**24**	**9**	**217**			
Yes	6	28	40	24	55	27	73	79	44	36	‡	8	·001
No	94	72	60	76	45	73	27	21	56	64			

Note: Percentages may not add to 100 because of rounding.

   * Degrees of freedom.

   † Groupings used in chi square tests.

   ‡ Very large.

Several points could be made to counter such a claim. First of all the assessment on which the statistical picture of language standards is based did not take into account the respondent's innate ability to learn to speak English, nor any personal circumstances that affected opportunities for learning rapidly; for example, whether an immigrant lives and works mainly in the company of English-speaking men or whether he continues to mix with his compatriots. A second point is the significance of the standard of education and the immigrant's socio-economic status before migration. This is perhaps shown in the contrast between the Polish and the Baltic groups in Table 26. It was pointed out in Chapter 4 that the Baltic group is conspicuous for its high average pre-migration occupational status and educational standard; the Poles were rated low on both these counts. A third and related point is the rural/urban background of the immigrants, which is also closely associated with the standard of English.[3] Finally, the age of the immigrant seems to have a strong influence on the ability to learn a new language. Comparisons of selected age groups indicate that the 'younger adults', that is, men aged 20 to 34 years, have a significantly higher proportion of respondents who speak reasonably good English than the 'older adults', that is men aged 50 years and over;[4] in fact, somewhere above 50 seems to be the critical age beyond which the immigrant cannot in ordinary circumstances master a new language. This seems to apply to all men irrespective of the length of residence in Australia, which was not proved to be statistically significant in conjunction with the language standard.[5]

Does this mean that there could be no plausible evidence to support an hypothesis linking birthplace and command of the English language in terms of cause and effect? This cannot be answered with any degree of assurance in spite of the evidence discussed in the preceding paragraph. For example, the relatively low educational standard and socio-economic status of the Polish immigrants arises from their ethnic background and is to some extent determined by it. Similarly the fact that the Italians tend to be poor English speakers because they mix mainly with other Italians may, in part, derive from their ethnic background.

It seems, therefore, that the discussion has to be inconclusive and that the whole range of other factors has to be taken into account to explain the relationship between English language standard and ethnic origin. The subjective factor—the immigrant's positive predisposition to adjust, and to learn the ways and the language of his new country—is probably the most influential. This may be shown in the following case of an Italian couple who live in Yallourn North. Respondent (aged 39) has lived in Australia for three years and only a year before the interview took place he was able to pay for the passage of his 33-year-old wife and their three children. In the words of the interviewer:

> This couple is one of the happiest I have met so far. The relationship existing between husband and wife was a joy to see. He was friendly and willing to talk in English to the best of his capacity. She was bright and cheerful throughout the interview and met every challenge possible to speak English. She speaks very well, especially when one takes into consideration that she had only 5 years of schooling and she has not been here a year yet (*Interview No. 227*).

This Italian woman has learned to speak English by regular attendance at English classes two nights a week in the local state school. She had tried to learn by correspondence lessons supplied by the Commonwealth Office of Education, but found this required too much time and effort which she could not afford while she had a large family to look after. Accordingly, about a month after her arrival in Yallourn, she started to attend the night classes.

In the area covered by this study there are English classes for the immigrants in every town and workers' hostel. The majority are held in local state schools and instructors are usually school-teachers seconded by the state Education Department. There are, however, exceptions to this rule. Thus, in Moe, a Dutch woman who has lived in Australia for nearly ten years, conducts afternoon classes for women in her home. In the SEC Ridge Hostel in Morwell a well-educated Greek teacher takes a class for Greek immigrants. He is able to help his compatriots to overcome the added difficulties which the Greek immigrants have to face—the mastery of a new alphabet. In the West Camp at Yallourn a local Y.M.C.A. secretary, himself an immigrant from the Netherlands, takes one of the two classes.

Some idea of the attendance and the characteristics of people who attend English classes is to be found in the following excerpt from a report prepared by one of the interviewers:

> The numbers attending classes fluctuate so much that it is hard to give a true estimate. In the class I visited in East

Newborough there were members from a Dutch, a German, and a Greek family. There were seven people altogether, but when all members attend there are up to seventeen. The two Greek girls had only just begun, but an elementary class could not be conducted for them, as nine is the minimum number required to establish a class. In the intermediate class in Moe which I visited there were ten present, two of whom were women. Many of the men told me that they alternated with their wives, as someone had to remain at home to look after the children. In the elementary class next door there were six present—a man and his wife, another man, and three women.

The age range is striking. In the Newborough class the members of the Dutch family present that particular evening were—the father, his grown-up son, teenage daughter, and his youngest daughter aged 10. In the Moe intermediate class there was a couple in late middle age. They realised the difficulties of learning a language at their age, but were still prepared to learn as they felt their happiness in Australia depended upon their mastering the language. In the elementary class there was a very old German lady who was experiencing insurmountable difficulties. After battling with the indefinite article she sighed: 'Ich lerne es nie!' This sums up one of the truths about learning English—the older one is the harder it becomes to master the language.

A command of the English language is of particular importance to social adjustment because it is related to friendly contacts, but there are several ways in which the immigrant can absorb general knowledge about Australia, its people, and their way of life. These include reading newspapers and magazines, listening to radio, and watching television, as well as the more formal medium of attendance at English classes combined with other types of instruction (films and lectures of an educational nature). Questions designed to measure the frequency of contact with such media were asked during the interview and the information was subsequently tabulated in conjunction with birthplace.[6] Table 26 highlights the concentration of immigrants with high exposure in the German, Baltic, and Dutch groups. By contrast, the birthplaces with low exposure are Ukraine, Poland, Greece and Italy, in that order.

The ethnic differences in this respect are obviously quite important but there is also another closely-related factor, differences in the immigrant's rural/urban pre-migration background. This factor was also found to vary statistically with the extent of exposure to mass communication media: the immigrants with a rural pre-migration background are less exposed than those of urban background.[7]

What of the actual content of the various media of mass communication? No attempt has been made to study this aspect except to list titles of newspapers and magazines read by subjects and wives. Table 27 lists some of the more popular newspapers and magazines in conjunction with country of origin and shows that the majority of the immigrants included in this study read at least one English language newspaper or magazine. In a group of 594 men and women only 43 persons did not read any English language periodical, and of these the highest proportion is to be found among the Italians, Greeks, and Poles. The most popular of the daily papers (all of which are published in Melbourne), is the *Sun* newspaper, which is read by 420 persons, followed by the *Herald* (201), and the *Age* (63). In comparison with the three metropolitan newspapers the number of readers of the local press is quite small: the Moe *Advocate* has 86 readers, followed by the Yallourn *Live Wire* (35), and the Morwell *Advertiser* (8). Of the weekly magazines the most popular are *Women's Weekly* (110 readers), *Australasian Post* (88), *Pix* (52), and *Weekend* (50).[8]

These figures and their distribution by ethnic groups must be treated with caution because they do equate such virtually immeasurable factors as the individual intensity with which a person reads a newspaper, the degree of comprehension, and the type and content of the reading matter. In some cases, as we found, reading a newspaper consists simply of looking at the pictures; in others a serious attempt is made to read and comprehend a news item or a feature article. Clearly more research is needed in this particular aspect of social participation, before the existence of definite ethnic differences could be even assumed.[9] All that can be said about the various media of mass communication is that they help the settler to improve his English, to arouse his interest in the affairs of the Australian community at large, and tend to draw him into more active participation in the affairs of his local community. This is illustrated in the following excerpt from an autobiographical essay written by a Maltese radio mechanic:

TABLE 27

English-language Publications Read by a Group of 594 Immigrants of Specified Birthplaces

Birthplace	Daily			Twice weekly				Weekly							Monthly	None
	Sun	Age	Herald	Truth	Advo-cate	Live Wire	Morwell Adver-tiser	Post	Women's Weekly	Women's Week-end	Pix	People	Woman's Day	Woman's Weekly Times	Reader's Digest	
Netherlands:																
Husband	34	8	11	—	15	5	1	7	6	3	3	1	2	3	4	
Wife	25	6	8	—	14	3	1	2	14	1			6	1	4	
Total	59	14	19	—	29	8	2	9	20	4	3	1	8	4	8	
Germany:																
Husband	18	12	10	1	7	2	1	4	1	2	1		2	3	2	
Wife	34	10	11	1	11	3	—	3	16	1	1	1	6	1	1	
Total	52	22	21	2	18	5	1	7	17	3	2	1	8	4	3	
Greece & Italy:																
Husband	32	7	15	5	2	—	1	4	1	5	5	2	—	—	—	
Wife	3	1	3	—	1	—	—	1	—	1	1	1	—	—	—	
Total	35	8	18	5	3	—	1	5	1	6	6	3	—	—	—	18
Malta:																
Husband	60	4	40	5	9	6	1	17	6	9	9	4	2	4	1	
Wife	37	2	17	1	8	6	1	6	14	7	2	—	3	3	1	
Total	97	6	57	6	17	12	2	23	20	16	11	4	5	7	2	12

Poland:																
Husband	27	1	12	1	4	2	—	6	8	7	2	1	1	—	—	—
Wife	13	1	9	—	2	2	1	4	8	4	2	1	1	—	—	—
Total	40	2	21	1	6	4	1	10	16	11	4	2	2	—	—	7
Yugoslavia:																
Husband	27	3	14	3	3	4	—	4	7	2	5	3	1	3	1	—
Wife	8	1	1	—	2	—	—	2	4	—	1	1	1	2	1	—
Total	35	4	15	3	5	4	—	6	11	2	6	4	2	5	2	—
Baltic countries:																
Husband	20	—	10	2	2	1	—	6	5	4	7	1	—	1	2	—
Wife	14	—	6	—	1	—	—	2	9	1	4	—	2	—	—	—
Total	34	—	16	2	3	1	—	8	14	5	11	1	2	1	2	1
Ukraine:																
Husband	25	3	8	1	1	—	1	1	1	—	1	—	—	1	—	—
Wife	12	1	4	1	—	—	—	3	4	2	—	—	—	—	—	—
Total	37	4	12	2	1	—	1	4	5	2	1	—	—	1	—	2
Other C. & E. Europe:																
Husband	22	3	15	—	2	—	—	12	1	1	6	—	—	2	—	—
Wife	9	—	7	—	2	1	—	4	5	—	2	—	1	1	—	—
Total	31	3	22	—	4	1	—	16	6	1	8	—	1	3	—	3
Total																
Husband	265	41	135	18	45	20	5	61	36	33	39	12	8	17	10	—
Wife	155	22	66	3	41	15	3	27	74	17	13	4	20	8	7	—
Total	420	63	201	21	86	35	8	88	110	50	52	16	28	25	17	43

Although I had some English schooling back in Malta and I could read English with ease I found it difficult at first to understand Australian speech especially when I heard some of my workmates address everything 'she is right', 'she is apples', etc. I listened regularly to the A.B.C. broadcasts of English for New Australians and received monthly the *Good Neighbour* newspaper from the Department of Immigration. Gradually I became very interested in all matters concerning Australia, such as new industries and other development projects and also foreign policy, especially recently in connection with Dr Subandrio's visit. I have maps of all States of Australia. I listen to the news daily and read about Australia as much as I can. I read the following newspapers and magazines: *Sun, Herald, Australasian Post, Walkabout, Radio, Television and Hobbies, The Scapular* (a religious magazine), *Live Wire, Advocate, Advertiser* and *Truth*. For the past 18 months I have been helping the Newborough Boy Scout Group and I am also a member of the local branch of the Democratic Labour Party.

The reading of books and periodicals in the immigrant's native language was scored according to the frequency with which he reads in his language, scores varying from 'Never' to 'Every day'.[10] The groups that have around 50 per cent of their members who read in their native language at least once a week are Poland, Germany, Ukraine, and Italy and Greece, but half of the settlers from Malta never read a Maltese language publication.[11] A comparison of those who never read publications in their native language with all others shows a marked statistical association.

There is no close association between native language reading and the rural/urban background of the immigrants such as was established in the case of other factors of social participation.[12] As could be expected, however, there is a close association between length of residence and native language reading;[13] at the longer durations of residence the frequency of native language reading shows a marked decrease. Presumably, with the passage of time, the need is satisfied to an increasing extent by the English language books and periodicals.

As to the content of native language reading, an attempt was made during the interview to list all foreign language newspapers and periodicals. Table 28 shows the distribution of such literature by language groups. It is evident that the German language publications have the largest circulation, followed by the Maltese, Greek, Dutch, and Polish periodicals. The supremacy of the

TABLE 28

Foreign-language Publications Read by Immigrant Households
(No. of Copies)

Language	Published		
	Australia	Overseas	Total
German	17	64	81
Maltese	3	59	62
Greek	46	6	52
Dutch	15	24	39
Polish	31	1	32
Baltic	20	7	27
Italian	12	13	25
Ukrainian	20	2	22
Yugoslav	7	3	10
Hungarian	3	—	3
Swedish	—	1	1
Other	i	—	1
Total	175	180	355

Note: Five of the families interviewed stated that they read various papers through the Continental Reading Circle in Morwell and the Magazine Library in Melbourne.

German language press is because it is read not only by the relatively small groups of German-born men (28), but also by the German-born wives of German as well as Polish, Ukrainian, Yugoslav, and Baltic settlers (41). Moreover, the men born in some of these countries speak and read German, which they learnt during wartime displacement. It is of some significance, too, that the very great majority of German periodicals are popular magazines printed in Germany such as *Die Neue Illustrierte* and *Der Stern*.

In terms of the number of copies of various periodicals related to the potential number of readers, the pride of place belongs to the Greeks who subscribe jointly to fifty-two periodicals in a group that numbers twenty-nine men and five women. Forty-six of these subscriptions are for six Greek weeklies currently published in Australia.[14]

With regard to the language spoken at home by the immigrant the pattern is quite clear. First are the ethnic differences, with a striking contrast in the proportions of immigrants who speak only their native language, ranging from 13 per cent in the case of the Yugoslavs,[15] and 16 per cent in the Dutch group, to 72 per cent of the Ukrainians. Secondly, there is a statistically significant association between the length of residence in Australia and the proportion of the immigrants who speak only their own language at home.[16] Thirdly, as in the case of native language reading, there is no statistical association between the settler's rural/urban background and the language spoken at home.[17] This does not necessarily mean that there is no causal connection between these characteristics. It may well be that settlers of rural background prefer to speak the ethnic tongue at home because their peasant values stress conventions and notions that are most easily expressed in traditional terms. The settlers of urban background, on the other hand, use the ethnic tongue at home because they see the career value of two languages for their children.

The last of the five factors that have a bearing on social participation is the immigrant's intention of teaching his native language to children. Table 26 shows that differences here among ethnic groups are quite striking. Some ethnic groups express a very strong desire that their children should attend classes in their native language: nearly 80 per cent of all Ukrainian and 73 per cent of all settlers born in the Baltic states have answered the question in this manner. By contrast only 6 per cent of the Dutch immigrants expect their children to attend classes in the Dutch language and civilization. It is of interest, too, that less than a quarter of the Maltese-born men and only 40 per cent of the Italians and Greeks have positive intentions in this regard.[18] The lack of such provision among Yugoslavs is conspicuous. Thus, to all intents and purposes, it is only among the immigrants from eastern Europe that any positive steps are being taken to organize language classes for children.

The east European groups in the Latrobe Valley have organized language classes on a formal basis with a syllabus and a system of incentives, as well as paid teachers. The Polish Association in the Latrobe Valley and the Ukrainian Association in Newborough run regular Saturday schools for children. Classes in Polish language, and the history and geography of Poland, are held in the Catholic school buildings at Moe, Newborough, and Morwell. Of these the Newborough group is the largest, with attendances of up to fifty children who are taught at two levels. Textbooks are supplied by the Polish Association in Victoria from Melbourne.

The Ukrainian Saturday school is also controlled from

Melbourne by the Ukrainian Association in Victoria. A group of forty children attend classes for three to four hours every Saturday. Children who make good progress in the study of the Ukrainian language and civilization receive book prizes. In addition, children aged from 12 to 18 are encouraged to enrol as members of the local branch of the Ukrainian Youth Association (S.U.M.). The Newborough branch of the association meets every Sunday afternoon. During the meetings, which last all the afternoon, children wear special uniforms consisting of khaki blouses and navy blue trousers (or skirts). Each meeting starts off with formal instruction in Ukrainian history, followed by competitions in reading and writing in the language. Members of the S.U.M. are encouraged to learn Ukrainian national dances and songs.[19]

Amongst the immigrants from the Baltic states the numbers are not big enough to warrant the organization of formal classes for children. Teaching is organized in small groups who meet in private houses. There is one such group in Moe, catering for the children of the immigrants from Lithuania.

The teaching of the language and civilization of the immigrant group to the children is a means of bridging the cultural gap separating the two generations. It would be too early to speak with any degree of finality about the effects of these measures on parent-child relations and on the social adjustment of the second generation of immigrants especially exposed to the disorganizing influences of a possible culture conflict. Nevertheless, there is a striking contrast between the western and southern European groups, on the one hand, and the Polish, Baltic, and Ukrainian groups on the other. The reasons for it are again rooted in the circumstances of migration. The Baltic and other east European groups consider themselves political refugees, and the maintenance of the language of the country of origin is looked upon as a duty to the country they lost. By contrast, the voluntary migrants from the Netherlands, Greece, and Italy may feel discouraged by the lack of opportunities in their old country, so they do not care about preserving the language and other symbols of national identity.

The elaborate efforts made by some groups to teach their children the tradition of their homeland are also a means of nationalist expression. Such efforts, however, do not seem to result in the inculcation of a strong chauvinistic feeling in the second generation. The 14-year-old son of a secretary of the local Ukrainian Association is following his father's footsteps as a group leader of the S.U.M. Yet when interviewed in the Moe High School this boy seemed indistinguishable from other Australian and immigrant children. The headmaster has singled him out for special praise as dux of his class and a leader in sport as well as in social activity in the school. It is clear, therefore, that the teaching of native languages to children does not necessarily prevent active social participation in Australian social institutions. This is summed up in the words of the Latvian engineer whose life history is published in Appendix A: 'As we have always spoken Latvian at home so my children also have a command of it, but otherwise they have been completely integrated to Australian society and Australian customs.'

Friendship Patterns

An inquiry concerning friendship patterns of the immigrants was concerned with three types of situation: work, visiting, and leisure. Although the definition of the work situation was completely unequivocal there was some confusion in the minds of our respondents as to the distinction between 'visiting' and 'leisure'. Some replied only to the question concerned with the visiting situation; others made it equally plain that the people they were friendly with outside work were the persons with whom they were spending their leisure and this also involved visiting one another. As the proportions given in Table 29 seem to indicate, the pattern of visiting and leisure was on the whole consistent and the data relating to both these situations are consequently reproduced here in full.[20]

The existence of pronounced differences among the ethnic groups in the friendship patterns of the immigrants is quite unmistakable, though in the work situation the differences between the various birthplaces are the least pronounced and in the visiting situation they are most evident; the leisure situation ranks just below 'visiting'.

The practice of ethnic groups with regard to choice of friends in terms of their country of origin in each of the three situations is shown in Table 29. With regard to the work situation it seems that the contrast here is between such groups as the Poles and Germans, who tend to associate mainly with migrants, and the British and Dutch, whose associations are with both Australians and immigrants.[21] The visiting and leisure behaviour of the Maltese, and, to a lesser extent, the natives of the Baltic states,

TABLE 29
Choice of Friends by Birthplace: Percentage Distribution

	British Isles	Netherlands	Germany	Greece & Italy	Malta	Poland	Yugoslavia	Baltic countries	Ukraine	Other C. & E. Europe	Total
(a) Friends—work											
N =	**181**	**43**	**28**	**51**	**83**	**46**	**30**	**21**	**29**	**22**	**534**
Mainly respondent's compatriots	13	5	4	—	7	2	10	—	3	9	7
Mainly other immigrants	29	30	54	33	40	54	33	33	45	27	36
Australians and immigrants	45	44	25	49	45	35	43	38	45	59	44
Australians only	13	21	18	18	8	9	13	29	7	5	13
(b) Friends—visiting											
N =	**183**	**45**	**28**	**52**	**83**	**46**	**31**	**22**	**29**	**22**	**541**
Mainly respondent's compatriots	21	38	25	35	53	26	29	45	55	14	32
Mainly other immigrants	9	4	18	13	10	28	19	18	14	32	13
Australians and immigrants	44	40	32	17	18	33	32	27	14	14	31
Australians only	17	11	14	4	5	2	3	—	—	9	9
Not stated	9	7	11	31	14	11	16	9	17	32	14
(c) Friends—leisure											
N =	**183**	**45**	**28**	**52**	**83**	**46**	**31**	**22**	**29**	**22**	**541**
Mainly respondent's compatriots	16	16	14	46	40	20	35	36	17	5	24
Mainly other immigrants	14	11	29	19	11	33	6	14	17	32	16
Australians and immigrants	39	29	25	27	19	28	23	23	31	27	30
Australians only	15	18	4	2	5	—	3	5	7	14	9
Not stated	16	27	29	6	25	20	32	23	28	23	21

Poland, Greece, and Italy, is to find their friends mainly among their own compatriots and other immigrants.

The ethnic pattern of friendships is clearer in the case of visiting and leisure than at work. Here the immigrant can choose his friends only from those in the gang or team to which he is directed by the management, which can thus, to some extent, regulate patterns of friendship by determining the ethnic composition of different sections. Therefore the pattern shown in the visiting and leisure situations can be taken as more reliable.

Indirectly the pattern disclosed here gives some indication of the extent to which the various ethnic groups confine the social participation of their members to one group, for, as has been shown, the possibilities for communication and social participation outside the immigrant's ethnic group are affected mostly by knowledge of languages. The reason why the groups with a poor standard of English have most of their ties within their national group is, therefore, evident.

Next, length of residence is an important factor in determining the extent of social participation outside the immigrant's ethnic group in visiting and leisure situations, but not in the work situation. A recently-arrived immigrant has a greater tendency than one who has been in Australia for some time to visit his compatriots and engage in leisure pursuits with them. It has been found that 49 per cent of the 'recent' immigrants (under six years of residence) as compared with 37 per cent of the 'older' immigrants (six and under fifteen years of residence) have most of their visiting relationships within their own ethnic group. Of those who have been in Australia for more than fifteen years only 6 per cent continue to visit mainly their compatriots.[22] The pattern here is quite unmistakable.

Membership of Voluntary Associations

The ethnic pattern summarized in Table 30 shows that there are very significant differences in the proportion of immigrants who are members of voluntary associations.[23] These proportions range from a maximum of 59 per cent membership amongst the Ukrainians, followed by the British and the Dutch (both 56 per cent), to a minimum of 16 per cent amongst the Italians, Greeks, and Yugoslavs. The existence of such a marked ethnic difference tells us as yet very little, for it does not indicate whether the ethnic group members have joined migrant or Australian associations. In this respect a comparison of these two classes of

TABLE 30

Membership of Voluntary Associations by Birthplace
(%)

Birthplace	None	Some	N =	Membership			N =
				Migrant Associations	Australian Associations	Migrant and Australian Associations	
British Isles	44	56	**183**	—	97	3	**103**
Netherlands	44	56	**45**	12	72	16	**25**
Germany	68	32	**28**	22	56	22	**9**
Greece and Italy	85	15	**52**	75	—	25	**8**
Malta	77	23	**83**	26	74	—	**19**
Poland	72	28	**46**	23	77	—	**13**
Yugoslavia	84	16	**31**	—	80	20	**5**
Baltic countries	59	41	**22**	33	44	22	**9**
Ukraine	41	59	**29**	71	12	18	**17**
Other central and eastern Europe	77	23	**22**	40	60	—	**5**
Total	61	39	**541**	17	75	8	**213**
χ^2	*			†			
d.f.	9			†			
Level of significance	·001			†			

* Very large.
† No test of significance possible because of smallness of numbers.

associations also seems to suggest an ethnic pattern (see Table 30). It appears that 71 per cent of the Ukrainians who are members of associations belong to Ukrainian associations, and a further 18 per cent belong to mixed Australian and migrant associations. By contrast, 97 per cent of the British and 72 per cent of the Dutch are in wholly Australian associations. Sixty per cent of all those interviewed do not belong to any formal associations.[24]

The implication of this pattern is clear. In the first place not only is the range of personal acquaintances and contacts for some ethnic groups (like the Dutch) likely to be broader but the potential involvement with the members of the other groups, and consequently their opportunity to exert some influence on the social structure of the wider community, is bound to be greater. In the second place formal membership of associations and the ethnic composition of such associations give an important indication of the extent to which the immigrant participates in his own ethnic system or that of the receiving society.[25]

The associations that have been set up in the Latrobe Valley mainly for the benefit of the immigrants range from informal groupings to formally constituted bodies.[26] The informal associations, which flourish among the Greek and Italian immigrants, are groupings larger than small face-to-face groups, have a regular meeting place, and are organized around recreational activities.

The Poulos Café in West Camp in Yallourn serves as an adequate substitute for a formal association of the Greeks in the district. As in Greece the coffee house is the most important single focus of the leisure behaviour of the male adult population, so is the Poulos Café for the Greek single men, mostly recent arrivals in Australia who live in one of the three SEC hostels in the Valley. Those who come and sip Turkish coffee, joking and gossiping with other men, also include some of the married Greeks who live in the district. Poulos Café has a store connected with it which also serves as a laundry depot, a newsagency where Greek language newspapers and books are on sale, and a travel agency for the men who wish to discuss travel arrangements for their wives, fiancées, and members of the family left behind in Greece. Mr Poulos Senior is also the head of the Orthodox Church Committee in the Latrobe Valley and he puts up notices whenever a Greek Orthodox priest comes from Melbourne to conduct a church service.

The Espresso Bar in Yallourn, though not as all-embracing

as the Poulos Café group, functions for the Italians. This seems to be a purely recreational club where the Italian men who live in the SEC hostel gather nightly to watch T.V., play games, and occasionally hear records of tunes currently popular in Italy.

On the more formal level there exists the Italian-Australian Social Club of Gippsland. It is of interest that—as its name implies—the club is open to Italians and Australians alike; it meets monthly (in Morwell or Moe) for socials and dancing.[27]

An example of a similar venture, for the benefit of both immigrants and Australians, is the Contra Club organized by a group of German migrants mainly to serve the social needs of younger people. Its activities were described in a local newspaper:

Aussies New and Old Mix in the 'Contra' Club

The Contra Club, started in Moe only a few months ago, seems to be solving the great problem of helping migrants assimilate more quickly into the Australian way of life.

Its membership is open to all nationalities, not only to Germans as some people seem to think.

At present the ages of members range from 17 to 25, but there is no age limit.

The aims of the Club, according to its president Mr Bernie Ipsen, who came from Germany about a year ago, is to bring together socially 'dinky di' Australians and immigrants.

By mixing in this way, New Australians learn to speak Australian more quickly and to understand Australian customs.

The Club meets every Wednesday night, at 8 p.m., in the Newborough Public Hall where records are played, informal discussions are held and trips are arranged.

The Club hopes to hold a cabaret ball or a similar function every three months.

It is also planning trips and 'fun' for week-ends when, said Mr Ipsen, the district is 'dead'.

The Club's first dance was held in the Newborough Public Hall last Friday and was attended by about 220. Prior to this, the Club has arranged a party, a trip to Mount Erica, Moomba Festival and to football games.

Co-founder of the Club with Mr Ipsen was Mr Peter Dathan, now Secretary, who arrived from Germany about five years ago.

Advocate, 1 July 1960.

Not all activities of immigrant and mixed Australian-immigrant associations are purely recreational. Some associations devote the energies of their active members and their finances to the relief of those of their compatriots who are in need through sickness, unemployment, or bereavement in the family. For example, the Polish Association in the Latrobe Valley has as one of its major aims these welfare duties to the Polish immigrants in the district, as well as the organization of celebrations on Poland's National Day (3 May) and other national festivals, and the support of the Polish Saturday schools. The dances and socials held frequently in the Newborough Public Hall and the Catholic school are the means of raising finance to support such activities. Similarly, the Ukrainian Association in Newborough also combines welfare and recreation to perpetuate among the immigrants and their children an attachment to the Ukrainian national traditions. The attachment of the Scottish immigrants to the traditions of their country is reflected in the existence of a vigorous Moe Scots Club.

Some ethnic associations evolve around a church or religious organization. Often these are informal and merely identified with the person of a priest, as in the Maltese community in Yallourn North. A Maltese priest who is attached to the Sacred Heart Parish in Morwell says Mass on Sundays in Yallourn North and also occasionally in Newborough. This is how one of the interviewers describes the way the Maltese community in Yallourn North participates in religious functions:

> The important social institution is the Roman Catholic Church, of which all are members. Of 35 people, 26 go each week, 6 once a month, 2 on special occasions and one never. A Maltese priest preaches in Maltese weekly in the local church, but the people miss the feasts, ceremonies and choral services they are used to at home. Although so many go to church, none of them belongs to any church club or society and only one has ever belonged to such a group in Australia.
>
> Only 7 of the Maltese interviewed have ever belonged to any clubs in Australia—two of them to Maltese clubs in Melbourne, and another two are the only active members from the group in any clubs. This may be partly due to the lack of organizations in Yallourn North and the feeling that once in a club you are involved in too much work. None has taken any interest in meetings about the proposed swimming pool, or the Progress Association, and they seem to have no interest in their Trade Unions.

This suggests that the Maltese group functions as an association set up for a definite purpose at the weekly church services and occasional festivals to celebrate feast days of Maltese patron saints. The association has no executive committee, no formal meetings, and its only officer is the Maltese chaplain who acts as a representative of the community on other bodies (for example, the Good Neighbour Council), and maintains regular and frequent contacts with all Maltese families in the district. In the words of the interviewer:

> Father Carruana has a great deal of social welfare work to do. He spends much of his time explaining social services, helping to fill in forms, interpreting for doctors and police, and trying to interpret the Australian way of life in an acceptable form to the Maltese. He has made a detailed study of their backgrounds because he finds these responsible for the many jealousies and differences between them and so knows how to approach each individual. He finds he is doing much that should be the province of a social worker, but it is essential to be able to speak the language and to have lived in Malta to understand the background.

The Lutheran Church in Newborough also acts as an ethnic organization, although its membership is of mixed national origin and includes Germans, Latvians, Estonians, and a few Finns. As well as meeting for church services, which are conducted in German and English, the congregation, with a committee of lay members, acts as a welfare organization, distributing aid to members who are in need, assisting recent arrivals in the district, and, in particular, looking after a few lonely German-speaking immigrants who live in one of the hostels.[28]

Sport, especially soccer, is the meeting ground of several national groups. Immigrants with continental European background consider soccer matches to be their favourite entertainment on Sunday afternoons, and flock in their hundreds to watch 'Germany' play against 'Holland' or 'Slavia' against 'Budapest'. Soccer clubs are mostly run on a national basis with a fair intermixture of English and Scottish enthusiasts, as well as a growing number of Australian players, mostly adolescents and men in their early twenties. Some idea of the national origin of soccer enthusiasts can be gained from the names of the two teams that were fielded at Moe one Sunday in August 1961:

Soccer match kept crowd on tip toe

The very large crowds watching the International Soccer series at Yallourn on Sunday saw the young Australia team go down, three goals to one, to the stronger Rest of Europe side.

In one of the best games seen in the Valley this season, with spectators vocally on tip toe throughout, the three o'clock match was a well merited draw: Germany 2, Holland 2.

In the 1.30 p.m. match, Australia v. Rest of Europe, teams were:—

Australia: Kaser, Walker, Schultz, Kovacs, Trantor, Allen, Evans, James, Ellis, J. Szabo, S. Szabo.

Rest of Europe: Slingman, Vangeninden, Alisauskas, Hargreaves, Bek, R. Mackey, Hunter, Langenberg, Chrixi, Ipenberg, J. Mackey.

Advocate, 18 August 1961.

The examples of several ethnic associations all suggest that these groups exist for specific reasons: to provide for a number of fairly well-defined needs of a spiritual, social welfare, recreational, and what could be called 'nationalistic' nature. Do ethnic associations last long? An answer to this question seems to be that they last as long as their members are in need of the various services the associations can provide. There is only one example of an ethnic association that has completed—within a span of barely four years—a full cycle of existence. This is the Dutch Social Club in Moe.

The establishment of the club is described in a report on an interview with one of its foundation members:

Mr Z. was one of the first Dutch settlers in Moe. He arrived in Moe in November 1951. His wife and family followed him six months later. Since his school days he had been engaged in voluntary social work in the Netherlands and had been active in a number of societies and clubs in his native country. He and his wife have always been very keen on acting in plays, etc., performed by dramatic societies.

As one of the first Dutch settlers in Moe he naturally was approached by the Dutch people who followed him and he gradually built up a number of official and unofficial contacts with the authorities—the local office of the Housing Commission and the Town Clerk. In 1954 he and a number of Dutch people got together and decided to establish a Dutch Choir. That was a tremendous success and the choir (male voices only) sang at special concerts and social functions all over Gippsland. The setting up of the choir, as Mr Z. puts it, satisfied men's needs for companionship, but there was still no outlet for women, i.e. there was no place or association where Dutch women, especially housewives, could meet on a social basis and find some entertainment. One of the complaints of Dutch women, and indeed most migrant women in Moe, is that there are no entertainments at all in Moe for women. Mrs Z. wanted to set up a Ladies' Club but many male members of the Dutch community were against it and in the end a compromise was made and the Dutch Social Club was established in 1955. Mr Z. says that in Holland the idea of a social club means essentially an association for mutual assistance and aid and almost always is linked up with insurance of its members. But in Moe the Dutch Social Club was mainly an association to bring together the members of the Dutch community and to help those in need.

The Dutch Social Club in Moe was formally constituted in November 1955 and reached the peak of its existence in 1956 when it had 150 members. It sponsored the following types of activities:

(1) the Welfare Committee collected funds to help families in trouble;

(2) the Moe Soccer Club was at first supported financially by the Dutch Social Club and all its players were Dutch. The club has changed its national character lately and is now known as the Moe Rapid Club; it has Dutch as well as English, Scottish and Australian players;

(3) the Ladies' Club—to provide regular entertainment and a meeting ground for Dutch women;

(4) the Dutch Choir now known as the Moe Male Choir;

(5) the Dramatic Society (known as 'Comedy Club') which in the years 1956-8 staged nine plays in the Dutch language for audiences averaging 400 persons, many of whom used to come from Morwell and the surrounding district.

One of the most successful functions organized by the club was a celebration on 5 December 1957 of the feast of St Nicholas (see Plate 3). On that occasion the Mayor of Moe, Councillor Stoddard, took part in the procession through the streets of the town followed by a crowd of children estimated at six hundred. Then the procession entered the R.S.L. Hall and St Nicholas distributed gifts to everyone present. The Dutch Choir sang in the Dutch language and a special entertainment was put on by the 'Comedy Club'.

The Dutch Social Club was disbanded early in 1959. In the words of its last president:

Members gradually started to drift away and there were fewer and fewer Dutch people who wanted to attend functions of any sort. It takes approximately two years for a Dutch family to settle in and once they get settled they join Australian clubs and associations. There is of course still a group of Dutch widows and one or two other people in need, or those who may be sick, and any collections of money for these people are these days being made by the Comedy Club.

This statement suggests some of the reasons why the club has outlived its purpose. The Dutch people in Moe no longer require a formal association to provide for their needs; some of them continue to find companionship among their own compatriots but they associate primarily with members of their regional and specific religious groupings rather than with other Dutch people as members of the Dutch community (see Chapter 9). It seems that the disbandment of the Dutch Social Club in Moe marks an eclipse of the Moe Dutch community as a national group, and, indeed, as there has been no 'new blood' from Holland since 1960 this may be an important reason why the Moe Dutch Social Club is no longer necessary.[29] Morwell, on the other hand, continues to attract new Dutch settlers who find employment in the SEC and the Gas and Fuel Corporation establishments, and the Dutch-Australian Club in Morwell continues to thrive.

How do the immigrants become members of Australian associations? This study has shown that the only way is through personal contacts and friendship with Australian workmates and neighbours; but progress is slow. A survey of several local associations in the Latrobe Valley revealed that very few immigrants have joined the more exclusive type of association, such as Rotary Clubs and Junior Chambers of Commerce. The Rotary Club of Moe, in April 1962, had no members born outside Australia and the British Isles. Two immigrants (a Pole and a Greek) who established themselves in business in Morwell were admitted to membership of the Morwell Rotary Club. Two immigrants, formerly of Dutch and German nationality, were introduced to the Moe Junior Chamber of Commerce.

By contrast the Apex clubs throughout the district make a real effort to attract immigrants of all nationalities. Nearly 25 per cent of the membership of the Morwell and Moe clubs consists of non-British-born immigrants and the man elected president of the Moe Club in 1961 is a former Hungarian. This is his description of how he became an Apexian, written two years before his election to the office of club president:

Four years after my arrival in Moe I met a man who became my friend, the first in my new country. He was a newcomer too—an Englishman. After a few weeks' friendship he introduced me into his Club, the Apex Club. Shortly afterwards I myself became a member of this wonderful organization. So I, who had no friends and lived the same isolated life as many are still living after seven or eight years in Australia, found myself in a group of young Australians, who accepted me without reservation as one of them. Through the activities of our Club I came to know more and more young men and through them I learned to know and love my new country. In due course I became an Australian citizen. Through the Apex Club I was appointed to the Good Neighbour Council as the Club's representative. Here again I met new faces, leading citizens of our community, who can always find time to assist the migrants in their problems, citizens who can see the potentialities of this great migration programme and carry on their self-accepted duties with cheerful dignity.

But I was not the only one to benefit fully from my contacts. The wives of the Apex members meet every month in each other's places. So my wife too had an interest apart from her monotonous home duties. In no time she had friends and her English improved practically over-night. I can advise most sincerely every new Australian to follow this route of mine as a road to happiness in our new country. Join whatever organization you like: there are so many different clubs and organizations which cater for everybody's need or hobby. It is an inexpensive but a very effective way to come to know our fellow Australians, to know and respect a nation which has undertaken such a migration programme, unique in its dimensions and which would present great difficulties to even bigger and richer nations.

It seems that the crux of the problem is—as the author of the above statement has put it—an unreserved acceptance by the Australians of the new member, an immigrant, as one of them. Often this is possible through common interest or hobbies. A Dutch migrant who is a keen naturalist and has made films of wild life describes how his hobby served as an introduction to several Australian associations:

We seem to fit in well in our new country according to the many friends we made. My film-projector and movies were my introductions to many societies and clubs and the list of memberships of my wife and myself is growing faster than we really intended. As members of several Australian societies we felt we should apply for our naturalization papers as soon as possible. So we were naturalized and the children grew up and mixed very well with their new friends. The daughter started nursing and passed all her exams with very nice remarks. She loves her career and is completely happy in her new country. The son rushed through his technical college and got three scholarships and a studentship. Two years more to the University and he can be what he always longed to be: civil engineer like his uncle John in Holland.

In brief we came to the following conclusions:

Australia is a beautiful country with opportunities for everybody who wants to work—specially for young people, to build yourself a career—a future.

The success of your new life is mainly in your own hands: when you mix with people, speak their language, and join their activities—they will meet you and help you in every way.

We will never regret the big step we took. We left many things behind—we gained more here in Australia.

Some immigrants are attracted to Australian societies and clubs through church membership. A Ukrainian immigrant in Newborough and his wife are both active members of the Legion of Mary, a religious organization in the local Catholic parish. He devotes a lot of his spare time to this work, which involves visiting people in their homes, attending regular weekly meetings and special church services.

Church work, such as singing in a choir, raising funds, and activities connected with children, are also attracting the immigrants, particularly the women, as the following excerpt from a report by one of the interviewers shows:

There are very few migrant women who have outside interests. Very often they do not have time for it, and even if they do they prefer to spend their leisure time at home with their husband and family, or to go on joint family outings at weekends or holidays. For many the only outing is the weekly shopping or a visit to the Infant Welfare Centre, and very often the husband thinks that this should be the extent of women's outings.

Many Roman Catholic women regard their church as an opportunity for meeting other women; the Dutch Reformed Church also provides a centre for women. The women's organizations in the area—e.g. Country Women's Association —do not have many migrant members, although the committee members state that they would like migrant women to join. However, the reason for this in most cases, the language difficulty, is a very real barrier and it prevents many of them from joining in various activities. Australian members could help more in this respect by not expecting too much from migrants in too short a time.

Activities connected with children—Kindergarten Mothers' Clubs, State School Mothers' Clubs and High School Parents' Associations seem to draw more members than other clubs because the parents are anxious to help with their children's schooling. Migrant mothers are active in helping stock stalls etc. and are interested in activities. The High School is anxious to discuss problems with parents, but not many migrants belong to the Parents' Association. Parents of children at the Roman Catholic Schools seem to have more contacts with their schools.

In some instances the immigrant participation in Australian associations takes place on a group basis. The building of the Newborough Public Hall is a good example. The Building Committee, which was set up in 1956, included five immigrants out of the total of twenty-five members. These five people (two Ukrainians, two Dutchmen, and one Pole) acted as spokesmen for their national groups, collected subscriptions from their compatriots, and organized working bees to help in construction.[30] On another occasion the Polish settlers in the Valley organized a collection in support of the appeal of the Lord Mayor of Melbourne to aid victims of the disastrous bushfires in Victoria in January 1962. The individual contributions by the Polish residents of Moe, Newborough, and Morwell averaged 12s. 6d. per head and the total of £153 17s. was far in excess of contributions collected by other ethnic groups in the Valley.[31]

The number of immigrants who are members of Australian associations is as yet too small to arrive at any generalization about the pattern of participation. It seems likely, however, that such membership does confer a higher status. As people move to higher occupational and social status they invariably tend to drop off those memberships which reflect their earlier and lower status. Thus, an immigrant tradesman who succeeds in establishing himself in business in the new country will attempt to enter an association which would reflect his higher status. The actual joining of such 'higher status' associations may reflect an aspiration on the part of one who wishes to advance in the eyes of his compatriots as well as the Australian people with whom he associates. This behaviour can be called horizontal social mobility and it takes

M

place when a member of an ethnic group begins to break his ethnic identifications and be accepted by the Australian people. A Pole who joins the local branch of the Liberal Party (a middle-class status group) will begin to reduce his relations within the ethnic group and increase his relations with the Australian people of a certain standing, thus moving to a different status within the society.[32]

Naturalization

Today I do not look back on the road I came. We only desire to see our children grow up in happiness, and to see them establish themselves in the country we adopted and which adopted us, and to become good citizens. For I believe that citizenship is not a matter of birth, but a sense of duty towards a country which gives freedom of movement and speech, good working conditions and good wages. It is a privilege to be a citizen of a country where a man is worth one man, no more and no less, where you can move wherever you want to, find work at which you are able to work, and where you can change your occupation without loss of face.

This statement by a Lithuanian settler and a resident of Yallourn sums up the feelings of many immigrants about the adoption of Australian citizenship. To many the ceremony of naturalization, with its formal renunciation of former national allegiance, symbolizes a break with the past. And if the past life has been an unhappy one (as in the case of the author of the above statement), then naturalization marks the beginning of a new phase in the life of the immigrant.

A visitor to the naturalization ceremony can sense this feeling as the new citizens take the oath and receive naturalization certificates from the Mayor (see Plate 3). Such ceremonies are attended by the local parliamentarians as well as representatives of the Good Neighbour Council and other voluntary associations. At a ceremony in Moe in 1960 all men who were naturalized received a little seedling of the wattle and the women a posy of flowers.

A statistical picture of the extent to which the eligible immigrants (that is, those resident in Australia for five years or longer) apply for naturalization is contained in Table 31. This shows marked ethnic differences but no consistent regional pattern. For example, the immigrants from the Baltic countries have the highest proportion of naturalized (76 per cent) of all

TABLE 31

Naturalization by Birthplace of Immigrants Resident in Australia Five Years and more
(%)

Birthplace	Naturalized	Not Naturalized	N =
Netherlands	64	36	**22**
Germany	20	80	**10**
Greece and Italy	50	50	**12**
Poland	25	75	**44**
Yugoslavia	52	48	**27**
Baltic countries	76	24	**21**
Ukraine	28	72	**29**
Other central and eastern Europe	64	36	**14**
Total	45	55	**179**

χ^2 27·4
d.f.   7
Level of significance   ·001

birthplaces, and the remaining ethnic groups from eastern Europe have relatively low proportions in this category: Poland 25 per cent, Ukraine 28 per cent. Again, the Netherlands has a relatively high proportion of naturalized (64 per cent) and Germany has the lowest proportion of all (20 per cent). It would seem, therefore, that any cultural affinity there may be between, say, the Netherlands and Germany, or Poland and the Baltic states, is not reflected in the numbers assuming Australian citizenship.

It would be tempting to explain the ethnic differences in terms of the extent to which individual ethnic groups participate in the wider Australian community. Yet there is no consistent pattern here either. For example, the fact that the Baltic states and northwest Europe have the two highest proportions of naturalized immigrants does not mean that they have a similar pattern of behaviour in regard to social participation. In fact their scores on the various indices having a bearing on social participation (for example, native language teaching to children, use of native language at home, choice of friends in the 'visiting' situation) are diametrically opposed. Or, again, the fact that the Ukraine and the Baltic groups have similar scores on the indices of social participation is not reflected in the proportions seeking naturalization; these proportions are almost exactly reversed.

This apparent inconsistency of behaviour has not been resolved in the present study. Clearly, further research and probing are required before the motivation is fully understood.[33] But one thing is certain and that is that naturalization is not a reliable index of social participation.[34]

People Who Do Not Participate

The preceding discussion has identified some of the ethnic groups that have relatively low scores on the various measures of social participation. We have seen that there is no uniform ethnic pattern and, moreover, that the scope for social participation in a particular group may be restricted to members of that group to the exclusion of others.[35]

But what about individual immigrants? What are the main factors that cause the individual to withdraw from social participation in the wider Australian community or to avoid the situations and relationships, described earlier, that bring him into contact with others? Two factors can be singled out for discussion. The first of these is homesickness or the difficulty experienced by an immigrant who believes that he can re-create in Australia the happier side of the social and geographical environment that he left in Europe. The second factor—or, rather, a group of related factors—is rooted in the disappointments experienced by immigrants in settling in Australia. These disappointments range from housing difficulties and ill-health to the real or imagined loss of occupational and social status. As the evidence collected suggests, the effect of the second factor may be more important to political refugees.

The ability to adjust to a new country is related to the expectations aroused before migration. Many immigrants whom we interviewed are not at home in the Latrobe Valley because they expect to find there several of the things they left behind in their country of origin. The majority realize, of course, that it is impossible to emigrate to Australia and maintain at the same time a close contact with their families, enjoy the social life of the community they left behind, have the same kinds of entertainments and all the other things of which they have retained pleasant memories.

Asked to name the things that they miss most from their country of origin (see Appendix C, Q.54), a third of all respondents named three kinds of personal contacts. Firstly, family contacts, a typical statement being: 'I miss my mother and father and relatives whom I visited regularly and shared celebrations with'. Secondly, women: 'It is hard to find a decent girl round here', 'I miss the companionship of girls who can speak my language', 'Girls will not go out with New Australians unless they speak good English'. Thirdly, freedom from language difficulties: 'I miss being able to talk to people—I feel lonely'.

Homesickness is also expressed in statements criticizing the general pattern of social life in Australia. About a third of immigrants of all nationalities said that they missed the social life of their close urban or rural communities in Europe, while some of the British immigrants criticized the lack of 'culture' in the Latrobe Valley.[36] Other immigrants from continental Europe spoke of things such as early closing of hotel bars ('I miss the wider social life associated with drinking and dislike the early closing of hotels', or 'I miss the civilized drinking in coffee shops and wine clubs') and the atmosphere of life on Sundays ('Sunday here is a cemetery', 'I miss the dancing after Church', 'I miss the general gaiety and holiday atmosphere of Sundays'). An excerpt from a report on the Dutch community in Moe sums up the difficulties faced by many immigrants in regard to social life:

> Quite a few families are not at home in Moe. Those who are older naturally have more ties to their old country and find it hard to relinquish previous ways of behaving. They try to recapture the life they lived in Holland, and when this fails they become very dispirited and unhappy. They seem to miss the bustle of city life, or the fact that there are always a lot of people around them; many people commented on the dullness of entertainment out here. Many felt, too, that they could never make friends as close to them as those they had left in Holland. They miss particularly a bright cabaret type of restaurant where a working man could take wife and children and pay a small price but obtain bright entertainment. Many families said that everything closes up on Saturday at 12 o'clock, and they were at a loss for entertainment—this is when they miss the gay music playing in the streets and the opportunity to go for a stroll, or window shopping. Women get very bored at home and sit at home brooding on the fact that there are no coffee-lounges where they can go with friends or while enjoying shopping excursions together.[37]

Next, there are those that miss some of the pageantry and tradition that forms such a large part of the life of the inhabitants of most European countries but particularly of southern Europe. This is how a middle-aged carpenter from Malta describes his recollections of life in Malta, stressing by implication how very different it is from conditions in the Latrobe Valley:

> Besides the Mardi Gras which lasts for three days before Ash Wednesday every town celebrates the feast of its Patron Saint. St George is the Patron Saint of my home town Curmi and his feast is celebrated on April 23. Celebrations last three days and begin with a solemn High Mass in the parish church. The day before people go to Confession and then receive Holy Communion at High Mass. There is usually a sermon by the Archbishop or his representative and then a relic of St George and his statue is carried around the town in procession. Thousands of people throng the streets and return to church for benediction with the Blessed Sacrament. For the following two days there is dancing in the streets, music and fireworks. Another important celebration is the Feast of St Peter and St Paul on June 29. The celebrations consist of services in all churches throughout Malta and on the following day there are traditional donkey races at Rabat. On the third day the agricultural show opens at Buskett and everybody flocks to the show. There is a custom that the newly-married couples spend their honeymoon at the Show in Buskett. People spend the night there under the trees singing folksongs accompanied by guitars, frying rabbits, eating fruit and drinking wine.

Finally there are miscellaneous things that the immigrants miss, such as certain sports (winter sports, soccer), food (for example, fish dishes), and such vaguely identified notions as 'snow', 'white Christmas', 'sea', 'climate', and 'twilight'.

The people who do not feel unhappy here are usually the younger ones and those who have fulfilled their expectations and have not set their hopes too high. Homesickness is not a lasting condition, but an impression gained during the study suggests that there seems to be a critical period in the process of adjustment of individual immigrants, usually between one and two years after arrival in Australia.[38] Once the difficulties of this period are overcome and homesickness loses its force the immigrant begins to notice some of the real advantages he may have gained through migration.

The second group of related factors that inhibit active participation is connected with personal disappointments and is often, as in the case of Displaced Persons, rooted in the events that led to migration.

Sometimes the disappointments and withdrawal from participation are aggravated by the age of the immigrant.

The example of Mr K. and his wife, both in their mid-sixties, shows how difficult it is for elderly people to make a good adjustment. Mr and Mrs K. left their native town in Lanarkshire in 1955. 'We were enticed by good reports of our elder son who has been in Australia since 1950 and also by the Australian migration propaganda in Scotland,' said Mrs K. Mr K. has not made a good adjustment in Yallourn. He does not get on well with his boss (he is a cleaner in the main office of the SEC) and would prefer to work in his old trade of kiln burner. The working hours (4-12 p.m.) do not suit him because he does not see much of his wife. Asked what are the things that he misses most of all he said: 'The constant activity, the way of life in a Scottish town—the entertainments and the ability to drink at any hour'. In reply to the same question Mrs K. said: '. . . the busy life and comings and goings of living in a large tenement house'. This is how the interviewer summed up her impressions of the couple:

> Mr K. was quite friendly but took the opportunity to air all his grievances about Australia and Australians. He sat huddled in a corner over a fire—a rather pathetic sight. . . . What struck me most during the interview was the hapless plight of the old couple. Both of them hate their work, the home they live in and their neighbours. They admit they expected too much of Australia—and they are now regretting their emigration. . . . Even though Mr K. would like to work longer he has been given his notice to retire through old age —and they will have to take out a pension on which they see no hope of saving up enough to return home to Scotland— which is all they feel they ever want to do (*Interview No. 605*).

In several cases lack of participation, and the consequent withdrawal and maladjustment, is linked with the difficulties experienced during the first few years of resettlement in Australia. This can be seen in the following example of a 40-year-old Yugoslav labourer and his German wife:

> Subject speaks poor English—much poorer than comparable migrants I have seen. His first years in the Latrobe Valley were very hard. He and his wife (who was pregnant at that time) lived in a shack although they were promised better accommodation. There was no electricity in the street for six years until the SEC put in a few poles. Then they had to pay for the making of the road and the footpaths. Wife says some Australian shopkeepers are very nasty to the migrants. She and her husband made few friends; she is homesick and

frustrated. After several years of hard struggle they have built their own home and furnished it tastefully. They have the material comforts but their social adjustment in Australia looks very unsatisfactory (*Interview No. 729*).

The frustrating experiences described in this example have probably been aggravated by a loss of occupational status suffered by the immigrant. In Yugoslavia he was a non-commissioned officer in the Army; then came the war, long imprisonment in a P.O.W. camp, followed by liberation and four years of service in the U.S. Service Units which were staffed by the Poles and Yugoslavs to guard American property in Germany. As a member of that organization he enjoyed a relatively high status in war-ravaged Germany. Now he is reduced to the status of a labourer and feels he is too old to learn a trade. Sometimes loss of status, and imagined or real discrimination experienced by the new-comers, breeds resentment and hatred of Australian people, as seen in the following letter written by an immigrant from eastern Europe who was reminded about his earlier promise to write a life history:

Received your letter dated 29.3.1960. I must remind you I am in no way indebted to you with my promise. First it was stated, I am required to write a short story. Second I had not promised anything to you or somebody else. Third my life story is in spite of my young age a very long one. As my parents still live behind the Iron Curtain and could be prosecuted, I cannot give much information. Myself had in mind to write a book under nom de plum. So I keep the story to myself. Besides I am accusing Australia like A. Dumas in 'Je Accuse' luring migrant here under false pretences. Until I came here I was a human being. In Australia I am not. The Human rights the Roman jurisprudence conceded, that by the law of nature 'Jus Naturale' all men were born free, does not apply to New Australians. I am reciting the most important chapter in Human Rights. 'Everyone is entitled to all the rights and freedoms set forth in this declaration, without distinction of any kind, such as race, colour, sex, language, religion, political or other opinion, national or social origin, birth or other status. . .

Until this is accepted we feel only tolerated slaves here in Australia. We are good enough to do the manual dirty work, but to rise, give us a 'Fair go' would be too much to ask. Why is a migrant doctor with a Nobel Prize unable to get a job??? Because he is a lot better than many Australians. He proved he is when he received the Prize. I learned a trade in three years. I never found anyone, who could do a job that I am capable of doing in spite of the fact that they learned the trade for 5 years. I knew a Professor speaking 8 languages he was forced with me to work carrying cement because he could not speak English. According to Australians he is an idiot. But they are as well. . . .

Other cases of complete withdrawal from social participation, even from the members of their own ethnic group, seem to be linked with war-time uprooting and persecution. The immigrants who behave in this way are invariably men from eastern Europe and their present attitude is a curious mixture of hatred of communism and resentment against Australia and Australian people. The following three examples taken from the interview files all suggest the same psychological mechanism at work.

A 50-year-old Lithuanian—was an independent farmer now labourer.
Respondent is desperately homesick, has children at a Russian University. He will not talk about them and wishes to remain completely anonymous. Never ventures far from his hostel room if he can help it. Mistrusts his fellow countrymen and Australians alike but is determined to stay here for the rest of his life (*Interview No. 826*).

A 58-year-old Russian labourer (ex-coal miner).
I was struck by the poverty of the dwelling and the fear, bitterness and resentment evident in the respondent's behaviour. He made a point of hating Communists and insisted that I write it on the schedule. He had a strange fatalistic attitude —probably resulting from experiences during the war and revolution in his own country—he remarked several times during the interview 'perhaps we'll all be dead tomorrow'. This man appears to have no contact with the outside world socially—except his (Ukrainian) son-in-law with whom, occasionally, he has a glass of beer (*Interview No. 311*).

A 36-year-old Ukrainian labourer.
I was struck by the pessimism and sensitive feelings of this rather intelligent man who has been frustrated in his efforts to integrate and is culturally starved. The hopelessness felt by the respondent: trying to succeed and climb yet tied to the environment, his job, etc. . . .

He is a strongly patriotic Ukrainian. Subject is an avid reader; especially of anti-communist literature. He has deformed opinions on the Australian way of life. Bitterness is the very note—e.g. he looks after the house—therefore rates are raised; he wants to borrow money for farm—can't; asks mayor, etc. for help on migrant integration—not forthcoming. Considers the Allies in siding with Russia in World War II as bad as the Germans. Has a brother who is a Communist in the Soviet Union.

All his effort goes into the house (wife's too). Has tried to make friends with Australians—rebuffed. Says the only way to do it is to go to the pub with them on a drinking spree—is not interested in this (*Interview No. 702*).

A related example of withdrawal from social participation is that of some of the hostel dwellers. It is true that to many of these, hostel life is a temporary and passing phase of the process of settling in. Some are saving hard to buy a block of land or, perhaps, to erect a dwelling on a block which they have already acquired.

But in the midst of the well-adjusted hostel dwellers there is a sizeable minority who, unjustly perhaps, have contributed to the creation of an unfavourable stereotype of hostel life. These men live an aimless existence in an artificial environment physically separated from the rest of the community. Some spend all their earnings on drink and gambling while others develop a 'could-not-care-less attitude' so characteristic of many men in this group. Several men, particularly of non-British origin, complained about being snubbed by Australian girls at local dances. This had led them to withdraw from outside social contact into their own national groups in the hostel and this naturally slows down their mastery of the English language.

The stereotype of a maladjusted hostel dweller, the depressing conditions, and the squalor of his life are not, as I have already emphasized, the dominant pattern in the places here described. But they leave a strong impression on the visitor to workers' hostels. This is perhaps an example of the situation in which 'exceptions confirm the rule' and justify a special mention of some of the less desirable aspects of hostel life. It is perhaps surprising that so many of our respondents have not become demoralized by the artificial life in hostels. The fact that some clearly have not succeeded points to a causal connection between the environment and the process of adjustment.

This chapter has highlighted some of the factors that have a bearing on the participation in the life of the community at large;

next, it has shown how the ethnic groups included in this study differ in the extent of social participation.

Two general points emerge. First is a relationship between the extent of social participation and the breadth of identification of immigrants with the new country and the new social roles performed by them. Second is the part played by the immigrant and the mixed Australian immigrant associations as agencies of social control.

Upon arrival in Australia the immigrant is forced to assume a new social role in the main institutional spheres of the social structure. If he is a southern European or an eastern European the immigrant usually comes from a peasant community based on primary, face-to-face relations, to an urban society in a secondary stage of organization. To make the necessary adjustment involved in such a change the immigrant has to learn his new social roles. The very large majority of immigrants—as we have seen—learn their new roles in immigrant organizations of all kinds. To the newly-arrived Greek construction worker his school of assimilation is the Poulos Café in West Camp where he meets some of the well-settled Greek immigrants and learns from them about Australian customs and rules of behaviour.

To a Ukrainian settler this educational function is performed by the Ukrainian Association through one of its committees or specialized groups.

If, on the other hand, he comes from an urban society of Britain, northwestern or central Europe—his social roles in Australia are not likely to be very different and therefore there is a less pronounced need for immigrant organizations to teach him how to perform the new roles. The case of the Dutch Social Club in Moe is an apt illustration.

These immigrant and mixed Australian-immigrant organizations perform yet another function in addition to their educational role. They act as agencies of social control and, therefore, are beneficial and necessary in the first stage of the process of adjustment. To maintain a stable personality the newly-arrived immigrant has to belong somewhere, to feel that he has status and influence and that he is recognized as representing something. This can only be achieved in such informal and formal groups as the home, the neighbourhood, the religious congregation, or a club.[39] The immigrants who do become members of such groups, where something is expected of them and where they have responsibility and a recognized status, will be ready to venture outside the group and participate in the life of the community at large (see Appendix A, p. 192). The immigrants who do not participate, the 'social isolates' and men harbouring a personal grudge or fear are—as we have seen—persons who have not satisfied the fundamental condition of successful adjustment and have not become accepted as members of their own groups.

SOCIAL PARTICIPATION AND GROUP AFFILIATION

The analysis of the data relating to the degree of social participation in the affairs of the Australian community revealed that the two non-British ethnic groups who differed most in almost every aspect of social participation were the Dutch and the Ukrainians. The Dutch had the highest and the Ukrainians the lowest proportion of their numbers who maintain visiting relationships with the Australian people. Again, the Dutch had the highest scores measuring the degree of exposure to Australian communication media; the Ukrainians had the lowest. By contrast, the Ukrainians had the second highest proportion of persons who were active members of migrant national societies; the Dutch had the second lowest proportion of 'joiners' of purely migrant organizations among the nine non-British ethnic groups included in this study.

Case Studies of the Dutch in Moe and the Ukrainians in Newborough

The pattern of contrasting behaviour seemed clear on the surface; but a further study of the non-quantitative material collected in the field raised doubts about the conclusion that the Dutch were easily the most 'assimilable' group and the Ukrainians were the least 'assimilable'—if the degree of social participation outside one's ethnic group can be taken as a measure of assimilation. The evidence collected by interviewers, conversations conducted with Australians, and the writer's observations seemed to suggest that not all the Dutch people and not all the Ukrainian people behaved similarly within their own group. In point of fact analysis of the distribution of the patterns of social participation within the two groups showed striking fluctuations ranging from no social participation to high social participation. Moreover, these differences seemed correlated with membership of some less formal groupings such as religious congregations. This seemed particularly true of the Dutch people, amongst whom the members of the *Gereformeerde Kerk* (known as the Reformed Church of Australia) had little contact with the Australian population, and others who belonged to the Presbyterian Church, or were listed as non-believers, mixed a lot with the Australian people.

167

This finding led to the decision that it was necessary to study further the pattern of group affiliation amongst the Dutch people of Moe and the Ukrainian people of Newborough, the objective being to discover the complex network of more or less informal groupings and cliques of social and/or religious character, the membership of which seemed to be a significant factor in adjustment.[1]

The main technique used in this study to identify the nuclei of primary groups in the two populations was the sociometric test (see pp. 42-4). The pattern of group affiliation revealed in this manner is discussed first of all with regard to the degree of social integration of the Dutch and the Ukrainian population. Next, affiliations based on the province of origin are compared, followed by a discussion of primary groups based on the membership of religious denominations. One such group—the Reformed Church congregation in Moe—is singled out for special examination.

Social Integration in the Dutch and Ukrainian Populations

Several approaches were used to examine and compare the degree of social integration in the two populations. The first and obvious method was to compare them on the basis of the proportion of their members who received more than a certain arbitrarily determined minimum of sociometric choices (see p. 43). A sociometric choice was registered when an individual was named in reply to one or both of the following two questions: 'Name three of your closest friends' and 'What three people do you see the most of socially?' The minimum of choices was fixed at five and on this basis the Ukrainians seem to be more integrated than the Dutch people: the proportion of persons in the Ukrainian population who received five choices and over—which can be assumed to be an index of popularity—is over 12 per cent, whereas the corresponding Dutch proportion is just under 4 per cent (see Table 32). An even more telling measure of integration is the proportion of persons in the two groups who received no choices. The proportions here were 25·9 per cent in the Ukrainian group,[2] and 37·7 per cent in the Dutch group.[3] This indicates that, unlike the Dutch, the Ukrainians are better integrated, and that there is a core of leaders who are known to, and respected by, a substantial majority in the group. This is also reflected in the membership of the *Hromada*, a local branch of the Ukrainian Association of Victoria. Out of forty-four males who are eligible for membership thirty-five, or nearly 80 per cent, belong to that

TABLE 32

*Frequency Distribution of Sociometric Choices by Dutch Adults in Moe and Ukrainian Adults in Newborough**

No. of choices received	Dutch		Ukrainian	
	No. of persons	% of persons	No. of persons	% of persons
0	158	37·7	21	25·9
1	104	24·8	16	19·7
2	72	17·2	18	22·2
3	45	10·8	8	9·9
4	24	5·7	8	9·9
5	9	2·2	8	9·9
6	5	1·2	—	—
7	1	·2	2	2·5
8	1	·2	—	—
	419	100·0	81	100·0
5 choices and over	16	3·8	10	12·3

* For definition of 'sociometric choice' see Chapter 9, n.4.

body. The majority of these are keen and active members of the *Hromada*, a fact which is seen in its manifold activities, including the construction of a substantial building to be known as Ukrainian Hall, the maintenance of a Saturday school and a group of Ukrainian scouts; organization of national celebrations and such fund-raising activities as dances and fêtes; organization of the Ukrainian Choir, etc. (see Plate 2).

The two Ukrainians who received the highest number of choices (Nos. 16 and 17) were a married couple whose popularity amongst all members of the Ukrainian population was unquestioned. No. 16 is a past-president of the *Hromada* and currently president of the Building Committee of the Ukrainian Hall. He also looks after the substantial collection of Ukrainian books that form the lending library of the *Hromada*. A likeable man, he and his wife are on very good terms with their Australian neighbours.

By contrast the two outstanding Dutch personalities—No. 318, who received eight choices, and No. 348, who received seven choices—could not possibly be described as leaders of the whole of the Dutch population in Moe. They were, for all practical purposes, leaders of certain sections within the Dutch population. No. 318 is a leader of the Dutch choir and a keen member of the Dutch Dramatic Society. The persons who chose him were mainly members of these two organizations. No. 348 is a leading member of the Committee of Management of the Reformed Church and nearly all the people who chose him were members of that church.

The preceding analysis of the degree of social integration in terms of distribution of sociometric choices has taken no account of other factors which may condition a preliminary conclusion that the Ukrainians are more integrated than the Dutch. The process of integration involves two things. First, it suggests a trend towards mutual identification by members of a group who share a set of common values; secondly, it assumes the existence of an easy flow of communications within the group without which a uniform set of values could not be shared. To satisfy these two conditions there must be, within a given group, a necessary degree of homogeneity.

An examination of the composition of the two groups in terms of age distribution, occupation, and length of residence in Australia brings out an extraordinary degree of homogeneity in the Ukrainian population compared with the Moe Dutch. In so far as the age distribution is concerned, 80 per cent of the Ukrainian people in Newborough are in the 35-49 age bracket compared with 43 per cent in the case of the Dutch in Moe.[4] Unlike the Dutch, then, the Ukrainian population consists mainly of middle-aged people. Again, there is an interesting contrast in the occupational distribution of males in the two populations. The Ukrainians are mostly semi-skilled labourers, but the Dutch are scattered in other occupational groups as well as a significant concentration in the skilled ('craftsmen') grades.[5] Finally, whereas 90 per cent of the Ukrainian people arrived in Australia in 1949 and 1950, 23 per cent of the Dutch in Moe did not arrive until 1954—although small groups had come at intervals throughout the post-war period.[6]

The striking degree of homogeneity in the Ukrainian population (to which must be added the fact that they all consider themselves political exiles and all left their country in similar circumstances) [7] is probably responsible for a relatively high degree of social integration in that group compared with the Dutch population at Moe. In other words, the preceding analysis suggests that structural factors in the composition of the population account for differences in group integration.

The second method of comparison of the degree of social

integration in the two populations was by means of an Index of Clannishness. This simple index expresses as a proportion the number of 'in-group' choices (that is, choices of the same birth-place) in the total choices of each respondent. Those who made no choices were excluded. A comparison of the Index values shows that the two groups are equally clannish.[8] It would appear, therefore, that in spite of the objective differences discussed above the Dutch people in Moe are no less inward-looking in their friendship patterns than the Ukrainians in Newborough.[9] A further analysis, however, in terms of religious affiliations reveals that there are no differences between the two denominations amongst the Ukrainians (i.e. the Roman Catholics of the Greek Rite and the members of the Ukrainian Orthodox Church), but the Dutch population contains one denomination which stands out as more clannish than the rest. The group which exhibits this significant feature of behaviour is the Reformed Church of Australia,[10] the members of which follow the teaching and tradition of the *Gereformeerde Kerk* in the Netherlands. The members of the Reformed Church differ quite markedly not only from the Ukrainian population but from the Dutch followers of other denominations.[11]

The preceding comparative analysis of the degree of social integration in the Dutch and Ukrainian populations has shown that, although the two groups are equally clannish, the Ukrainian people are much less differentiated and more closely integrated than the Dutch. The Ukrainian community of Newborough seems, then, to be truly a community in the sociological sense and not just a collection of people with a common ethnic origin. Close ethnic ties in the Ukrainian community are reinforced by the godparent relationship or the institution of the *kum*. This institution recreates something of the pattern of kinship ties that was disrupted by the war, deportations, and flight from the Ukraine. It is noticeable that religion is not a barrier in the selection of godparents, and, once formally established, the ties linking the parents of a child and his godparent and the latter's spouse are as strong as the ties of blood.[12]

No such strong factors of integration are to be found amongst the Dutch in Moe. They seem to be split into a number of smaller cliques (such as the Reformed Church congregation) who behave differently. It will be our task now to identify more closely some of these cliques and consider whether the membership of such groups has an effect on the extent of social participation.

N

Province of Origin and Social Participation

An analysis of the sociometric choices made by the Dutch immigrants[13] shows that the settlers from Limburg are conspicuous for the tendency to find their friends amongst the immigrants from the same province of origin, followed by the people from Friesland, North Brabant, North Holland, and South Holland. More often the tendency is to associate not only with people from the same province but with persons from the same town or village in the Netherlands.[14]

There is much in the history and linguistic structure of the Netherlands that explains why the people of these three provinces are relatively more clannish. Limburg and Brabant were not added to the Generality Lands of the United Provinces until after the Treaty of Munster in 1648 at the conclusion of the Thirty Years' War. Under Dutch rule these territories, with their predominantly Catholic population, gravitated towards the neighbouring Belgian and German provinces. This tendency was finally recognized in the Treaty of London in 1839 when Limburg became part of the Germanic Confederaton. It was not until 1867 that the London Conference ruled that Limburg should be incorporated with the Netherlands.[15]

The predominantly Calvinist Friesland has also shown extreme individuality throughout the course of the history of the Netherlands. This dates back to the constitutional crisis of 1648-51 when the provinces of Friesland and Groningen alone backed the Stadtholders (William II and his successor William Frederick of Nassau Dietz) in opposition to the powerful majority of the States General dominated by the provincial States of Holland.

The dialect spoken by the Frisian people is also different from the speech of the people of the central provinces. The speech of the Frisians is closely related to English,[16] and at one time extended as far west as North Holland, but today is spoken only in the province of Friesland and on the islands off the coast of Friesland; it is, in fact, a separate tongue from the Low Saxon and Hollands —'Dutch' dialects spoken in the central provinces; from the seventeenth century the Frisian dialect has also existed as a fully developed literary language.[17] The distinctive linguistic characteristic of the Frisian people was often commented upon by the Dutch in Moe. Limburg and North Brabant, too, have peculiar dialects which mark their inhabitants off from the rest of the Dutch people.[18]

Religious Affiliation

Religious affiliation among the Dutch people in Moe has already been found responsible for the differences in the degree of 'clannishness'. A more refined method of investigating such differences is to consider numbers of in-group choices (i.e. choices in the same denomination) for each religious denomination.

An index similar to that described above was used, by expressing the number of choices in the same denomination as a proportion of total choices for each subject. It was found that the Reformed Church group had the highest degree of clannishness in their own denomination[19] and differed from all except the Roman Catholic Church in this respect.[20] But it should be remembered that the Reformed Church is an exclusively Dutch institution, and therefore in-group participation for these people means participating exclusively with their compatriots. In the Roman Catholic Church, however, in-group participation can mean mixing with people of other than Dutch origin; there is some evidence that a sizeable proportion of the Dutch Catholics make friends with Australian Catholics in Moe.[21]

The Reformed Church stands out, too, because it has the lowest proportion of adherents who never attend church.[22] In view of the features of the Reformed Church which have been demonstrated, the composition and pattern of group affiliations in the congregation will now be examined in detail.

The Moe congregation of the Reformed Church is affiliated with the Reformed Church of Australia and New Zealand, which is based on the teachings of the *Gereformeerde Kerk* in the Netherlands. That church was founded in 1834 when a group of ministers broke away from the *Hervormde Kerk* (the original post-Reformation Dutch Reformed Church) and returned to the stricter orthodoxy of an earlier period. The founders of the church claimed that the teachings of Calvin and the Bible were too broadly and too liberally interpreted. They attempted to follow more closely the teachings of Calvin as set out in his *Institutes of the Christian Religion.*[23]

Throughout its history the *Gereformeerde Kerk* in the Netherlands has encouraged the emigration and group settlement of its members in the United States, Canada, and, more recently, in Australia.[24]

The first *Gereformeerde Kerk* families arrived in Moe in 1951, and, until 1955, used to meet in one of their homes for Bible reading and hymn singing. During that time there was some discussion in the group as to whether or not they should eventually affiliate with the local Presbyterian Church which at that time had—and still has—a Dutch-born Minister. There were some in that group who were in favour of affiliation but the majority were against it. For a while a Calvinist (that is *Gereformeerde Kerk*) Minister from Melbourne visited Moe at intervals, but early in 1956 a new Minister was sent by the mother-church in the Netherlands to look after what was now a congregation of about thirty families. This man resigned his appointment early in 1959 and was succeeded by an American-born Minister of Dutch ancestry who had trained in the Calvinist Theological College in Michigan, one of the early overseas foundations of the *Gereformeerde Kerk*.

The minister of the Moe Reformed Church has the responsibility of supreme spiritual adviser; he conducts two services each Sunday, visits families regularly, and gives spiritual advice and support.

There are several officers elected by the congregation to assist the Minister in his duties and, above all, to maintain strict orthodoxy amongst the adherents of the church. These include the Deacon who assists in conducting services and three Elders. An official handbook has summed up the functions of the Elders in Reformed Church congregations:

> Calvin also achieved a notable reformation in the government of the Church by the appointment of Elders to rule over, and teach and visit the members according to the New Testament pattern. . . . The Elders supervise the entire life of each member, encouraging the development of their Christian life, and correcting the erring.[25]

The Elders are elected by ballot by the congregation and hold office for two years. It is their responsibility to spend a couple of evenings with each family every year, going through their whole religious practices and beliefs to see that they are up to standard. They seem to do this much more frequently, however, so that if ever a family is in any sort of trouble it has always plenty of opportunity to share and discuss it.

The Moe Church is completely self-sufficient financially. All wage-earners are expected to contribute 10 per cent of their net earnings for the needs of the church. The contributions are voluntary, though the pressure to pay up is very heavy. Besides the regular contributions, each Reformed Church family is

expected to make donations towards the expenses of running the
theological college in Geelong, the training centre of the church.

In addition to the regular weekly services, other spiritual and
material needs of the members are provided for in three main
committees established within the church. Their functions and
structure are described by an interviewer who worked mostly
amongst the Reformed Church families:

Youth Group

The Youth Group at the moment consists of two sections, six
children in the over-fourteen group and twelve in the under-
fourteen. The group has two main purposes. Firstly to keep
the younger members of the church together and secondly to
further their Bible study at a level which is comprehensible
to them.

At the moment the main emphasis seems to be on Bible study.
At their fortnightly meetings the children are given prescribed
texts of the Bible to discuss; and any general points which may
arise out of this. I have never been able to talk much to the
children themselves about this but have heard from
ex-members that this is very strictly disciplined and most
discussion is about the moral and spiritual aspects of various
habits of Australians and the world in general. For example
the over-fourteen group listens to a recording of a popular
'hit' and then they discuss moral aspects of its content.

After a supper break the children have a game or two but this
is seen as of very secondary importance to the Bible study.
At one time this group had attempted to have associations and
affiliations with other groups in the district but this is now
discontinued. The present leaders see the function of this
group as too dissimilar from the others for such arrangements
to be satisfactory.

Ladies Guild

This group is designed with a similar purpose to that of the
Youth Group, that is, to keep churchgoers together and to
further Bible study. Mrs B., the President, also aims to give
the women more general knowledge as she feels they are
quite ignorant of world affairs, history or anything outside
household tasks.

At the moment they meet once a fortnight for prayers and
hymn singing. Also, one woman is assigned to give a talk on
some well-known personality such as Florence Nightingale or
Elizabeth Fry, someone who has led a good, Christian life.

Sponsoring Committee

In 1955 when the Reformed Church was constituted in Moe the members became concerned about the small numbers in their congregation and looked into the possibility of sponsoring migrants. This was first organized on a state-wide scale under the name of the Reformed Immigration Association Scheme or RIAS. This did not function effectively and in 1957 the responsibility was delegated to each congregation. The Moe group formed the Sponsoring Committee, consisting of four senior members of the church including the Deacon. As it has functioned over the past three years these had contact with churches in the Netherlands who gave them lists and references of prospective *Gereformeerde Kerk* migrants. The committee selected those they thought suitable and put them on the boat, brought them to Moe where they had accommodation arranged, the larders stocked with food, a meal cooked and bedding ready. They also did what they could to arrange suitable employment for the men.

The figures for families sponsored in this manner are:—

1958	22 families
1959	38 families
1960	22 families

At the moment migration to the Valley has virtually ceased and the Committee is in a state of relapse, although they continue regular visiting of the most recently arrived to offer them friendship and religious counselling.

The church has been extremely disappointed with this programme, as most of the families leave the district very

TABLE 33

Sociometric Choices of Members of the Moe Reformed Church (Gereformeerde Kerk) Congregation

	Groups			
	A	B	C	D
N =	**25**	**12**	**10**	**16**
Choices				
Total No.	91	34	33	39
Dutch	79	34	23	29
as % of total	86·8	100·0	69·7	74·4
Ref. Church	68	29	14	14
as % of total	74·7	85·3	42·4	35·9

quickly. Some families appear to be insufficiently informed about conditions in Moe before arrival while others complain about heavy subscriptions to the church and strict supervision of their private lives.

An analysis of sociometric choices (see Table 33) in the Reformed Church congregation reveals four groups of people that differ from one another in the extent of their in-group participation. Group A includes office-bearers in the congregation past and present, their wives or husbands (twenty-five in all). Group B includes the persons sponsored by the church who for the most part are recent arrivals (twelve persons). (Two of these are office-bearers and so are included in Group A as well as Group B.) Group C consists of unmarried members of the church who are known as regular churchgoers (ten persons). Group D consists of persons not included in any of the above groups (sixteen in all).

Group A. Nearly half of all adult members of the church belong to Group A.[26] Out of ninety-one choices made by members of that group, seventy-nine are Dutch and the remaining mostly Australian neighbours; sixty-eight of the Dutch choices are members of the Reformed Church; eleven non-Reformed Church choices were mostly business associates and close friends.

The majority in this group appear to be people completely devoted to their church, keen to give up a substantial proportion of their earnings for the maintenance of the Minister and other needs of the congregation. But the interviewer is frequently struck by a measure of suspicion shown to outsiders:

> No. 222 was friendly but hard to talk with. As he was an ex-Deacon of the church I had expected him to be glad to talk about it and his work but . . . although not openly loath to talk about it he did not seem able to. . . . Many of these church men . . . wanted to talk but just did not have any facility of expression, seemed . . . just unaccustomed to any discussion such as I was trying to encourage. Their whole approach seemed quite incongruous with what would be expected of an Evangelical church. A sort of self-sufficiency with no need of the outside world except as a means to get money to live.

Another leading member of the church (No. 259) confirms the impression of the researcher that there is a good deal of latent dissatisfaction with the way the church has developed:

> He feels the people are becoming more and more narrow and isolated, flocking together for security. Originally the aim had

been evangelical and to move towards affiliations with other churches.

Group B. At the time of the sociometric survey only six married couples were in the category of recently-sponsored immigrants. As recent arrivals they seem to be under a strict tutelage of the Elders and the members of the Sponsoring Committee and, as a consequence, mix almost exclusively in the church and have few outside contacts. To the researcher they present a picture of neutral, withdrawn people of impassive appearance. Most seem glad to be in Moe and are ready to accept the church's protection.

> Mr R. and his wife are an elderly couple who were sponsored by one of the founders of the Moe Church. They made sure there was a 'good *Gereformeerde Kerk*' here before they decided to emigrate. Mr R. came into conflict with his employers when he arrived here over working on Sunday and refused to do any work on Sunday unless it was urgent. He is now working on his own so that he can do as he pleases. Their life is ruled by the church . . . passively they obey all church teachings.

Only one couple in that group were critical of the discipline imposed by the church:

> Mr V. receives regular visits from church members. I have a feeling he does not really appreciate these and would prefer to be left alone. The only family he sees besides church members is one with whom he travelled to Australia.
>
> Mrs V. is often visited by members of the Sponsoring Committee, but like her husband seems to prefer to remain a little removed from them. Does not join in other women's morning coffee meetings but does belong to Ladies' Guild.

Group C. This group has a much lower proportion of Dutch and Reformed Church choices than Groups A and B. On close inspection of the choices made by Group C it was found that the younger members of the church, though on the whole strict in their attendance at church functions, do not necessarily mix with other members of the same group. They tend to give as friends people they have met in their work. For example, two daughters of a leading member of the church, girls aged 19 and 21, are shown as good church members but give as friends Australian girls in the place where they work. Similarly No. 264, a young man aged 20 and a member of one of the founding families of the church, described as a 'strict church member', names as his closest friends three of his Australian workmates.

Group D. This group includes fifteen persons who described themselves as members of the Reformed Church but seem to be on the fringe of the congregation. An interesting fact about this group is that they have the lowest proportion of Reformed Church choices but not an equally low proportion of Dutch choices.

Some people in this group have other obligations, such as a young family, and they are too busy to keep up friendships even within their own group. For example Mrs G. (No. 382, whose husband is a Baptist) is described as follows:

> The family try to have Bible readings three times a day—a practice they observed in Holland and which they try to keep up here, as it is part of their church rules and is compulsory.

Another subject, No. 391, is not anxious to mix socially. Says he sees all the church people on Sunday, which satisfies him socially, but his wife visits within the church circle.

A number of people in this group complain about the tensions and conflicts within the church.

> Although No. 95 attends Reformed Church regularly she is very much a fringe member. . . . She said the quarrels and dissension within the church are not unique and that churches of this nature in Holland had similar troubles. She does not like being involved in these and has steered clear of close association in both countries for this reason.

Some members of this group are not happy at all about the discipline imposed by the church. This is how the interviewer described one of her informants, No. 238:

> Mr H. was extremely nervous and anxious in a manner which may have been due to expected arrival of two Elders of the church during the interview. When they did come his English became almost incoherent and he was obviously very ill at ease and dreading their visit. Mr H. and his wife recently moved from Geelong where they mixed solely with Australians. . . . They have made no friends in Moe even though they attend the Reformed Church. They either do not wish to belong to the clique or have not been accepted by the other members.

The evidence presented here points to several areas of disagreement and stress within the Reformed Church. It seems that the relationships within the church are not as close and stable as the high proportion of in-group choices would suggest. This is how an interviewer who lived for three months with members of that group sums up her impressions:

I have a feeling these relationships are based more on convenience or for security than on respect or regard for each other. Nearly every family I spoke with liked to think themselves superior to another in some way or another. Even within such a small group as this there is great class consciousness, e.g. when No. 18 was trying to work out his friends, his conversation went like this: 'Of course we are all friends in the church'. Nearly every interviewee said these exact words—and it seems to be one of the basic principles they follow, many a sermon being given on the subject. 'I will put No. 259 as he has the most similar background to me in Holland and sees things on the same level as I do. The rest of the members are only workers of little education. People with whom I really have little in common.'

If these impressions are accepted as correct (and they have been confirmed by other members of the team), then it will become necessary to modify our original concept of primary group affiliations which was defined as resting on the assumption of mutual identification and spontaneity in a face-to-face group. The Reformed Church in Moe lacks these two attributes.[27] Instead of spontaneous mutual identification there is strict discipline enforced through an hierarchical group structure. Strict orthodoxy in the practice of Calvinist precepts must be observed by all members of the group; those that do not conform to these rules are ostracized, and, if they persist in this stand, face ignominy and expulsion.[28]

This last point raises, in turn, an important question which has theoretical as well as practical implications. Reference is made here to the functions of ethnic primary groups in transmitting the culture demands of the absorbing society. The foreign-language church has often functioned as a 'marginal' institution (to extend R. E. Park's terminology to institutions) which protected the immigrant from personal disorganization and homesickness but at the same time retarded his adjustment to the culture of the absorbing society. The Reformed Church in Moe seems to do more than that. It is not only protective, it not only retards the process of adjustment, but actually stands between the migrant and his new environment.[29] This is in direct contrast to the Ukrainian Orthodox Church—also a foreign language church.

Analysis of sociometric choices of the adherents of the Ukrainian Orthodox Church in Newborough shows that this particular group is not as self-contained, doctrinally and socially, as the

Reformed Church in Moe. It has been shown earlier that the two religious denominations in the Ukrainian community in Newborough (the Catholics of the Greek Rite, and the Orthodox groups) do not differ significantly in the degree of their clannishness. This has been confirmed in interviews with the Ukrainians in Newborough. The evidence collected suggests that, though separated doctrinally, members of the two denominations mix socially with one another to a considerable extent. There has been no attempt made to set up separate social organizations within each denomination that would compare with the Ladies' Guild and the Youth Club in the Reformed Church. On the contrary the *Hromada* seems to be the only and all-embracing social (as well as political) organization catering for all Ukrainians, irrespective of their religious affiliation. Its office-bearers and rank-and-file membership are composed of both Greek-Catholics and Orthodox people, all of whom work and act in complete unanimity. The researcher is left with an impression of a closely-knit ethnic community in which nationalistic objectives and ethnic group goals override religious differences. The contrast in this respect between the deeply-divided and differentiated Dutch people in Moe and the Ukrainian community of Newborough is striking.

This chapter has employed several methods in an attempt to compare the Dutch people in Moe and the Ukrainians of Newborough in terms of the degree of social integration in the two populations. These methods included an analysis of the proportions of persons in the two populations who received more than a certain number of sociometric choices, an application of the Index of Clannishness, and an analysis of in-group choices, both for the two populations as a whole as well as for persons from each province of origin and adherents of each religious denomination.[30] The application of these methods has shown that the Ukrainians in Newborough are more closely integrated than the Moe Dutch. Moreover, it has been demonstrated that many Dutch people are divided and largely segregated into groups based on province of origin and religion, and that no such divisions exist amongst the Ukrainians; the latter, therefore, can properly be termed a community. The Dutch people of Moe, on the other hand, have few common ties that would override differences of religion, provincial dialect, and related cultural characteristics. The Dutch population of Moe is simply a collection of individuals of common ethnic origin who happen to live within the boundaries of a local government unit. In the absence of organized corporate life at this level the researcher has descended, as it were, to a lower level of social organization to discover nuclei of regional and religious communities, or primary groups that play a crucial part in the process of adjustment.

An examination of one such closely-knit community, the Reformed Church in Moe, has served to emphasize that the primary group is a true unit of ethnic relations. Hence a clear insight into the functioning of primary groups within larger ethnic collectivities is crucial for an understanding of the process of integration to the larger social structures. It is obvious that the immigrants who become members of such large social structures, such as factories or territorial communities, make their decisions and concert their actions within those structures not by direct focus of attention on the central authority but rather by identification with some individual or individuals with whom they have primary group relations and who serve to transmit to them ideas from and concerning the larger structures.

CREATING COMMON VALUES

I know that there are Australians who are not in favour of this migration programme and there are also many who are indifferent towards it. But I always remember that this migration programme has been initiated and maintained by great men, with vision and faith in the future of Australia, men who were and are able to emerge above the average man in carrying out their duty towards their country and never for a moment forget the way Australia must go to achieve a position amongst the nations of the world.

I honestly try to become a good Australian citizen and I endeavour to fulfil my duties as such. However, if I fail, there is still one consolation for Australia. I have given six young citizens to this country, six of the many hundreds of thousands of young children, who are as fair dinkum already as any of the Australian children. One can build a nation on a young generation, and if for no other reason than this, what is happening in Australia and outside it is not a matter of indifference to us. Let us therefore unite in mutual respect and understanding, and build Australia into a greater place in which to live.

Not all the settlers in the Latrobe Valley have been as articulate in their expression of love for the country of adoption as the Yugoslav engine-driver from Yallourn North whose words are quoted above. Some have not struck their roots as yet in the Australian soil; others have clearly not succeeded and are on the point of returning to their native countries. But an overriding impression is of the people who are doing their best to strike roots and contribute their share to the building of 'Australia into a greater place in which to live'.

This is true even of the immigrants who do not appear to participate in the life of the community at large and—as shown in Chapters 8 and 9—mix mainly with other immigrants of the same ethnic origin. The Yugoslav engine-driver exemplifies this attitude. He has made a very good occupational adjustment but outside his work his contacts have been mainly with other immigrants, mainly Poles and Yugoslavs, who helped him to build a fine house. Yet, although his psychological orientation has been mainly to his compatriots and other immigrants, he clearly sees it his duty to bring up his children as good citizens of Australia and thus repay a debt of gratitude to his adopted country.

The pattern of his life has a symmetry and contentment that more pretentious persons rarely find. There are his children, his good wife (a Triestini), his friends, his SEC job, and his forty acres of land on the outskirts of Yallourn North, where he grazes half-a-dozen cows and runs an excellent vegetable garden. His is a hard-working life but he takes equal pride in his SEC job and in his land, which only a few years ago was a barren paddock covered with stone and a few decaying eucalypts. Inner diversity and organic wholeness is here, all within the range of his influence and appreciative, perceptive life. His is an example of organic integration in which a strong predisposition to change combined with successful economic adjustment in the first generation will probably be followed by a smooth transition of the second generation of immigrants from the values of the old world to the standards of behaviour of the new. The children of our hero are not likely to face the disturbing experience of a culture conflict, for in their upbringing the conduct norms and traditions of their parents will be blended with the norms of the Australian society.

The success of this organic process of merging between Old and New Australians, and the link formed in the process by the children of the immigrants, is primarily due to the spirit of tolerance and willingness to accept the immigrants shown by Old Australians in the Latrobe Valley. True, there have been, as there must be, misunderstandings and frayed tempers. But these have been isolated instances and their total absence during the economic recession of 1960-1 suggests that Australians and the immigrants can get along in a spirit of mutual tolerance and with a desire to find the highest common orientation.

Several factors have contributed to this satisfactory state of affairs. First, the local press has acted in a highly responsible manner, criticizing in editorial comment Australians and immigrants alike, giving praise where it is due and, above all, avoiding blanket generalizations, based upon an isolated instance, in which a whole group is condemned. Second, the churches and local voluntary organizations have contributed their share of goodwill towards the immigrants in helping them to solve their problems and, above all, in giving wholehearted support to the good neighbour policy laid down by the federal government. Finally, the fact that not only the immigrants from overseas but also a very large proportion of Old Australians in the Valley are newcomers to the district has perhaps contributed to the creation of a common orientation among the people who share similar problems of settlement in a new, rapidly expanding area.

The challenge for the Latrobe Valley is to maintain this spirit of pioneering and to attain social stability without slackening off technological progress. The social experiment of Yallourn, Yallourn North, Moe, and Newborough is being repeated in Morwell and at Hazelwood, and there is every indication that it will also be successful. After a time, however, a stage of development must be reached when the existing towns will cease to grow at the present rate. Several problems of settlement will have to be solved, houses will have been built and amenities provided. But unless this development is accompanied by a corresponding extension of educational facilities at a higher technical and possibly tertiary level and an increase in employment opportunities in light industry, the communities of the Latrobe Valley will not be stabilized. The present unbalanced pattern of development shows that the Latrobe Valley cannot absorb its young people functionally and in numbers large enough either to provide a living for a good number of them or to assure stable and permanent families. The people who stand to lose most in this process are the immigrants, for a break up of family life encourages feelings of impermanency, of mobility, of not belonging, and not being a part of the community.

In many respects the Latrobe Valley and her settlers is a microcosm of Australia today. But the reader is warned against hasty generalizations based on this study. It would be wrong to conclude that all the British, Dutch, Italian, Polish, Latvian and other settlers in Australia behave like their compatriots who have been included in this study. Perhaps the most important finding of this study is that the immigrant's ethnic origin is not the only, and most certainly not the decisive, factor determining his behaviour. There are other factors that may be as important as, if not more important than, the immigrant's culture imported from his country of origin: his rural or urban background, demographic status, the nature of kinship ties, period of residence in Australia, place of residence, not to mention certain personality characteristics, though the latter have not been analysed in this study.[1] Thus, the features of behaviour that have been analysed here are not necessarily to be found in other immigrants throughout Australia. It has to be borne in mind that the settlers in the Latrobe Valley are a very special group whose adjustment is conditioned not only by the factors just mentioned but also by the ecological setting of industry and residence to which special attention was devoted in the earlier chapters of this book. It should be the task of Australian sociologists to test whether, and under what conditions, the findings of this study apply to comparable industrial areas throughout the country, places that are as truly remarkable and as exciting as the Latrobe Valley.[2]

Appendix A

The Life History Schedule

The following notes are for the guidance of persons who have undertaken to write their life histories. It would be desirable if the writers followed the sequence of headings given below though it is not absolutely essential. The writer's native language or the English language can be used.

1. *The family background*

   Description of parents' background: father's occupation and social position, housing situation and property. Brothers and sisters. Some more important events in the life of the family: annual celebrations, religious feasts, births and deaths of relatives.

2. *Childhood and schooling*

   Early memories of childhood: play, illness, holidays. Early school days. Secondary school: subjects taken, attitudes to teachers and school mates. Aspirations of adolescence and emotional disturbances. Interests outside school: sport, reading, youth associations. Writer's observations on the system of schooling in his native country.

3. *Earning one's own living*

   Description of occupational training and where received: apprenticeship, adult education, university training. Difficulties encountered in training. Source of financial support. Interest in politics, social work, literary, music, etc.

4. *The War*

   Writer's occupational situation and geographical location at the beginning of the War. Chronological account of events. Writer's participation in fighting. Persecution and flight.

5. *Emigration to Australia*

   Decision to emigrate. Contact with Australian authorities. Circumstances of departure from Europe. Conditions on the migrant ship. First impressions of Australia.

187

6. *The process of resettlement*

Finding work in Australia. Housing situation of the writer and his family. Learning a new job. Workmates and friends. Learning the English language. Participation in social and political life. Naturalization. Interest in Australia and the country of origin.

7. *Marriage and family*

Courtship and marriage. Children—their birthplaces and care. Problems associated with bringing up children before and/or after migration.

The Life Histories

From London to East Newborough

I was born in 1913 in Woolwich, second largest borough of London. My father was employed at that time by the Port of London Authority in the docks at North Woolwich and surrounding dockyards, with whom he remained until reaching retiring age. We lived in Woolwich in a rented house from the time I was born until the family moved to a new Council Estate house in the suburb of Eltham, December 1921. This area had been developed by the Borough of Woolwich as a garden estate, with all-electric houses, the first such estate in England. Remained in this house until I left to be married (1939). Mother and Father both interested in politics, and were members of the Woolwich Labour Party, both of them at various times holding executive and committee positions, on both political and social committees. Family consisted of myself, the eldest, and three sisters, all still alive, no other children being born.

Birthdays of family were usually the time for celebration, as was Christmas, when the family always have spent at least one day together, until, that is, we were split by emigration: I came to Australia, one sister went to Canada, and another to U.S.A.; the youngest sister still lives in Eltham with her husband and family. All of us are married and have children.

Can vividly remember our holidays, taken when we were small at Brighton, Sussex, and as we grew older taken mostly at Ramsgate, Kent. We had a holiday of fourteen days at the sea every year. At the age of 5 years I commenced school at Bloomfield Rd Primary School, Woolwich, a school controlled by the London County Council. After moving to Eltham in 1921 I attended the

Gordon Girls' School, also an L.C.C. School. From here I passed by competitive examination at all years of age to the Woolwich Central Girls' School, where I remained until 1930, leaving there to enter H.M. Civil Service, with the Board of Education, then situated in King Charles St, Whitehall.

While at school in addition to normal subjects taken, I took courses in French, some German, domestic science, shorthand and typing. I remember my school days as a normally happy time, had the usual likes and dislikes of various teachers and school mates. Played hockey, cricket, netball, and tennis while at school. Cannot remember any great emotional disturbances during this time. During my last year at school I also attended evening classes in the subjects I would be taking in my Civil Service exams. I was at all times greatly encouraged in my studies by my parents, particularly my father. I was also encouraged to read good literature by my parents, who on the occasions of Christmas and birthdays, always included some good books as gifts, a system that I have followed with my own children. This type of reading, taken over a prolonged period as it was, I feel sure gave me a very different outlook on life. I feel that too much good literature is crowded into too short a time while children are studying for various exams, and they consequently do not grow to appreciate it. Far from finding any defects of the schooling system of the London County Council, I have nothing but praise for it, and consider it to be far superior to the type of education that my children are receiving here. Education in London, and I believe in the whole of England, is completely free, by that I mean that not only does a child attend school free of charge, but there is no charge for any kind of books whatsoever, in all my years at school the only book I can remember having to buy was a French dictionary. From the age of 12 years, I was a member of a Girl Guide Troop, with whom I remained until I was $16\frac{1}{2}$ years old, this troop gave me some very happy hours. I attended church with this troop, but apart from that did not consider myself a regular church attender.

My entire working life before I married was spent in the Board of Education, that is, from May 1930 to June 1939. The work was interesting and varied. I received a good clerical training, dealing particularly with statistics and coding work. This latter stood me in good stead, for at the time of the Munich Crisis in 1938, I was lent by the Board of Education to the Admiralty for special duties. On another occasion when a new Ministry, that of the

Unemployment Assistance Board, was formed, I was again lent to another department for special duties relative to the formation of a new Ministry. I made many friends during these years, and until coming to Australia, regularly met many of them. I earned very good money during this time, and always assisted at home, by allowing a regular amount out of my pay to my mother. I completely kept and clothed myself, and regularly saved money. Through my parents I had always a deep interest in politics, and at the age of 14 years I joined the Labour Party League of Youth (the official junior branch of the Labour Party in England), but although a financial member my parents would not allow me to attend any meetings etc. until after I had left school. This organization, in addition to giving me a sound grounding in political matters, also gave me a good social life, and incidentally, some of the happiest times I can remember. There was quite a large group of us, and we went around together as a club, both socially, in sport, and in politics. We camped together every holiday weekend, played tennis, cricket and netball, hiked, ran dances, whist drives, bazaars, and helped organize elections. We often attended as a group various types of theatres in London. We organized study circles, debating groups etc. It was through this organization that I met my husband for the first time. We were married in July 1939, exactly six weeks before the start of World War II, having then known each other for about seven years.

Before marriage we had started to purchase a new house at New Eltham, also in the Borough of Woolwich. This house we moved into as soon as we were married, and this was where we were when war was declared. My husband, a carpenter by trade, had to register for National Service, and was conscripted in April 1941, and since the only money I would receive from the Government was 28/- a week, I had to go out to work again.

I obtained work with the local Borough Council, working as an Administrative Clerk, in the Town Clerk's Civil Defence Dept. at the Woolwich Report Centre. This work was very interesting and absorbing. I dealt in the main with the organization of the paid personnel attached to the 88 wardens' posts throughout the Borough. In addition, I became a voluntary worker on one of the Civil Defence Mobile Canteens, and later in the war, a firewatcher at the New Eltham Public Library. All this in addition to running a house and working all day. Our house sustained slight damage, mostly to roof, doors and windows as a result of enemy action, nevertheless it was still habitable, and we were lucky not to lose it completely. I resigned from this job at Christmas 1943 as I was then expecting my first baby. He was born in March 1944. In June 1944 the flying bombs made life pretty nearly unbearable, and so I applied to be evacuated with my baby to a quieter area. I was sent to Connah's Quay in North Wales, and thoroughly enjoyed the time I spent there. The people there were very friendly and I was sorry to leave eleven months later. My husband was eventually demobbed in November 1945. He started work again as a carpenter, and was still employed in that capacity when we decided to emigrate. Before we made this decision however, our second child, a daughter, was born in April 1949.

Our decision to emigrate came about as a result of my husband bringing home a copy of the Melbourne *Age* that he had obtained from a friend at work, who was also intending to emigrate to Australia. We were fascinated by some of the advertisements, particularly those regarding foodstuffs and the 'positions vacant' columns, and from this arose our feeling that it might be to our children's advantage to emigrate. We were the first of our family to leave England, but our parents did not try to stop us, they felt we were the ones to make the decision. We applied for papers on 31 October 1949, and actually landed in Australia less than seven months later.

The State Electricity Commission of Victoria were our sponsors, guaranteeing us a house upon arrival, and work for my husband. We have remained in the same house since the SEC installed us in it nearly nine years ago, and my husband is still employed by them.

Our first contact with the Australian authorities was at Australia House, but our interview only extended over approx. half an hour, and we were only seven months from date of application to arrival here, so we hardly saw enough of anyone there to be able to give a definite opinion. We were always received politely, but we would have appreciated far more accurate information regarding this area than we received. We were shown photographs of Yallourn, and told that was where we were going to live. We were more than horrified to find ourselves in East Newborough knee deep in mud, with no roads, footpaths, street lights, sewerage, shops, schools, doctors, or halls in our near area. Just what we would have decided had we known of the true conditions, I feel unable to say now, but that picture did help us to decide to emigrate. It all looked so neat.

We sailed on R.M.S. *Orontes,* not an all-migrant ship, and at that time carrying 1st class passengers as well as Tourist. But the accommodation was good, the food simply excellent, and the ship itself perfectly clean and well-maintained.

The first thing we both remember of Australia was standing outside a butcher's shop in Fremantle, and gazing open-mouthed at the quantity of meat in the window; we had been accustomed to a very small meat ration, and it hardly seemed possible there was so much meat in the world as we saw displayed in that window. The next thing of course, was the fact that clothes could be bought without coupons, and we had a good spending spree.

As I have already said, we had no housing problem when we arrived or worry about finding work. Both those items were already arranged for us. But the area, just recently carved out of the bush, nearly broke our hearts, but we realized that to sit down under it would not improve it. Most of us from England had been used to roads being built in new housing areas before the houses went up, sewerage was always available, and shops, schools, etc., went in at the same time as the houses. This do it yourself business was something very new to us, and therefore not too well received. However, some of us got together and decided to form a Tenants' Association, as all the houses here were the property of the SEC and our occupancy of them the result of working for them too. This Association was formed in July 1950, and I was elected the first secretary. We decided to press for all we were worth for roads and footpaths first, then school and shops, and we proceeded along these lines. The Association also tried to cater for the social side too, in spite of the fact there was no hall available to us, and all our meetings had to take place in the open air, using the porch lights of houses to read our minutes, and take notes. We arranged trips to the sea by bus for our members, and at this time we had a 100 per cent membership. A Christmas party for the children of members was arranged for our first Christmas in Australia, and we hired the R.S.L. Hall in Yallourn for this purpose, and ran buses in for the children and their parents free of charge. Some two hundred children were entertained that day. A monster bonfire night was also organized on our first 'Guy Fawkes Day' and included a torchlight procession by the children.

We sent deputations to everyone we thought could assist us to get our area properly developed, and I well remember waiting in the pouring rain with the president of our Association, Mr Bill Dool, when the members of the Victorian Cabinet came to inspect this area. We were fortunate in being able to meet at this time Mr W. O. Fulton, the then Minister of Health, and he always placed his good services at our disposal, and helped us in innumerable ways. Having been amongst the first of the migrants in this part, we always felt very sorry for the new arrivals, and after talking this over in committee, it was decided to seek permission from the SEC for some of our committee and their wives to enter the new houses awaiting new tenants and light fires, tidy up, and make up the beds that had been lent to us by the SEC, as we came here straight from the ship, and had no time to buy furniture. This we still feel was one of the best jobs we did, as the sight of a clean made bed, and a warm fire did much to help people forget other things. All this work was of a voluntary nature, and we rarely lacked for help. All were willing, and all worked.

Gradually other organizations came here, the churches sent ministers, and helpers, roads, etc. came, a hall was erected, a fine school came, and shops, practically a small town grew in less than ten years out of the bush. Now there are sports ovals, sports clubs, and a picture theatre, almost everyone has a car, and is able to see more of Australia. The interest we have in Australia stems largely from the fact that we feel we have helped to make one small portion of it grow.

From Haarlem to Moe[1]

Everything around is still peace and quiet except in 34 Keizer Karelstreet one can hear the tinkle of an alarmclock, which is switched off after having rung for a long time. Only just awake and already I realize that this is our last day and that we will sail towards our new future tomorrow. There is a lot to be done today, so better get stuck into it; first get the children out of bed. This causes no difficulties this time. Straight out of bed they run towards the windows: 'O look Mam, it has snowed'. Yes if you wash quickly and get dressed you can still go and make a nice snowman today.

The contractor has promised us that he would take us to Rotterdam tomorrow: this saved us a lot of time and trouble. Just have a look around for anything I might have forgotten, yes that cot there. All 6 of them slept in it. Strange to know that one has to leave all this behind tomorrow. But after all we wanted it ourselves so better not think too much about it. The sale of the house is settled. The house (on a rent-basis) with all inventory 1,500 guilders . . . 600 guilders had been taken by my husband and son who went half a year ahead, the other 900 guilders were meant for me and the 5 children to buy clothing, suitcases, some kitchengear and crockery. But we missed out, we still had to hand in the money.[2] Because what my husband had done was illegal, he ought to have told the Labour Bureau, so we missed out. Yes, as long as my husband was in Australia and I in Holland I got a subsidy, was then called to the office and received a coupon to go to a second hand goods-shop with the 5 children and there I could choose some things for them and myself. My husband used to work at the Department of Social Service so . . . ? he was *also* a public servant which is highly respected but with a family of 8 it was still a life of poverty. But I am talking too much. Tomorrow we are going to Australia. I have no great expectations, I do not have to become rich, if only I can give the children what they need, clothes and shoes and if I occasionally can put an apple into their hands then I will feel rich already. Is everything ready for tomorrow? Yes, we will be collected at half past seven; if only we were on the boat on time.

Next morning 6 o'clock, everybody is present, people from the whole street are there to say goodbye. The car arrived on time, never will I forget this moment, I did the rounds for the last time and then handed over the key to my brother, who was going to look after things; everything was turning around in front of my eyes but I had to control myself for the children. Once more before the corner we waved farewell and then it was all over and we went on to Rotterdam.

Once on the boat, we were brought to the dormitory—everything looked clean and fresh, I had never seen such a boat before, and I thought it was marvellous. After I had found a suitable place for the suitcases I went up again with the children to wave a last farewell to all the people who were so dear to us but on arriving on deck we discovered that the boat was sailing already and we could hear the last tones of the 'Wilhelmus'.[3]

Now everything was over and we would go and enjoy the trip. But oh where was my cabin now? Quite hopeless, in all the excitement I had forgotten our number. But one of the stewards came to the rescue so it was not long before we were back in the dormitory.

It was announced that a meal was served for the children aged
1-6. I found the table where my youngest one of $2\frac{1}{2}$ years could
sit during our trip. On that table was absolutely everything that
appeals to small children. We were not used to that. When
Daddy brought home his wages, it had usually been spent before
I had touched it. Then we used to do the shopping and with
that was one jar of jam for the children and for Daddy's sand-
wiches $\frac{1}{2}$ lb cheese to last him two days. On Saturdays we used
to get 2 lb meat and 1 lb of dripping and that was that for the
whole week.

As far as clothing is concerned, for the kind of people we were
it was unobtainable. I have 3 sons and 3 daughters and from the
old clothes of the eldest I made a dress or a pair of pants for the
youngest and so you went on to make ends meet.

When I saw all this lovely food in abundance I had to think
back to all this. The first days I hardly dared to touch anything
but the steward said 'Go ahead, help yourself, that is what it is for'.

The journey was beautiful but one did not get much rest, when
you are a mother on her own making a journey with 5 children, the
eldest of which is 15. You needed to have eyes in the front and the
back. A space was fenced for the little ones but it was not enough.
There were 1,200 people on board more than half of which were
children and I preferred to keep them with me. The ports in which
we berthed were fantastic, specially at night with all the lights,
illuminated gondolas with all sorts of merchandise. For a farthing
one could buy the most beautiful things (if only one had the
money). But we enjoyed the spectacle all the same. Only 14
more days and we were in Melbourne. . . . Never in my whole life
have I seen so much water as in those last days. The journey was
over, another $\frac{1}{2}$ hour and we would enter the harbour.

Australia a New Future. There was screaming, whistling and
shouting, one could hardly hear oneself. After a long search I
found my husband and son. It was a happy reunion after half
a year. It was a Sunday and we could not leave the boat till
Monday. That night it was beautiful weather and we thoroughly
enjoyed it. After having talked all night about all sorts of things
i.e. about things that had happened during the past 6 months,
we decided to have an hour's sleep and it did not take us long
before we slept like logs. My husband and son were allowed to
sleep on board the ship. After a few hours we met in the dining
room. The service and the food was again excellent. The weather
was quite different from the previous day, it was pouring down.

That was why we went by taxi to Flinders Street. It was 10 o'clock in the morning, what could we do! Our train to Moe did not leave till 5.50 that night. We first took our suitcases to the luggage department. I thought it was a pity that we could not board the train at once and thought . . . how is that possible, there are sure to be more trains per day. But in the first place I *knew* nothing about distances and could not understand nor speak anything. For all I had learned in Holland, I had forgotten. What could we do now? Come on Dad, lets look first for a place to sit down. The children were hungry and naughty. It did not take long before we walked into an enormous store (yes, now I know how it is called: Myers) . What a beautiful store, it is not exaggerated but one can buy anything there from a pin to an aeroplane. Time went quickly that day and before we knew it was 5 o'clock and we had to go to the train. I thought: one hour and we will be there but *that* was disappointing. It was $2\frac{1}{2}$ hours from Melbourne to Moe.

The little one had fallen asleep and we were not far from it. But the closer we came to Moe the more nervous I got, what would the houses look like? My husband had written that we lived on a hill. I had imagined myself—Australia, a warm country, our house on a hill, so a house with a thatched roof, cane furniture and everybody wearing summer clothes. It was 4th January so summertime, but it was still cold and the rain poured down (by now we know that Gippsland is the worst part but at that time we thought that it would always be summer here) . On the boat we had made a little song about it the chorus of which went as follows:

> Australia the promised land
> Australia extends its hand
> Australia it is there so fine
> the country of the sunshine!

The train stopped; where were we now? It was already passed 9 o'clock and we could not see a thing anymore and that was Moe 8 years ago, small and primitive. We were given a cordial welcome to Australia by our Dutch friends who had been looking so well after my husband and son. My husband did office work in Holland but in Australia one has to take on any job at all when one wants to be a *good* migrant (and as 500 people had been sacked that moment at the paper factory amongst whom was my husband, he took a job with a contractor who was laying sidewalks. When you are not used to this sort of work, it is not easy and he had to

give up. He was severely ill for 6 weeks). We were welcomed
with a lovely Dutch cup of coffee and a beautiful Australian laid
table. This was one of the first things that was very strange to
us, especially pumpkin, one has to learn to eat that. All the lovely
meat, pudding and when one thinks one is finished then you get
a cup of tea with lovely homemade cake. Yes the Australians are
excellent cooks. And now the great moment had come . . . we
were going home . . . home . . . to our own home. I could cry with
joy. The roads were very bad and the street lighting was even
worse, with 2 torches we moved bit by bit to 62 Wirraways
Street. . . .

But that was not a house, but a superb residence, compared to
our house in Holland. 3 Bedrooms (mattresses on the floor), a
lounge, that would most likely stay empty for the first 2 years, a
beautiful dining-kitchen and there was an electric stove. I could
not believe my eyes, this stove belonged to the house, what a
luxury. But that was not all, we had a beautiful bathroom, yes
a bathroom with a bath. This is in Holland only meant for rich
people, they think that a labourer does not need such a thing, if
he comes home tired and dirty from work, he can wash at the
kitchentap and if one can spare the money you might go to the
public bath house once a week.

And now what a joy, even if you want to have a bath every
day, how rich we are! Yes those things are wonderful in Australia.
There is also a laundry with a copper and 2 troughs with taps.
These things do not exist in Holland. There I had to boil my
washing on the gas stove in a little kettle and then I had to scrub
it with the board and a scrubber and that lasted *all* day before it
was hanging on the line.

And what beautiful gardens all the houses have! O, what
wonderful freedom and nature in Australia, these thoughts passed
through my mind. When we were in bed (on the floor) it did
not take long before we were all in dreamland. But every time I
woke up I could feel the rocking of the boat and it was all like a
dream. We slept long the next day. I think it was because of the
difference in time of 9 hours between Holland and Australia and
we had to get used to the new time. It often happened that we
had a nap in the afternoon. We had lived in Moe for a week and
we discovered 7 more Dutch families. When going for a walk we
met one of them, after a chat they asked us if we were interested
in joining in the English language lessons on Tuesdays and
Thursday nights. It seemed a very good idea but my husband

worked at the SEC in Yallourn on a shift system, so he had no
chance to join. But my eldest son and daughter, 15 and 16 years
old joined me and we kept it up for three years. Thanks to the
teacher and the Mothers' Club; they gave us fresh courage—
courage and confidence in a new future. We all loved the lessons
and tried to follow it as well as possible (one is never too old to
learn). I had been to the lessons for about a year, the lesson
started at 7.30 but by the time the children had bathed and were
in bed it was always late and I sneaked into the classroom and
wanted to sit down. They were discussing the use of the preposition
'between'. The teacher looked at me and said: Mrs de Zaayer,
where is your nose (he thought of course that I would not know).
And I thought: that I can tell you exactly: 'My nose is between
my eggs'. I looked astonished. What was so funny. I had to laugh
too because of the others, and bit by bit he told us that it was
not eggs but eyes.

I always liked to enter a shop and to ask for something for which
I did not know the word. In Holland I always used cleansing
milk[4] to clean my face at night but I did not know how it was
called here so I entered a chemist's and asked in my 'double-
Dutch': 'Could you please give me a bottle of toiletmilk' and I
told them that it had lemon in it. They asked me whether it
was meant for the toilet but I told them, looking seriously, that
it was for my face. The man turned around and it seemed as if
he laughed; anyhow I went out of the shop and there on my own
I started to laugh heartily. We liked it here but still . . . ? I can
never tell what it was. The only thing we had was linen and
kitchenware, so at night we usually played cards in the kitchen
and then suddenly . . . the tears started to flow and I had to have
a good cry. What was it . . . homesickness? No, not that . . . But
I missed something here, I wished there was a repertory society
or something else, that would give one a break. But could we not
start a club together with all the other Dutch people? One of our
best friends was also all for it, moreover he had belonged to a
repertory in Holland. We put our heads together and so the
Dutch Social Club came into being, and as all our children, big
and small, play some music, we can look back on many nice
evenings. The repertory is 5 years old now. We started with
'The Jantjes' and played it twice with great success. The most
beautiful play was 'Thy will be done'. Plays like that I like best.
Something seems to stay behind. Yes one should not sit still, should
try oneself. It is so easy to say after a year: 'I do not like it in

Australia', those people are failures. One can not judge in a year.

We are almost 9 years in Moe and have seen the place grow, so many things have improved in that time and building is going on. Another 5 years and Moe will not be a country village any more but a nice country town. Our path was not always paved with roses during that time. We had lived in Australia for one year. My husband worked with the SEC. I was woken up one night by a lot of stumbling and noise. I got out of bed and what was wrong? My husband had been brought home, he had had an accident, had broken his leg badly. During that time we got to know the Australians. As long as my husband was home we hardly got any money (all this has improved since). But they did *not* leave us in the lurch. They had a collection for us at the SEC and a crate with potatoes and vegetables and a piece of meat was delivered home. *That is how the Australians are* when they know somebody is in trouble. I myself have been in hospital ten times which cost a lot of money. It was not only doctors' bills but also commitments on furniture and everything we had to buy. And yet I have *often* been told: 'I do not understand . . . you come here with nothing, and within 2 or 3 years you have a house full of furniture and some money in the bank, or a house of your own'. Yes, it is difficult to answer.

We in Holland like sociability.[5] So when a migrant arrives in Australia he sticks to his Dutch customs, that is: Dutch meals, Dutch sociability. Enjoying nature does not cost money so one can save a bit. In that way a migrant is richer than in Holland. We were used to a life like that—but—we still eat a lot better than over there. A party without a pot of beer or a glass of wine is no good, it is part of the fun, it creates the atmosphere. If my husband feels like a beer, then we get some in the house. Being sociable does not have to cost a lot of money: we often have a wonderful night with a cup of coffee and a biscuit and some music. But one has to look for a thing like that here. Sociability is sought here in Australia away from the home or in front of the T.V. It struck me that all people who own T.V. miss a lot of homeliness. Last week we were invited to an engagement party. As soon as we entered we had to sit down and be quiet because there was a good show on. We were there at 8 o'clock and during the show we had a cup of coffee. At eleven the T.V. show went off and the party was finished. But under all conditions 'when you are in Rome, do as the Romans do'.

Another month and I will be an Australian too but that does

not mean that I have forgotten my home country. No, one will *never* forget. But that beautiful small Holland is very poor and there is no more room for us and no future for our children. And still I have the hope of spending a holiday in my home town either by winning a lottery ticket or by chance circumstances. I still am of good heart; yet I often build castles in the air and tell myself: What would you do *if* you won a prize. I would not keep it all for myself. I would go to Holland in the beginning of January for 3 or 4 months. To my hometown Haarlem between Amsterdam, Lisse, Hillegom, Bennebroek, all the places of tulips, daffodils, and hyacinths. When I close my eyes, I can still see them; like coloured carpets, red, blue, white, mauve, yellow, pink. I will remember that all my life. Just like the 'Tulipweek'— people come streaming from all countries to see little Holland in its array of flowers, cars, bikes, scooters, pedestrians all decorated with garlands of flowers. Yes, when that time gets nearer, April, May, then my heart often yearns to that precious bit of land. And that is why it is my dearest wish to see it once again but then under better circumstances than when we left it.

A family with 6 children of which only the father works in which one lived day after day in a daily routine whether it was Monday or Sunday the circumstances remained the same. The only difference is that one does not work on Sundays. One walks in Sunday outfits, the children with patched clothes and shoes. And when we went for a walk with the children and they saw an icecream man and Daddy was in a generous mood then they all got a 10 cent icecream and their day was made. But Father and Mother thought: 'We could have bought 2 loaves of bread for that money!' I am talking here of 9 years ago, circumstances have changed a lot. Thousands of Dutch people have migrated to Canada, America and Australia . . . now there is plenty of work and wages are high . . . but for how long? Housing is hopeless, especially in the big cities; 3 or 4 families in one house. What a pity it is that such a rich country has to be so poor. Culture is highly appreciated, social services are marvellous. This is one of the things that are difficult for a family here in Australia. Take only myself. I have been in Australia for 8 years and have been in hospital ten times, although we are in Latrobe Valley, we still have to pay a lot and that is one of the things that make one poor. In Holland we belonged to a Medical Benefit Fund and paid a certain amount every week. When one had to go to hospital for a big operation, the operation and 6 weeks hospitalisation were free and medicines and doctor's visits were also included. I hope, Editors, that you do not mind that I write about this but my experiences of the last years have made us poor.

Our children, 3 girls and 3 boys have become independent during that time. One is married, 2 girls in Melbourne, yes that is another thing one has to get used to. In Holland the children generally stay home until they get married. When they have work out of town they come home by train at night. It is a pity, with the children homeliness also departs. My whole family is musical. We do not have T.V. but an accordion, 3 guitars, mouth organs and love singing, I would not change for anything. It is a pity that there are so few jobs in the small towns, especially for girls, but I know it is a developing country. Australia needs young people, but once they are here are forced to go to the big cities for jobs. And when one wants to keep the family together you are forced to go with the children. It is not easy to get used to during the first years. And on top of that there was the language barrier but we soon finished that one and we accepted with both hands the English lessons that were given free of charge. That was a lovely time. Via the lessons we came into contact with the Mothers' club and social evenings. I will never in my life forget the friendliness and helpfulness and the patience with which the Australians treated us and are *still* treating us. It was difficult for both sides, we had to learn another language but our friends (if I am allowed to call you that) had to understand what we were talking about . . . After having lived in Australia for 8 years many things have become clear to us. There are even things that annoy me. Some weeks ago there was an argument on the bus. Two Australian ladies were annoyed by it. I know myself that it is not pleasant to sit next to people who start talking in their own language, while they have been here for years. Then it is better to keep quiet. We have come to Australia and have to adapt ourselves. And I want to be very frank: now that I have mastered the language more or less I would not want to go back unless on holidays. But a trip like that costs £400.

My father is here on holidays and returns next year. He is 78 and thinks this a lovely country and a country with a future. His only wish is that I will take him back. But something magic would have to happen: we do *not* have as many worries as in Holland but one has to work for one's money here just as well. It is 13th December 1961, another few weeks and it is 1962.

Dear friends, I with my family and my father, wish you all merry Christmas days and a happy New Year.

The Story of a Maltese Trade Union Official and Political Organizer[1]

The underwriting are my hints of the past, this includes my family.

My father's occupation was a Master Builder—Stone dresser. As far as I know my father's hobbies were speaking with other fellows about trade and at home always watching the birds and other things that for him were precious. He was very very proud of the family especially my mother, watching her working (she is dress maker Male and Female) dresses shirts and suits because we were in need of money to bring the family up and happy and they can even pay debts on the house they built for ourselves. My father used to own a quarry. In the family we are four brothers and one sister, all except one is married. The oldest brother he is living with me he is single and he is or was, as we call it 'Black Sheep'. Until he was 18 years of age he was very quiet and obedient to my father and mother, but everybody knows if you start go out with people who are worse than you are you become worse than others. He joined the Merchant Navy in 1935. Soon afterwards the Spanish civil war starts and he was in Gibraltar and they called every ship on the alert. According to one of his mates now living in Canada both were drunk, they crossed the border and were arrested, they were released a few hours later and he stopped on the ship (it was a cable ship laying cables in the Oceans).

Sir, I start school at the age of 4 in Elementary school a 'Government School'. As a pupil a year later I was stage two similar to stage one and within six months I was graded up again to standard one because I reckon I was a little bit intelligent. Year after year I always passed all my examinations till grade five, that's the last stage or class in my village, then my father and mother decide to send me to a college St Mary's College in Cospicua[2] one of the oldest cities of Malta; by this time I was about eleven years old— a better school and education. Father used to pay me besides bus travelling books and uniforms ten shilling a month that is big money for that time. I was very smart because all my brothers weren't very educated and I start reading about civil war and even some books about politics—that was about 1937-38. I always liked this kind of habit like. Although I was very smart my attitude to my teachers and especially to my parents was very good. In my first year in the College I won an Atlas Book. I still own it—*The Oxford Preparatory Atlas.*

Well after 2 years schooling the Head Master sent for me and he asked me whether I would like to sit for an Examination (Dockyard Exam:) I told him that I like to but I am young. My age was 13 years I was 2 years too young—that's according to the Law to sit for that kind of Exam; he said not to worry I fix everything for you, so I agreed. He told me keep your mouth shut and I fix everything. I expect what is coming but I wasn't worried about it; he sent a false birth certificate. Well time came, and I sat for the exams. When I entered the room for the Oral, I was asked how old I am and straight I told him 15 Sir. He start looking around and said to the other teacher it doesn't looks like 15 years. I told him that I am very short for this age and they start laughing, everything went through. We start the Exams in December 1939 when as you know troubles of wars start all over the world. We finished the Exams and Results came out who passed and who's not. We were about 700 boys and only 300 needed, 200 for Apprentices and the other 100 we called them qualified. I became '175A' and I passed the Exam.

I tell you the truth, I prayed God not to pass because I always hated dockyard. Sir I think God heard me because they delayed because of war trouble. After the Results for about 3 months nothing was heard when we are going to start. That was in March 1940 so there were some protests from the Apprentices about the delays but by that time war starts and I remember it was June and everybody says Italy against us. I was very happy because I said well they will make the dockyard out of action and they wouldn't send for me. Well although I was near enough 14 years I did not realise what is coming for us. It was 10-11th June 1940 and that day my ears every second of the clock was on the Radio listening about wars. Well, it was about 10 o'clock in the night of 10th June 1940 we heard on the wireless that H.M.S. *Glorious* Aircraft Carrier was sunk and everybody said the Italians sunk it and even there were lots of lives lost. I was very sorry because most of the people I know them including their wives and children: I remember women running around screaming and crying. Well as you can guess what a moment it was. I did not bother very very much, because all what I want to hear is the News whether Mussolini is in favour or not. Every body in my country was very sad and sicklike. It was a bit of loose time for me that day because everybody was wondering what's coming on

P

so I stopped all day mostly outside to hear news and peoples' ideas. It was about 11.40 p.m., if I remember it was Monday 10th June 1940, we heard the local Wireless (they call it 'Rediffusion') that Mussolini at about 12 o'clock he is going to announce which way he is going. After a while we heard: 'Viva, Viva Mussolini!' and he declared war on England—that means even on Malta.

I remember everybody screaming carrying little babies from one house to another and so on. I left home like a fresh carnation —I entered home I found my mother crying and wondering where we go because where we used to live it was a military place all over. About 300 yards away from us there was and still is a petrol Installation; about 3 miles on the other side is a seaplane Base, about 4 miles over the other side an Aerodrome 'Halfar' a Fleet Air Arm Base so they decided to go to a place they called Zurrieq. Well as far as I know there was no safe place in Malta because more or less every where was a military place whether aerodromes or seaplane bases or Military workshop so Malta was all over a military place.

Well we start from where I left you about the Exams. It was July or August and the Dockyard was nearly destroyed and they announced that this year there will be no Apprentices available because most of the Dockyard workshops are out-of-action. We spent about 6 months in Zurrieq all of my brothers even my father they can't stop home without going working and it was a bit far for them to go to work so they decide to go back to our house in Birzebbuga my home village. By that time I was 13 years 11 months. One day I was reading the daily paper *Times of Malta* and I found a job advertised 'page boy needed' that is 'telephone boy'. I went in and we were about 25 boys for two jobs. They gave us a date to sit like for an Exam—I was a bit nervous when I saw that people and they only need 2 boys. Well after three days we received a letter—the only two who passed was myself and another fellow friend—his name is William Fursman, he is Maltese—Father English and Mother Maltese too. We went on to see when we are going to start. I remember there was the Mess Secretary Wing Commander O'Conall and when he dropped his eyes on me he told me how old are you fellow. I start scratch my head. I told him 13 years 11 months; I told him that I was born on 17th Sept. 1926. He did not believe me so he asked me for Birth Certificate—I went running for it because I did not want to lose the job if possible although it was not a very good job but better than doing nothing. Well we started on 1st of

Sept. 1940 as a page Boy. He said do you know any Tailors because we have got to fix Uniform for you. I went on straight eh is this a military uniform and he start laughing so to pull my leg he said Yes. So I told him better if he find somebody else and he said what's wrong with that. I told him that I do not like services uniforms on me; he said no it is a uniform just because over here there will be lot of V.I.Ps. Well that's alright with me.

We start working—we've got to work 12 hour shift from 7 a.m. to 7 p.m. one day a week off. Our work was to receive telephone calls and deliver them to Officers in the Mess including delivering letters and hang on who is on day and night flying. For me and my friend more or less it was a sad thing when a pilot is lost because we've got to go and tell their wives about the tragedy as well; One time it was about 3 or 4 a.m.—I forget the day, it was in 1940—one of the pilots—I still remember his name, pilot officer Ball—was killed while he is landing after night patrol so I received the signal and I went to the Commanding Officer. He asked me to find out where he lives so then I go and tell his wife about it. First of all it was very early in the morning—it was about by this time between 4 and 6 a.m. everybody still asleep—so I went on and start push biking around the house till I decide that its not too early. It was about 6 or 6.30 a.m., I knocked the door and I was going to say Good-Morning but neither for me nor for her it was a good morning it was a sad morning. After a while she said can't you speak? I said with a smooth voice Yes, but I stopped again, well this is all within minutes after, I said your husband died while he is landing crashed. She started screaming and crying like a mad woman and it was my first scratch I got from a woman because she came like an angry wolf at me, today I realised what she felt.

Well, I spend in this job from 1st Sept. 1940 to 22nd November 1941 then I read on the papers that the Air Ministry needs Apprentices and I decide to sit for the Exam—less trouble and a better job like. I start with the Air Ministry on 26th November 1941 as Apprentice Electrician—I was still under age, supposed to be 16 years, but I was 14 years last birthday. I spend 5 years 10 months Apprenticeship 10 months more than usual Apprenticeship. My wages were for the first 3 months 1-6d a week and I used to hide 6d in my shoes so when I go home I give 1 shilling to my mother and then she will give me 3d pocket money that makes 9 pence pocket money although you can't buy anything with it at that time because everything starts to be scarce. I start

my apprenticeship at a seaplane base 'Kalafrana'—there was a
Power Station, workshops, stores, and Hangars. For the first few
months I do not want to do anything because when on Fridays
I used to go for pay when I see the envelope I'll get very sad—
my wages in the Officers Mess as page boy were 11/6d a week
including food and uniforms. Well then I decide to start learn
the trade otherwise when Exams comes I'll be backwards and I
would not get any increase in pay so I worked hard and hard.
Well the first day I start, there was an old man—he was Mechanic
Fitter very very skilled—and he called me in and told me some
words—afterwards I realised what these words meant. He told
me what you see and what you hear and make yourself—you don't
know nothing—in one word close your eyes and ears and even he
told me to keep secret what I see and I hear in case I need them
in the near future. It was a good idea—very good too. From there
after about 1 year I was transfered to an underground Petrol
Installation 'Char Dalam' there is even a cave and Museum there.
Over there I was not better off because the Foreman he did not
like me—why I do not know—we used to fight every minute of the
day. Well time passed and in trade I was better than him because
I worked hard and even studied very hard at home. In 1947 there
was a chance to go for a course on High tension Under Ground
Cable 6.6K.V. I was very interested so I filled a form and I sent
it. No reply. I enquired again and they told me we didn't receive
any applications from you. I made another one and other one till
I found that this foreman used instead to sign them himself.
Then I sent a personal one to the Superintendent Engineer and
I explained everything, and after a while it came granted. I went
for the Exams including practical and I passed. When I passed I
signed like a contract to stop for 7 years with the Air Ministry
and then they will hand the certificate to me but I broke the
contract and I lost it but still got the ability for me just the same
—no difference at all.

By this time I start playing soccer and even looking or go around
with girls—as you know either women or sports one of them; both,
you can't do, well, that's how it is. In 1945 I was about 19 years
of age I won or we won (I was captain of the team) the Anglo
Maltese Cup, a beautiful Cup.

By this time I was already taking a great part in Union—though
I was young in age I was chosen as a shop steward and I used to
fight hard. After the first Election held in Italy that was in 1947
sometime, I was chosen to play an International Match 'Soccer'

under 21 years, and I had a good time. We played near Palermo nice gardens and girls too. I was watched very much by our Manager. When I returned to Malta I met this present wife, I said well I'll pass the time with this, but this was going, I found later, to be my wife. I was twice champion of my village, including district, for billiards. I received 2 medals one from the Queen, it was Princess Royal, and another one from her husband Prince Phillip—this was after they married. One of these medals was a charity Match for the Polio boys and the other one it was Cup Tie —we won Cup and Medals—I was playing with Valetta F.C.

These days were very hard life for me—sports, Union, politics and women. In 1946 they start committees in every village for M.L.P. 'Malta Labour Party' and I was chosen in the committee and I was even chosen delegate to represent my village. In 1946-47 political meetings start and I took active part running propaganda here and there especially in the farming area. When I was going to get married, that was in 1948, I decide to drop everything behind but the devil came around and the Split came.[3] It was a hard knock to the working class because everybody knows that the other Parties are too right or too left. Nationalist Party under the Leadership of Henry Mizzi was pro-Italian he was even, during the war, interned in Uganda, and the other although it wasn't strong enough it is too against working people including Union Constitutional Party under Miss Mabel Strickland which owns the press in Malta, *Times of Malta* and *Berka*—the latter is in Maltese. The Labour Party make a success—they elect 24 or 27 members out of 40. It was a hot peak. In 1949 after 2 years of solid Labour Party they split, some of the people say it was a family affair. Well I remember one time the Prime Minister, now Sir Paul Boffa, he told his deputy, he was Mr Dominic Mintoff, Minister of Reconstruction, to take his post as a Prime Minister because he is more energetic and young and he is stronger to fight and he said No. I reckon the trouble occurred when the Committee sat to elect the Deputy Prime Minister. It was between two great people (1) Mr Dominic Mintoff, Minister of Reconstruction and (2) Dr A. Colombo, Minister of Finance. Both these two people are clever—everybody knows about them. Dr Colombo made for the first time the Malta National lottery and it was a great great success too. From then onwards war started in the political group. In 1949-50 they split and Dr Paul Boffa and Dr Colombo were excluded from the Party.

They were bad years till 1954 when Dr Boffa resigned from

Politics and Dr Colombo changed his life and went for priesthood. They were during the solid Labour Party in Cabinet as follows: Prime Minister Dr P. Boffa.—Deputy and Minister of Construction D. Mintoff. Finance Dr A. Colombo; Education Dr Godwin Ganado; Minister of Justice Mr A. Schembri-Adami; Minister of Customs B. Camilleri; Minister of Emigration Mr John Cole, now in Australia. Then Boffa, Colombo, Schembri-Adami, John Cole, and Ganado formed the Malta Workers Party. They made a success and after 4-5 years once only the Deputy Leader was elected; and finished the Party.

On April 24th 1949 I married—it was Sunday and I was still playing football, 'Soccer', but I advised my Club that I am going to get married so I am not going to play that game more or less —no more from Saturday night. I found the Club Manager waiting for me home and he told to play. I insist no but more or less I was forced and I decide to play. You can guess how stupid I was. I am going to get married in the afternoon and the same day I went to play a hot and fast game. It was the Cup tie Final —we won the game 3:2. I was supposed to get married about 4.30 p.m. but at 4 p.m. I was still at the Club; I took my wedding clothes and all from the Club to the wedding ceremony—good fun.

Well time passed along and I was still hot on politics. By the time we were looking for a family—my wife was pregnant with the first Boy John—the peak of the election was on. Once there was a meeting by Nationalist Party and I started asking questions one after the other to the Prime Minister. After a while I was taken off by Police to the Police station, after a while I escaped and started on questioning again. I heard one of the Police inspectors saying where is the ——? catch him, and I start to struggle to avoid being in their hands and I went up a hotel stairway till I was running from one roof of the building to another. Somebody told my wife and family and they came to see where I was. Some of the police asked my family where I was. All this trouble for nothing more or less. Well when ever there is a meeting no doubt about it you will find me in the first rank. One time I went for a meeting in a strong seat place of my opposition and the Police inspector in charge in this meeting knows me very much, he looked at me and said Frank, what you doing here, this is a strong place to handle, I said I'll be quiet Sir and he said I hope so, so I moved away from his sight till I get the best place where I can go on the platform and tore the Nationalist banner—do not forget this Party is pro-Italian anti-

British—and I succeeded although I was kicked like a ball by these supporters. There were a lot of friends during these days and they used to tell me you're mad and never came with me. They even asked are you earning any money—they knew that it was only a hobby that's all. One of them he is living in Melbourne even now—his father is ex-Sergeant of Police. When he saw me the first time he asked me whether I'm still in politics. I said No over here is too quiet and even I lost interest. Although I used to make trouble during Political meetings I never was in Court.

Well my wages as electrician were before I came here £6.13.0 a week—very good money—I compare this money is better than here because over here the cost of living is very dear. About my emigration to Australia I cannot say why I emigrated—even myself I do not know what made me come to Australia. Well after doing everything needed to come to Australia, we must see the Australian authorities for the what they call final check. He was very happy when he heard me speaking and when he saw my family although he started looking at one of my children because he was a bit dark; but every thing was alright.

A week before I left I was called to the Emigration Office it was a call from the Director of Emigration Mr Axisa and he asked me to be spokesman on the ship for the Maltese Migrants at first I did not accept this because my Cousins, both living in Queensland told what happened to them, although I am different to them— I am smart and I would not care less what difficulties I will meet —I can handle them, so then after long conversations with Emigration people I accept it. Well time came to embark—it was about 9 a.m. on August 24th. I start my troubles on the ship— you'll find lots of obstacles especially when you've got people illiterate and different nationality. We left about noon—we find it hard from the first—heavy seas and more than 90% of the people were sick. For a way I was happy—no troubles of fighting—but other troubles for I want the doctor, others hot water, others this and that but everything was going good up to Port Said. Well I found it terrible, even myself; in the afternoon they tried to avoid to give us cup of tea or coffee. Food was very poor on the ship although I managed a bit, but still food not the best. The ship including the crew were excellent—I can't grumble—they helped me very much. There are people in Melbourne—when ever they see me they say if you wasn't there I'd be dead because of the sea. In about 27 or 28 days on sea I never slept more than 2 hours during the day or night. In one place there was an old woman one time she gave me all her belongings and said to me Frank I am dying, this little basket is for you and the other one give it to my husband. There was gold rings and so on. I start laughing she said its true, Frank I am very sick. This woman lives in Brunswick. When ever I go to see her sometimes for her I am the Messiah. I used to give her 1 small bottle of orange and 1 biscuit every hour of the day. She and others offered me money. I always reject them. I say no money I must help you. They still love me and whenever they see me they adore me. One of them she died a few days after we disembarked the ship in Melbourne I was very sorry for her especially for her 3 small children.

Australia I think is very good country but I reckon it is run mostly, according to what I read in the papers, by Americans. My idea is they can do better for the country because I want to look for the future of the country and family. If war starts, I reckon and most people can see it, that Australia is far away from most of the leading countries. I mean by this that if war starts according to this new warfare business Australia wants to defend herself because nobody could help here. As in the last war, this is natural I defend myself and not other countries. Secondly in Australia there is lot of resources like coal, uranium, gold, zinc and many others. They cannot open them during the war, they must prepare for the future as we can see the world always with trouble in I think there will be no permanent peace in the world so we must prepare in case. I've got a bit of experience of the last war. England use to send a lot of Convoys to Malta and most never reached the island safely, that's because we were cut off from the world or I make it simple we were surrounded from the point of Gibraltar to Suez Canal on both sides by Germans and Italians so if ships arrive from Suez Canal area it is very hard to bring them in through Malta because they were attacked from North Africa or Crete-Greece and if it comes from the other side of Gibraltar the same—Pantelaria, North Africa or Sicily they were all under German-Italian hands—this is my experience. As far as I read about Australia during the war unarmed Japs can land when ever they want to; that time Americans helped them but this time I doubt whether they help or not because of these new weapons.

I've got as far as they look 3 healthy children
    John born in Malta 26th July, 1950
    Michael born in Malta 6th June 1953
    Lewis born in Yallourn Australia 2nd September 1956

The eldest looks to me very clever energetic and quick in action I hope he keeps going as it is. Michael is very nice not so clever energetic and quick in action although time might change him, Lewis exactly like John energetic but he is small only 2 years but he gives me a clue that he will be like his oldest brother. The eldest sometimes asks me when we are going back home, I say oh sometime we go and have a look around, Son. Well but in Australia I am not interested in politics, Union or any other organizations but I always keep my eyes open for these Communists because they promise plenty and give nothing.

Sir,
I hope that you are happy about my old life and I hope that you will give me answer about what I said to you.
I wish you answer me. You might find I'm not a very good English writer but you understand.

Yours Faithfully
F.G.

From the Agony of War and Slave Camp to Freedom and Peace in Australia[1]

Childhood. I descend from a purely Polish family. My father was born in a middle-class family. His father lived in a country town where he had a chemist's shop from which he supported his wife and two sons. His income was not big, for, as my father would say, the people of the town were poor and sometimes he had to help them.

It was a time of poverty and enslavement. Poland, in fetters, was constantly fighting against the aggressors who cruelly oppressed the nation. My grandfather's shop was returning just enough to support the family.

I understand from my father that the standard of education was the lowest in the part of Poland occupied by Russia. He himself, in spite of adverse circumstances, managed to complete his secondary education. He had to learn the Polish language and other subjects related to Poland in secret schools, where the teachers of Polish youth were risking life and freedom. My father always used to call them heroes.

During the first World War my father served with the Polish Legion and was granted the Cross of Valour. In liberated Poland, for want of an office job, my father worked in a munition factory, as a foreman. After a few years he was promoted to the position of supervisor of the nickel-plating shop.

My mother, a Polish woman born in a very patriotic family, received the same education as my father, i.e. she studied in similar circumstances. She also lived in the Russian-occupied area. After she married she worked during the 1st World War in a hospital in Warsaw, but after a short while she stopped when my sister was born. In liberated Poland she was dedicated to house-keeping and bringing up the children.

I was born in a memorable year, a year of defeat and of great victory: 1920, during the bolshevik war when the Polish soldiers in ragged uniforms and torn boots, hungry, abandoned and without any help, were fighting against the aggression of Russian communism. The victory was ours! And I was fortunate enough to grow up in a free Poland.

Later I was to know the fetters.

There were six children at home: three girls and three boys. My two sisters died young, one of measles another of scarlet fever. Four of us remained. I was the only girl and probably that was why my mother loved me so much. I was the oldest. My parents were doing well and my mother had a domestic help. We lived in a 3-roomed flat. It was rather small and my mother was worried, but housing conditions were very difficult after the war. After 150 years of foreign occupation the country was like a weak baby trying to stand up. Our flat, although small, was beautiful. It had nice furniture, plenty of sun and lots of flowers on the balcony. In summer we would go to the country for whole two months. It was indescribable joy. The village in the district of Pulawy, on the Vistula, was the most charming place, which has remained in my heart and wandered with me thousands of miles right to Australia.

For whoever has seen the Polish countryside cannot but love it as I do. Who does not love those enormous forests, those orchards, those cottages so unlike any others, those warm, clear, fragrant evenings, and the singing of nightingales?

In autumn in Warsaw, I would go with my brothers to the park to gather chestnuts. In winter we would sledge and skate, and sometimes gain bruises. It did not matter as long as sledges were there. The childhood care-free years quickly passed. It was time for school.

The School. I was seven. Since I was never sick, apart from an occasional cold, when I was seven I looked nine. I was tall and strongly built. I remember people saying to my parents that I was clever. Already at that time I loved singing and music. I never liked noisy games with my schoolmates. I preferred to be alone. As a child I had many dreams but not one of these came true. Instead, all the horrible things tumbled on me and stifled my thoughts and my desires. Of my dreams there was soon not a trace left. But all this was yet to come. In the meantime I had before me thirteen years of happy life. It would have been better for me not to live than to see what was to destroy the joy of my life.

During the first years I was not a good pupil, always just getting a pass. But from the third year on I became the best in the class. My teachers loved me. My schoolmates disliked me and envied my every praise and distinction. I did not regret this particularly because, as I said, I could do without friends.

The subjects I liked most were history and singing. I enjoyed excursions, educational films and gymnastics and I played basketball well. In a word, I liked everything and found everything interesting, only mathematics would drive me to despair. This was a great disappointment for my parents who wanted me to study in this direction. But I was attracted by history and music. I had a very good voice. I finished primary school with a good result all round. The last day at school will always remain in my memory as will the act of passing the school banner on to my successor. The headmaster and teachers wished us good luck for our future life. On a nice June day I said goodbye to the school, alas forever. During my last year at school a great event took place: the death of Marshal Jozef Pilsudski, mourned by the whole Polish nation. Gone forever was our legendary Leader, loved by every Polish child for his work and for the independence he won for Poland. The loss we suffered was so great that immediately after his death, a storm began to gather over Poland and more and more frequently one heard the word war.

Another blow I suffered was the death of my father. His prolonged illness exhausted all our savings. Then he died. How tragic is death! The death of someone dear always leaves sorrow. The death of a father of young children spells a difficult future and hard work. Our situation changed abruptly. My mother had to sell all her valuables. She had to get rid of the domestic help. For a few months there was only sorrow and weeping in our house. Two of my brothers were in primary school. The third, aged three, was at home. I had just started to study at a business college. After a while my mother had to go to work which was difficult to find. Finally, she got a position in a nursery school. Her salary was barely enough to pay the rent and to live very frugally. I had to leave the college after a few months to stay at home to look after my brothers. So came to an end the wonderful dream of my childhood. I was always so busy I never had time to take a walk in the park nor to learn music. Only after my mother re-married did things improve for us, but not for long. *The Outbreak of War.* It was 1939 and that autumn brought war. So many deaths everywhere! And tears, and fires and noise, and hunger and cold. After a month of most heroic struggle Poland fell following the attack by the enemy from the east: Russia.

The Polish soldier fighting against Hitlerism was sure of the eastern frontier and did not suspect that Russian pledges [of non-aggression] were only a trap. Also Germany and Russia tore the country asunder once more. But the Polish soldier only lost a battle! For the war was going on and Polish troops were fighting, from the first day to the last, in foreign countries, for 'our freedom and yours'. The war took us by surprise because nobody believed Germany would criminally attack at night without declaring war. We Poles never attack first, but we defend ourselves when attacked. Our motto is: We do not want what belongs to others, but we want to keep what is ours. Shortly before war broke out I went through a six weeks' course of first aid. I was attached to the Red Cross in the sector of Utrata Rozrzadowa and we were to help troops as well as civilians. Alas, our work did not last long, for on 2nd September our station was bombed. Three hundred soldiers were killed as well as a number of civilians. This caused panic. We lost contact with our superiors and re-establishing it was out of the question. One terrible air raid after another. One could not poke one's nose out of the shelter and the exploding bombs were deafening. On 3rd September, at 5.15 there was another air raid which lasted only for half an hour. During this time I lost all that was our house. Only a heap of rubble was left. None of my family was killed, however, for they were not in the house. We were left without food and without clothing save what we had on.

On 8th September, the whole of Warsaw was afire. Hundreds of the enemy's planes were destroying my beloved city. There was no rest—bombs everywhere. People left the city in panic, carrying with them their belongings. My family and I were among them, trying to get to Rembertow. Behind, Warsaw was burning like a torch, illuminating the road which was dark and crowded. There were thousands of adults and children, many weeping, some lost, all terrified. The troops retreating to the east could not move because the roads were so packed. It looked as though everybody had left the town. But these were only a few weak people the rest remained to defend Warsaw with utmost heroism. We stopped at Milosna. It was impossible to proceed because the roads were littered with corpses of men, horses and cattle, some decomposing in the sunny, warm days of the golden Polish autumn. Drunken German pilots were slaughtering the defenceless civilian population with machine guns. The war was raging over the whole of Polish territory. The Polish troops fought bravely but the Germans were advancing rapidly towards Warsaw. On 12th September I saw them for the first time in my life; I also saw their crimes. A handful of our soldiers fought for six hours against a whole German division. Hidden in a forest they defended access to the capital until they were all killed. Their blood soaked into the Polish soil they loved and died for. There were many dead and the school was packed with wounded. All men were arrested, including boys over 14 years old. For me this was the day when I encountered the enemy, the day of [the German] 'New Order'. After many days of fighting, when no help from the allies was forthcoming, Warsaw capitulated. We returned to Warsaw, which looked as if it had suffered an earthquake. Piles of rubble where houses used to be. Graves, many graves in the streets. Among the graves, half-mad people seeking their dear ones. The crosses on the graves usually bore names. Among the fallen heroes one could find boys aged sixteen or seventeen.

Under the German Occupation. The houses that remained were almost all without window panes, some without water. There was no light, no fuel and, worst of all, no food. The streets were full of the hated German soldiers, against whom we swore to fight till death or victory. The winter, enemy of poor people, came very early. After we returned to Warsaw it was out of the question to find any accommodation. Finally we moved into a building which had been used as railway office, and of which some rooms remained. Our family occupied one of these. We had not a single bed, or table or chair. We did not even have a spoon or knife, or blankets. We were in utter misery. The shops were closed, and there was nothing to eat. There were German kitchens at a few points where they were giving out 1 litre of soup and half a kilogram of bread per family. But in order to get that it was necessary to queue from six o'clock in the morning and by the end there was nothing left. After a few weeks the shops were re-opened and we were able to buy a few necessities. Our magnanimous rulers issued ration cards on which almost nothing could be bought, except 250 grams of bread for two days for an adult person. Children were getting half that. Briefly, the enemy started to rule by starving the people. But we were tough and we had no intention of dying as quickly as the Germans would like us to. We Poles can manage even in the worst of situations. Prolonged fighting tempered the Polish nation and we became harder than steel. Even Hitler was not able to break us. The new order imposed a curfew at 8 p.m. After that nobody could leave the house. Those who did were shot or, at best, arrested by German patrols.

Christmas 1939! It was our first in captivity, a cold, hungry and fearful one. There was no heating, no Christmas tree with candles, no carols sung aloud and there was nothing on the table at which we gathered as usual. Midnight Mass was forbidden. This Christmas will always remain in my memory and it will be remembered by all the people of Warsaw. We got a bloody present from Germans: 110 men were executed in Wawer, near Warsaw. It was the first official mass execution. On the snow lay the innocent victims of Hitlerite murderers who were killed only because they were Poles. The families were not allowed to bury them. Later, they were buried in a mass grave. In this execution I lost a person dear to me.

People were frightened at first, then swore vengeance. A long, difficult fight began. Thousands fell in this fight, but the gaps were being filled by new people and the ranks of the Polish Underground grew stronger every day.

The German occupation was a hell for the Polish people. There was no fuel, the food rations were totally inadequate and clothing was not available. Infectious diseases like diphtheria and typhus were rampant. There were no doctors and no medicines which were commandeered by the Germans. We had no soap and no hospitals, which were only for Germans. Parks, picture theatres, cafés, hotels and theatres were for Germans only. Every night houses were searched. During one of these searches we were robbed of money which my mother had kept at home. It was useless to try to recover it, we were lucky we were alive. We had almost no light. The electricity was scarce and we used an acetylene lamp but carbide was almost as hard to get as food. Whenever somebody left the house he was never sure he would return, because the Germans were rounding people up in the streets. Those caught, both men and women as well as children from 14 years up, were either deported to Germany as forced labour, or put into Pawiak prison and subsequently sent to concentration camps, whence nobody returned. Pawiak was the hardest prison, for political prisoners. In this prison, even during the Russian occupation Polish patriots were being killed by the Czar's hangmen. Under the Germans Pawiak was the most fearful torture place. There was no return from Pawiak and there were only two ways out; one, a short one, was death; the other, prolonged suffering in a concentration camp and ultimate death.

The schools were closed. Only old people would go to church because the young ones were afraid of the mass arrests which had previously occurred. During the devotions, when the church was full of people, the Germans would block all exits and then drag out brutally all but the very old, without any distinction of sex or age. That was why younger people stayed away from the communal prayers which we needed so much to strengthen our faith. For the weak ones were losing faith and there were some who doubted the very existence of God because He could not watch so much evil, so much blood spilled and so many tears shed. Prayer gave us new strength and faith that the enemy would eventually fall, that he would lose his right hand and would never again use it to grab somebody's property or to take somebody's life, that he would choke to death with the blood he has spilled. Months were passing, months as long as eternity, and there was no change for better. On the contrary, after the war with Russia, everything became worse. Arrests did not stop either day or night. The Germans, sure of their front in Russia, had, for the time being, the power of life and death. In vain we hoped for aid from our allies. The enemy was raging. Hundreds of people were murdered every day. Two or three executions took place daily. They were no longer secret, for the names, the places and the dates of birth of those executed were displayed on posters. The food was supplied by people who, running a deadly risk, went to the country to buy it at exorbitant prices and to resell it at a profit. Thanks to these people it was possible to buy something when one had money. That is if the Germans did not raid the markets confiscating all food and arresting the people. Similar raids were taking place almost daily: in markets, in trains and even in shops.

The Jews were separated from the rest of the population by a concrete wall, on top of which was strewn broken glass. The lot of these people was even worse than ours. They were squeezed, several people to a room, and had no food. The Poles were forbidden to enter the ghetto and those who dared to do so were shot on the spot. So these people were dying of hunger. The Jews were, like ourselves, rounded up in the streets, but there was one difference: for them there was only one destination; the camp of Treblinka and death, while some lucky Poles would be only deported to Germany, where they would face hunger, hard work and humiliation. The youth from 14 years old were captured in the streets, in the churches and even in the schools. Those arrested were deported on the spot, without being given a chance to see their parents. Their families never knew what happened to those who did not come home at night.

Sometimes, after a few months, a letter would come saying that they were in Germany on forced labour. This youth had no chance to complete their education, for during the years they would normally spend at school, they were forced to work hard on the land or in a factory, without ever reading a book. The enemy wanted us to be ignorant and their aim was the destruction of our intelligentsia. This was perhaps the greatest tragedy for the Polish nation.

After the fall of the Jewish uprising, which lasted nearly six weeks, there was silence in the ghetto. There was emptiness where hundreds of thousands of people had lived. Some houses were still smouldering but there was not one life left. Some were murdered in the ghetto, others were deported to concentration camps. We knew that the same kind of future awaited us. Some people with weak nerves broke down and did not believe in a better future. My stepfather was one of these. After the fall of Poland he was afflicted with a peculiar psychological illness, he could not eat; he could not sleep at night; he did not leave home except when going to work; he could not stand the Germans or their language; he even did not like to look through the window onto the street. Like my father he was in the Polish Legion (in World War I). The fall of the country was a mortal blow to him. He did not live to see the end with the Germans running away and their place taken by the new enemy: Russia. He died on 22 April, 1943. It was Good Friday and a double sorrow for us. A week after the death of my stepfather, my mother went with some friends to the country to get some food. On their way back they came across German patrols and they had to flee. Alas, they were seen and the Germans pursued them with shots.

One woman was killed. My mother fled across a river and into a large forest and escaped. The river was shallow but, as mother later said, as cold as death. Hidden in the forest she had to wait —soaked, cold and hungry—until the following morning. She could not proceed because she had lost her way. In the meantime I was awaiting her return. She did return! She was barely able to stand and there was fever in her eyes so I called a doctor immediately. Three days passed before the doctor found she had pneumonia. One blow after another exhausted my strength. However, I had young brothers who wanted to eat and a sick mother who needed my help. It was a woman doctor, Dr Jaworska, who performed, with God's help, the miracle to save the life which was half gone. For two months my mother fought with death and I was with her. Sometimes I would sleep only 3 hours in 48. One of my brothers was helping me but he could not do much, because during the day he was working in a factory. The two others were still children and could not help. The family was supported by my brother and myself.

The most difficult thing was to get medicines for my mother. I would run from one pharmacy to another with tears in my eyes. Alas, the medicines were simply not there at any price. Dr Jaworska helped me and procured the injections which were to return health to my mother. This was but the first of a whole chain of sufferings which awaited us. Three months after the death of my stepfather and the grave illness of my mother my brother did not return home after work. A terrible night followed, a night of waiting. Nobody went to sleep. My younger brothers were crying. My mother was on her knees praying that her son might return. I was completely numb, unable to cry, to move or to pray, although my mother kept asking me to pray for his return. This was one of the most tragic nights in my whole life. In the days which followed we made investigations. But they were useless and we could find no trace of my brother until one of his friends told us that he was caught in a round-up which took place while he was returning home after work. His friend who was with him on the same tram managed to escape. All our efforts to find him were in vain. On 14th August I saw in the street a man who was sticking up posters, red as blood. My heart was beating so hard that I was unable to make a step. Some people were reading the wet poster which was a death-roll. I remember only that when I did look at it, I saw the third name from top was that of my beloved brother, who was one of the executed

Q

hostages. He was 20 when he was killed, on 14th August, 1943. I saw his name only for a short moment. I remember that I uttered an inhuman cry and then I fainted. When I recovered my senses it was 20th August. I opened my eyes. It was night and a candle was burning in the room. I did not know where I was and I did not recognize my home. There was an ice bag on my head and my limbs were so heavy I was unable to lift them. In the dark corner of the room I saw a woman. She was sitting at a small table, and looked as though dead. Her eyes were closed and she looked very old. I was so frightened I screamed. The woman came to me and then I recognized her as my mother and I knew I was at home. She wept very much and complained that I wanted to leave her as her son did. She knew he was dead and it made her an old woman. She told me that on the 14th, two men brought me home, that I had been in bed for six days, unconscious the whole time. She called a few doctors who tried to put me in a hospital because I had Meningitis, but there was no room. I was not given a chance of survival, but apparently I was destined to live. Five weeks passed before I got up for the first time, and then I had to learn to walk. My life was terrible and I was resentful that the doctors had not let me die. The solitude in the house after I lost my brother was unbearable. Everywhere I could see his image and I had to think of his last hours, of his suffering, his anxiety to live, of his longing for us. It was more than I could stand. Today, fifteen years afterwards, I still find this memory heart-rending.

After the death of my brother I thought only of vengeance and I was prepared for everything. My mother's health was bad. She would sit in one place staring and unmindful of what was going on around her. Sometimes she would sit like that for six or seven hours. If somebody interrupted her she was angry. At night she hardly slept at all, but she would pray and cry and call my brother to come so she could see him once more. Sometimes she would talk to him as if he were there. Since I did not sleep very well myself, I heard everything and I was terrified. I feared I might lose my senses and I thought my mother was showing signs of mental illness. She forgot that she had three children left, i.e. myself and my two younger brothers. So I had to look after them. They had to eat and to get some food it was necessary to have a lot of money, physical strength and cool head. I was only 23 then but I felt as if I had lived for ages. During the day I was too busy to feel any pain, but at night everything came back and I could not sleep. A year passed and we got hopeful glimpses of an early end. Every week a friend of mine from before the war, who was a lieutenant and who had worked since the beginning in the Underground, would bring me a bulletin.[2] From it I could follow all the fights of our boys and all the crimes of the Germans, which then reached their zenith. Defeats on all fronts were driving them mad and their whole fury was directed against us. Hundreds were executed every day now. The hooter of the Black Maria could be heard in the streets of Warsaw several times a day. The round-ups were going on now day and night. At night they were breaking into homes dragging out people in night-gowns. These people were then taken to Gestapo Headquarters in Aleja Szucha, where they were tortured. Some died during those inquests, others survived only to be executed publicly next morning. The Germans tried to suppress our patriotism with terror. They meant to scare us into meek submission. But Poles are not slaves, they know no master and they will not allow themselves to be put in fetters. The enemy's fury gave us strength to fight for we knew it was his agony. We had to live to avenge our murdered brethren. Our hands and hearts longed for a fight which would be decisive. *The Warsaw Uprising.* The Russians started to bomb Warsaw at night. It was the civilian population who suffered most. During the day—German raids; during the night—Russian bombs. The food was becoming ever scarcer, for the Germans were confiscating everything. The cost of living became high beyond belief. One kilogram of bread cost then 26 zlotys, one kilogram of lard—400 zl., one kilogram of potatoes—6 zl., one egg—11 zl. The friend who used to bring me the bulletin was murdered in Aleja Szucha, after four days of torture. No longer reading the bulletin I had no inkling of what was going on in the city. But I could see Germans running away. Their troops, together with their allies: Rumanians, Hungarians, Ukrainians. Trucks full of wounded soldiers, deprived of medical help. The trams stopped running. The taxis disappeared because they were used by fleeing high civilian officials. From the windows of our flat I could watch those masters of our life and death. I was longing with all my heart to fight them, to bite them with my teeth for my murdered compatriots, for our misery, for my sick mother, for my brother buried in a place unknown to me or maybe cremated. This was the longing of every Pole, including the children. In the streets the crowds were watching the retreating troops. There were no raids, for the Germans had no time. In the streets one could see quite a few young men in long, black raincoats. Later I found out they were members of our Underground Army who were occupying key points. The loudspeakers were appealing every hour, in Polish, to the inhabitants of Warsaw to join the German forces to defend the city together. They said that another 'Miracle of the Vistula'[3] should happen as in 1920, and that the Soviet Army should break against the walls of Warsaw. The same people who bathed in our blood and tears, who acted as our hangman during five years, now called for our help. But their appeals were in vain. The murderers of millions of our people retreating, to be replaced by others, the red ones, no better at all. I knew there was going to be an uprising. People were buying as much food as they could get. We did not know when it was to be, but there was something in the air which presaged struggle.

For the fourteenth time in history the population of Warsaw would rise to get rid of the fetters and to give blood and life, so those who survived might be free. The Soviet troops were only a few kilometres from Warsaw and we expected that they would help us to drive out the bloody hangmen. But our hopes were deceived this time as in 1939, and nobody helped us when thousands were falling every day in an uneven struggle. Our so-called friends stood idly by watching the death of the best sons of Poland and the destruction of a great city.

The Germans were still strong enough, and we were unarmed and hungry. Only our hearts were ready for the greatest of sacrifices. The uprising surprised me in the street, far from my house. My mother lived in Praga and I was caught by the uprising in the City. To go back to Praga it would be necessary to cross one of the bridges over Vistula and it was out of question. That morning, when I was going out, my mother asked me to come back soon. I did not know it was goodbye for ever. From 1st August to 7th October I was in the city. Not being a writer I shall never be able to describe the tragedy of the population of Warsaw; even the best pen could not do so. I think I shall not go to hell after I die because I have been there already. I was hungry and dirty, in rags, misery itself. I lived on what was available, and I would pass hours without water. I worked wherever there was a demand for hands. I was not active in the army organization but I think the work of the civilian population was as important as the struggle of the army. Everybody was taking part in the struggle: men, old and young, women and children, ghost-like people covered with their own blood. The wounded were running away from the underground hospitals to go on fighting, for we were short of hands and the enemy outnumbered our forces and was armed with heavy weapons.

Thousands were falling daily and we had to bury them in the backyards or in the streets. Others were buried under the ruins of destroyed houses. The city was never conquered, but they had to give up fighting because they had no ammunition, no food, no water, no light, and no medicines. The capitulation took place on 2nd October, after the whole town was reduced to rubble and nearly 300,000 inhabitants lost their lives.

On the 7th October I was dragged out, with others, from the basement of a ruined house and driven to Pruszkow. But before this we were subjected to a search, during which we were robbed by the German soldiers. I was robbed of my watch, a ruby ring and a wallet with about 30,000 zl. in it. I was left only with what I had hidden on my bosom and this was of great help in Pruszkow. Pruszkow was the first stage in the wandering of harassed, half-mad people who had lost everything. From there they could only go to Germany as forced labour or to a concentration camp. But we had only our lives to lose and nobody cared much about that. We had lost everything. All we had remained under the ruins. What could be salvaged was railed to Germany.

We were placed in the railway workshops, surrounded by a high wall and heavily guarded by police. The shed No. 4, where I was, was packed with 600 people; men, women and children, several of them sick. One was lucky even to find a place to sit. One would not move from that place and at night one would sleep there on the bare concrete floor. There was no water and nobody washed. Nobody changed their clothes. Some, including myself, were wearing summer dresses. At night, in spite of being so crowded we were cold, and sleeping on bare concrete made our bodies stiff. The first night I was so tired I slept insensible to cold; as long as I could sleep it did not matter where or how. The uprising had lasted 63 days and there had been no opportunity or time to sleep. But the following nights, until 17th October I could not sleep. I just sat shivering with cold. At 6 a.m. there was breakfast: half a pint of coffee (for those who had their own containers) and a quarter pound of stale bread. For dinner there was a pint of a cabbage soup. The cabbage was rotten and stank but the soup was hot. But I was not fortunate enough to get any because I had no container. Three times daily we were mustered. In the morning the men would be taken to Warsaw to

dig trenches; many of them would not return in the evening.
Two days after my arrival to Pruszkow I met a friend of mine who
was working as a nurse. She had a special pass and was allowed
to leave the camp. She helped me, buying for me bread at 100 zl.
a kilogram. The lavatory consisted of a deep trench above which
was a board on which 20 women could sit. If one lost one's
balance one could drown in the excrement.

Deportation to Germany. On 17th October I left Pruszkow.
We were issued with a pound of bread and two spoonfuls
of beetroot jam wrapped in paper. Then we were assembled and
marched, at snail's pace, towards a goods train. We were loaded
70 to a wagon. It was so crowded that nobody could sit down
and we had to stand all the way. There was not enough air and
the little window with bars was the object of struggle. Everyone
wanted to be near the window, and the strongest won. Finally we
arrived in Czestochowa. It took two days and two nights, for the
train stopped frequently for long periods. We were not allowed
to leave the train during the halts and the police watched that
nobody approached it. During the 48 hours, we were allowed
3 times, four at a time, to attend to our physiological needs. It
had to be done on the spot, under the eyes of a policeman who
was watching us with a machine-gun ready to shoot. We were
dying of shame, but the Germans did not care. When our journey
was over we left the train half dead. We were put into a camp
on the following day. There was an inspection and bath. We
had to take off our clothing which was taken to be disinfected,
while we waited for our turn in the bath. It was so cold that we
were blue. After the bath, we were shaven and smeared with
some stinking liquid. Then we got back our clothes, crumpled,
stinking and half burnt. We waited there three weeks for transport to Germany. Food was inadequate and we were hungry but
we had straw mattresses and two blankets, and we could sleep.
The reveille was at 5 a.m. and after cleaning up our quarters
there was, at 6 a.m., breakfast consisting of 200 grams of bread
and a cupful of coffee. For dinner we would get a litre of soup,
and for supper—the same as for breakfast.

We had two masters: a German from Poland named Binek and
a Ukrainian born in Kolamyja named Steliga. For a bed not so
well-made or for the toilet badly cleaned we would get a couple
of kicks and a few slaps in the face. Also we could be deprived
of a meal. Every day of the week, except Sundays, our masters,
with dogs, would drive us to work in a sheet-metal shop, where

we were being prepared for future work in Germany. On 19th November at 2 a.m. I said good-bye forever to my country. Sorrow was parting my heart and if I am still alive it is because the windows and doors were closed and because my companions talked me out of it, for I wanted to break the window pane and jump out of the train and to run away or perish, but on Polish soil. But my companions were watching me and kept trying to persuade me that we would return when the war was finished. I did not return, however. The new enemy was oppressing my country, plundering and deporting people to Siberia. I was so afraid that, in spite of great home-sickness, I decided not to return. It took us three days to reach the point of our destination, Augsburg. After a week in a transit camp we were assigned to work. The transit camp was situated 2 kilometres from the town, in a valley. The barracks were surrounded with an earth-wall. The mud was ankle deep. In the camp there were only 12 Poles, the remainder were Ukrainians and Russians. Two families lived in one room partitioned with blankets. Everything was filthy. The toilets were blocked and if one wanted to go there one had to put on boots because the excrement was ankle deep. The meals were cooked by Russian women. Throughout the week I ate some stinking Russian borsch and half rotten potatoes. For supper there were three potatoes per person and curds made from skim milk. In order to obtain a ration it was necessary to give in a coupon. The latter were there to prevent anybody from getting a double ration.

I lived together with 44 girls from Warsaw in one big room. There was only one window in the room and an iron stove which never burnt for want of fuel. The barracks were of weatherboard and between the boards there were thousands of bugs, which did not allow sleep at night. A few minutes after the light was switched off I was all covered in bites. They were very painful and itching. It was the first time in my life that I had seen anything like it. We tried to defend ourselves by putting the straw mattresses on the floor and by keeping the light on, but it was no use. The bugs kept falling from the ceiling straight on our faces. Finally, I went to the office and asked to be sent away from the camp somewhere where I would not be bitten by bugs. Even the hardest work seemed preferable. My knowledge of German helped me and within a week I was sent to work in Würtemberg. With me went 5 other girls from Warsaw. We went to a small village named Adolefurt, where there was a fortress and in it a munitions factory. They used to call us bandits from Warsaw. The building where we were to live was near the gate so the guards could keep an eye on us all the time. But it was reasonably clean. We had iron beds painted white, fresh straw mattresses, three blankets each, a table and two benches. There was another reason too for great satisfaction: central heating and hot water. This was simply paradise. We were issued with drill clothes and wooden shoes, as heavy as our life. Besides that we had no other clothing and no linen. It was December and winter was beginning. The reveille was at 5 a.m. and before we had breakfast we went to work. We worked from 6 a.m. to 6 p.m. At 9 a.m., there was breakfast: one cup of coffee with saccharine. We were given one kilogram of bread for seven days. Everybody would eat that in one day, and for the remainder of the week there was nothing. The dinner consisted of two or three potatoes, unpeeled, and sauerkraut in water. The sauerkraut gave us indigestion. For supper we had a cup of peppermint infusion and some potatoes with mustard sauce or curds.

I worked 12 hours daily in a bunker, cleaning and packing powder. There were 28 Armenians working there, as well as 6 Polish girls from Warsaw and one Russian girl who was a primary school teacher from Leningrad. Among the Polish girls there were 2 postal clerks, 2 models, a young girl aged 16 and myself.

Thousands of planes were flying over every day and one air raid followed another. During the alert nobody was allowed to leave the workplace, not even the Germans. Only when the first bombs were about to drop would we be allowed to think of escape. Of course if we were surprised by the bombs, there would be no escape and we would all go up with the dynamite.

During the week we could not leave the precincts of the factory; the gates were watched. Only on Sunday, from 2 to 8 p.m. were we free to move about within a radius of 2 kilometres. Crossing this line carried a fine of 10 marks. I had a letter 'P' (for Polish) affixed to my dress. During twelve hours every day I would carry hundreds of bags of powder of 35 kilograms each on my back. After a month of this work I had no strength to go from my barrack to the bunker. I stopped working, I could not make the norm. Whereupon I was accused of sabotage and was arrested by police for questioning. The doctor to whom they sent me found me weak but fit to work in the open air. For the remaining weeks I was clearing snow from the streets of the factory. The work was not easier, for one had to work twelve hours in cold as low as 20 degrees centigrade below zero. But by then, the Front was only 20 kilometres away and we could hear clearly the shooting and this gave us strength to hold out.

On 2nd April, it was Easter Monday, at 7.45 a.m., our factory was completely destroyed by bombs. We were all saved because we were still in bed and our barracks were 5 minutes walk from the factory. We ran away. When we reached the nearest village, nobody believed that we could have remained alive. For four days we had nothing to eat and we had to sleep in the open in the vineyards. Some Poles who were working in the village stole bread for us. One day it snowed and we had to find a shelter. There was a tool-shed near there and we broke into it and slept there one night. But the next day a German woman came shouting, and threw us out of the shed and called police. They put us with people from other bombed factories and evacuated us to a place near Switzerland. There we were assigned to work. I was to work for a gardener, but after 3 days there I was liberated by the French troops. During those three days we worked from half past five in the morning till late at night. There was a Polish boy from Cracow working there. He was 18 then, but when they first brought him to that work, he was only 14. He showed me his back which was blue from the constant beatings he was getting from police called by the gardener, who accused him of loafing, being cheeky and not working hard enough. The police would take him to the kitchen and beat him up. During the four years he spent there, he was beaten eleven times, the last time a fortnight before the coming of French troops. I was treated worse than a slave during those three days.

Liberation. How great was my surprise when, on Sunday, nobody woke me up: nobody was calling me to work. By nine o'clock I was somewhat alarmed. I got up and went to the kitchen. They had already eaten their breakfast and the kitchen was cleaned up. My boss's wife greeted me with a smile and said, 'Good morning, Miss Lydia. Did you sleep well?' I was dumbfounded and could not believe my ears, while she continued: 'Your breakfast is in the oven. I did not want to call you for breakfast because you were asleep. You are free now. Last night the French troops occupied the town and ours did not defend it.'

Free! I was so overcome with joy that I could not move. Then I wept and found it difficult to believe. The town was 3 kilometres from my work-place, so it was not until noon that I saw the French and I believed in the liberation. Not one German could be seen in the town and one had the impression that they had all died during the night. But there were many French soldiers and people of many nationalities. The French were distributing tinned food, cigarettes, soap, chocolate and wine. They had special sympathy for the Poles. He who was never a slave cannot understand what it means to be free. For me, it was the happiest day in my life.

Later I lived in a camp but it was overcrowded there being 1,500 people in a few barracks. So some were billeted in private houses. The food was very good in comparison with what I had while working for the Germans. The French were doing their best to help. In 1945 I was married. My husband was an ex-political prisoner from a concentration camp. I knew him back in Poland and it was a great surprise to see him again. He was in the camps of Auschwitz, Dachau and Schonberg. In 1946 my son was born. My husband was very active in the Y.M.C.A. He was teaching boxing at which he was pretty good. He also formed a soccer team. This work occupied all his free time. My son was the joy of my life. Life would have been quite bearable if it was not that we lived among our enemies. My husband worked as a welder earning 200 marks per month. In addition we were getting food from U.N.R.R.A. and later from I.R.O. The American and English parcels were also a great help. Polish-Americans were sending us special parcels and clothing. We did not want to return to Poland. We intended to do so before my son was born, but the news we were receiving frightened us. It was not the Poland for which we had waited and for which millions had died. We had waited for a free, democratic Poland, whereas she was now at the mercy of our enemy. So, for the sake of our son and of a quiet future for ourselves, we decided, although it was a very painful decision, not to return to our fatherland, dominated as it was by the red enemy and suffering utter misery. We wanted to begin a new life, free, among free people. We chose Australia, a free and prosperous country which we knew only from stories. We looked forward to emigration, we were impatient to go there as quickly as possible and to help build that young country and to forget forever places the remembrance of which would bring tears to our eyes.

Our relations with the French authorities were very friendly. We had many amusements. Artists, good revues, concerts, and pictures were brought from Paris. Every Saturday and Sunday there was dancing for the French, but Poles were always admitted.

On Sunday there were soccer matches. Our club, 'Polonie', of which my husband was president, was one of the best teams, and it was a cause for great joy whenever they won against Germans. Then every member of our team would receive a parcel from the French authorities; the Germans were furious. It was a victory. The Germans had no longer any power over us, because we were put under the French authority called P.D.R. They would greet us with a smile, but it was the smile of a lurking reptile waiting for an opportune moment to strike a deadly blow. They cursed Hitler while inwardly they were staunch Hitlerites. They know how to mask themselves. I hated them so intensely that I longed to leave them and to cast them out of my sight. For when I saw them I could not help remembering all I had gone through, all my misery, my ruined country, the death of my brother and millions of other Poles. I had to hate them for all that and for my being unable to return to my country, where their accomplice of 1939 continued to murder the harassed Polish nation. I hated them also for the torment and personal humiliations of my husband in the concentration camp.

The day came when we went before Commission. After two days we were passed. A few weeks later, we were passed by another, Australian, Commission. There were no difficulties now. The conversation with the Australian Consul made a very pleasant impression on me. Saying goodbye he wished us luck in our new country which was to give us freedom and work. On 14th July, 1949, after three weeks in a transit camp, my family and I left without sorrow the country of our persecutors. The three weeks we spent in beautiful Naples were a little tiresome. Bad food, exorbitant prices in the canteen, children's ailments and waiting for the ship spoilt our humour. Nobody knew what was awaiting us in Australia. We were impatient to see that happy country and those lucky people who never experienced violence. *On the Way to Australia.* On 15th August we went aboard the ship. I was terribly frightened by the immense water. I was also very sorry for my country, in which remained my mother, my brothers and the bones of one who fell victim of Hitlerite crime. On 16th at 7 a.m. we sailed. For the last time I bade farewell to my country. The mainland quickly disappeared behind us and I was blinded with tears. Europe was left behind and we were steaming towards a new country and a new life.

During the first days aboard all was novelty. There were so many people speaking different languages. But our quarters were not too comfortable. There were 60 women and children to a room. Men were much better off because they were alone while we had to look after the children. Besides, the women had to clean the cabins, shower-rooms, toilets and corridors and to wash and iron, so they had very little time left. The men worked in the galleys, dining rooms and offices, so that everybody was occupied. The food was very bad and there was not enough fresh water, so that on the Red Sea it was on only three times a day, one hour at a time. The heat and the shortage of water was driving us mad. One could not buy a drink either because drinks were reserved for the ship's personnel. At night one could not breathe in the cabins. Mothers were fanning their children who, although completely undressed were crying, gasping for air. The bed-sheets were saturated, the ventilators did not work and we were in despair. We were not allowed to remain on the deck after 11 p.m. Again, as during the occupation, there was a curfew hour. A policeman guarded the exit to the deck. One night it was so bad that we were literally facing suffocation and the captain came and decided that it was really impossible for us to remain in the cabins. So we were allowed to sleep on the deck. But it was not much better there, and we all waited impatiently to leave the tropical zone. I was so tired with the heat that I could not watch the Suez Canal. My husband felt very well. He worked as a male nurse in the ship's hospital, played cards and talked with people. I watched two funerals: of a woman and of a child, and I was terribly upset, and was still so when my son contracted measles and was taken to the hospital, and I was not allowed to see him. I was desperate for he was my only child and I feared to lose him. In the Indian Ocean I became sea-sick. The sea was very choppy and our ship was rolling so much that it was difficult to stay in bed. Things were being thrown from one end of the cabin to another, making a terrible noise, which we could not stand. For three days I was so sick I thought I would never see Australia.

There were two fires which started in the boiler-room, but fortunately, they were quickly put out.

My son remained in hospital until we reached Melbourne. The first land I saw was Australia. There was a stop of half a day in Perth and my eyes were opened wide as I watched this country unknown and so different, where I was to start a new life. Our next stop was in Melbourne where I left the ship. One day before we disembarked I got back my son. He was to be sent to a hospital in Melbourne while we would go on to Bonegilla. I was in such despair that there was no room left in me to enjoy the nearing end of a tiresome voyage. At the last moment I got back my son. He had changed very much during those seven days in the hospital. The high temperature and dieting robbed him of his strength so that he could not stand on his feet. And he grew very thin. That was why I greeted this country with a sad face. The day of disembarkation there was a lot to do and everybody was waiting impatiently to set foot on land. In the port there were a lot of journalists and photographers. Having left the ship and passed the customs inspection I found myself in the train. It took the whole day to get to Bonegilla where I was put in a barracks occupied by eight families.

Australia: Peace and Happiness. The first supper in Australia tasted wonderful. For the family allowance we were receiving before my husband went to work, we could buy fruit and chocolate for our son whose health was improving every day. A few days later we received clothing which was badly needed by some. After a month, my husband got a job and we had to part. I went to Cowra, where I lived for the next two months. From Cowra I went to Sale where I lived for nine months. My husband came home only for weekends. He was not earning much and it was very expensive to keep two houses, so we could not save much. It was simply impossible to find a private accommodation and for a whole year I had to live in camps. Only after a year did my husband find a room in a private house for which we had to pay £2.2.6 per week. On top of that I had to work without pay: laundering, ironing, cleaning and looking after children. I had no time left for my own family but, nevertheless, I was happy because I was with them. The fact that I did not know English was making my life difficult. Nobody understood me and I could not understand anybody. Shopping presented the most difficult problem. A word badly pronounced would not be understood by people. We must have looked very funny to them. The people with whom we lived were not very nice. The landlady treated me almost as her property merely because she let us the room for which we were paying. So, with our savings we bought a block of land, three miles from where we lived. It was in the bush where cows were grazing. There was no water and no light and the shops were three miles away. But it was all unimportant now that we had our land. We borrowed £200 from the bank and my husband built a bungalow of two rooms. We dug a well 12 ft. deep which supplied our water. My husband was building in his spare time and some of his friends were helping him. So it took only six weeks to complete and by Christmas we were in our own nook.

The beginning was very difficult because we needed everything and had no money to buy things necessary for the house.

What made me most happy was that every day I learned a few more English words, and my son was speaking good English with other children. As my English improved I was able to make the acquaintance of some Australian families. It is thanks to these people that I can manage in everyday life.

We lived for six years in our bungalow. What we missed most was the bathroom. The water was already there, because the migrants themselves and their wives were digging trenches in order to facilitate the installation of water and electricity. The tall grass, which made us fear snakes—disappeared. Where there was only bush before, the houses of migrants were mushrooming. Today, the place is so densely settled that it is impossible to buy a block of land anywhere near the main road. We have light and water and some streets. In 1956, we started to build our house. Our savings were not enough but the bank helped us again and thanks to this I have been living for the last two years in my own, four-roomed house. The building took my husband a year and a half. He worked in his spare time and I was his only help, for there was no money to hire anybody else. It was hard work. We had no rest and no pleasures. I moved into the house when it was not quite finished. But it is almost finished now. Inside, we have not much furniture because we are still paying off the bank. Besides, there are improvements to the property to be made and prices are very high today. After paying the bills nothing remains from my husband's earnings.

My husband likes his work and has many Australian friends with whom he is very popular. As a sportsman of long standing he is a member of the local club. Now he has more time for leisure and he goes swimming and fishing or hunting, which he likes very much. He has more amusements than I, for I only have pictures and reading, although I like music, theatre and the hum of a big city in which I grew up. The place where I live is very nice but awfully quiet. On Sunday I only go to church. At home I listen to the radio. During the week I have no time to be bored because I have a big garden where I work in my spare time. I gain great satisfaction from this.

My son is going to a Catholic college now. He is in the second year and is progressing satisfactorily. He is the best of his class in English, which gives us great pleasure. He is almost like a born Australian and likes everything his Australian colleagues like—sport above all.

Today we lead a happy life. We have a house and work and we are healthy. We have freedom and enjoy the friendship of people born here. I am happy that I have left far behind the unpleasant memories of the German occupation.

I am happy and I want to work for this country in which my family and I have found peace and happiness.

My husband and I want to secure a happy future for our son and a quiet tomorrow for ourselves, far from the Communist terror. We want to live in a free, democratic country. And we want to put all our strength at the service of this nation to make it powerful yet peace-loving.

The Story of a Latvian Engineer[1]

I was born in 1914 in Riga, Latvia, i.e. during World War I. My father, a tradesman, was called up in the Russian army. So till 1919 my mother supported my sister and me. After the declaration of peace my father was discharged and on his return started working for the Latvian public service, where he remained till Latvia was annexed by the Soviet Union in 1940.

I started school at the age of six. I spent two years in pre-school, then six years in primary school, after which I spent five years in the State technical high school. Latvian schools not only imparted general and specialized knowledge, but also endeavoured to bring up the pupils as conscientious citizens of the State. Such non-political youth organizations as the scouts, Y.M.C.A., Junior Farmers, Junior Red Cross and the Junior Anti-Alcohol Association helped the schools in this patriotic upbringing. At the age of twelve I also joined the scouts, and was later active as a leader till 1940 when the Russian occupants closed it down.

After finishing the State technical high school I worked for a year as a trainee in order to gain my diploma and technician qualifications, and then continued working as a technician. At the age of 21 I was called up for National Service, for one year. After being discharged from National Service I again began working as a technician and also enrolled in the University of Latvia to study engineering.

As my material means were satisfactory and my future seemed assured, in 1939 I got married. My wife, whom I had known from my school days, had graduated from the Teachers' College and was working in Latvia as a teacher; later however, she was matron of a Children's Home.

At the start of the Second World War, when the internal political situation worsened, I was again called up in the army for further training. On returning from the army, I did not take up my studies again that year.

In June of 1940 the Soviet Union occupied Latvia, and a few months later annexed it. In connection with the nationalization of private property and various decrees issued by the new regime, I was dismissed from my job. For a few months I worked at any job available, but then, due to the shortage of specialists, I was again employed as a technician on some nationalized enterprise. My wife continued working as a teacher at the Riga Children's Home. During that time, working conditions had changed. Workers were required to participate in various political discussions and gatherings as well as carry out their normal duties. Every non-attendance was regarded as an anti-State activity and was followed by various reprisals.

From the very first days of the occupation many of Independent Latvia's public servants and social workers had been imprisoned and had disappeared without a trace. One of the largest onslaughts of this kind occurred in June 1941, when, within a few days, thousands of Latvians were imprisoned and deported to Soviet slave camps. This brutal onslaught which was not confined to any particular class, and which spared neither babies nor the old or infirm increased discontent with and hatred for the ruling regime, this was most noticeable when Germany declared war on the Soviet Union.

German forces entered Riga in July, 1941. The people looked on them as liberators, in the hope that an Independent Latvian State would be reinstituted in the near future. But these hopes were dashed when the German Civil administration was set up. Living conditions showed no great change, only the occupation forces had changed and instead of persecuting classes they persecuted races. During the German occupation I continued working in the same job, and a year later again took up my studies at the University of Latvia.

At the start of 1944 as the German army retreated, the front was again near Latvia's borders, and in the autumn it reached Riga. Intensified mobilization began, and German military institutions called up Latvians to serve in the Latvian legion and various other auxiliary forces which the Germans had formed. Being a specialist, I was one of the lucky few who escaped joining the Legion. At that time the German administration began the evacuation of places of employment and of the population. Thinking back on the terrifying year of Soviet occupation, a great number of Latvians fled to parts of Latvia as yet untouched by the war, and later on to Germany, hoping to get to areas occupied by the western powers, or else they stowed themselves away in fishing boats, bound across the Baltic for neutral Sweden.

So also did my wife and I, and our four year old son, find ourselves in Germany in October, 1944, and were put into a camp for foreign workers. Living conditions in the camp were poor. We lived in barracks, several families, including small children and babies cramped into one large room. Our movements were completely restricted. The camp was bombed in allied air-raids several times. I was sent out from the camp to work as a labourer on the erection of temporary dwellings and the clearing away of mines. I worked at this job till the arrival of the American army.

Soon after we were transferred to an U.N.R.R.A. camp. The food there was noticeably better. A few months later, when west Europeans who had been doing forced labour began to return home, a new problem arose, because we east Europeans, whose countries had been occupied by the Soviet Union, refused to return home. It seems that no one had conceived of such a possibility. For quite a while families were repeatedly 'screened', before the reasons for our refusal to return to our native countries were understood and we were then accepted as 'Displaced Persons'.

As the days spent in the camps turned to years, we tried, as far as circumstances would permit, to lead normal lives. We established schools, theatres, choirs, churches, attended English and French lessons and various courses to learn new trades. We also took great care with the upkeep of the camp and its surroundings. As far as possible we found salaried jobs either with the camp administration or the American army units. At that time I worked in the camp administration, as head of the Labour Office, but when, in 1947, the camp was moved, I joined the 'Labour Service' group founded by the American army. My family and wife and two sons (the younger was born in 1946 in Germany) stayed in the camp.

As neither we, U.N.R.R.A., or its successor I.R.O. could regard this life in camps as a solution to the D.P. problem, the question of emigration arose. Emigration began in the second half of 1947, when a few western countries began to accept immigrants,

R

at the suggestion of I.R.O. At first it was only possible for single people in very good health to emigrate, but later this also became possible for whole families.

In our area, Bavaria, Australia began to accept families at the start of 1949 when we also decided to take advantage of this and submitted an application for migration. A few months later we were called to an interview and medical examination by the representative of the Australian Immigration Department at Schweinfurt. The whole family had to undergo a very careful medical examination. If any member of the family had the slightest defect in health the whole family could be rejected. The Australian Government representative also interviewed every member of the family. During this interview I signed a contract, agreeing to work for two years in any job in any place chosen by the Australian Employment Office, and I also signed a promise to support my parents, so that they would not become a burden to the Australian Government. Although we all had the interviews at the same time, my parents were only able to come to Australia in 1950, that is, a year after my family and me.

In 1949 (July), after repeated medical checks and checks of documents, we left the transit camp in Germany to go to a transit camp in Italy near Naples. We were there for a month. There the family was separated and we lived in large communal rooms which were very crowded due to the large number of emigrants. This facilitated the spreading of children's diseases. The kitchens and dining rooms were remarkably dirty. The children, particularly, took badly to the strange food and parents were forced to supplement their diets from the canteens. As there was no money, it was raised by selling clothes and valuables on the camp's extensive 'black market'. In the middle of August, after yet another medical and document check we began our voyage to Australia.

We were booked on the former army transport ship *Nelly*, which now sailed under the Panama flag. Life on the ship was very crowded, for there were about 1,500 emigrants aboard. Families were again separated and usually met on the deck and in the dining rooms. In spite of that, the start of the voyage was satisfying, particularly after the month in Italy. Our misfortunes began a week later. The ship's engines began to break down and the ship stopped several times, which lengthened the voyage. Children's diseases also broke out and measles reached almost epidemic proportions. The children were vaccinated but as the serum soon ran out, only a small number were fortunate enough to receive the injections. Near the end of the journey drinking water was also rationed. These poor conditions during the voyage were partly to blame for two deaths. We spent the time on board doing various set tasks, or learning English in groups we ourselves organized. After a voyage of 32 days we reached Melbourne in mid-September 1949.

From Melbourne we were taken to Bonegilla migrant camp. Even here conditions were unsatisfactory, particularly as regards family living quarters. In the barracks, many families with small children all lived together in one big room, and as a result many children again became ill. Both my sons also fell ill, the elder with scarlet fever, and the younger with measles. The latter caught a cold while in hospital, got pneumonia, and was transferred to a Melbourne children's hospital when complications arose, and was only discharged after six months. I attended English classes in the camp and did various odd jobs until I was settled in a job. After three weeks the Employment Office put me to work at SEC in Yallourn. For the two years under contract, that is, the first two years in Australia, I worked as a labourer. I lived in the Commission's Workers' hostel where conditions were quite satisfactory. I got on very well with my workmates, both Australians and immigrants, some of whom had already been working there for some time. My Australian workmates tried to help me out in various ways, particularly at the start, when I had the usual language difficulties. I spent my spare time in the hostel learning English and furthering my technical knowledge by correspondence. The Y.M.C.A. also had a branch in the hostel with a library, various games, recreation rooms, and regular film showings.

Six months later my family was transferred from Bonegilla to a camp at Sale, which enabled me to spend the weekends with my family. At that time I began to search for a home for my family near my place of employment. After a long search I found accommodation of two rooms and we moved in.

When my contract expired I first worked as a surveyor's assistant, and then as head of the Building Section's laboratory. I am still employed in the laboratory. With this new job, I was given the right to rent a Commission house at East Newborough, which greatly improved our living conditions. Later, it became possible for me to buy this house. After living in Australia for five years, I applied for Australian citizenship and a year later my family and I were naturalized.

The question of my children's education was also favourably solved. My elder son, after finishing the local high school, enrolled in the Architecture Faculty of the University of Melbourne. My younger son is still studying at high school, so that he too can go on to the University after finishing.

As, besides our two children, we also supported my parents (my mother died in 1954 and my father in 1961), my wife has worked since our arrival in Australia, at first in a textile factory, but since 1961 as a head teacher in a kindergarten, gaining the right to work as a teacher on the basis of a certificate issued by the Latvian Education Department and approved by the Australian Education Authorities.

As my living and working conditions have been satisfactory I have changed neither my job nor home. Having spent thirteen years or so in the one area with the one employer it has been possible for me not only to mix in Australian society but also to join local social organizations. I have been an active worker for the Y.M.C.A. and have been secretary of the local branch since 1958. I have also been an active member of the local Lutheran Church and have been treasurer for six years. Mixing in Australian society has not deterred my being active in Latvian social and welfare organizations. As we have always spoken Latvian at home, so my children also have a command of it, but otherwise they have been completely integrated by Australian society and Australian customs.

Looking back on my life in this country, I can say that I have no regrets at having chosen Australia for my second homeland.

Appendix B

SAMPLING PROCEDURE AND NON-RESPONSE

The statistical universe from which the sample was drawn consisted of 2,150 overseas-born males who at the time of the survey constituted 48·4 per cent of the total male workforce employed by the State Electricity Commission at Yallourn and by the SEC contractors at Morwell.

Once the limits of the universe had been decided, the next step was to stratify it. It was necessary to group the members of the universe into strata by means of what were considered the most important variables in selecting a sample of immigrants. Two such significant variables were chosen. The first was locality or place of residence, which was considered an important factor in view of the observed differences in the ecological characteristics of the seven places. The second factor, and an obvious one for this study, was country of birth. At first no less than twenty-five different countries of birth were classified in the analysis of the SEC labour files. These categories were subsequently reduced to nine. The other variables used in the preparatory classifications were date of birth and date of commencement with the Yallourn SEC. From these last two variables age and length of employment were calculated as at 30 June 1958.

All this information was collected from the SEC records on to cards, one for each employee, with his full name, address, country of birth, date of birth, and date of commencement with the SEC. The data were then tabulated and tables were prepared summarizing the information and cross-classifying all male employees into birthplace groups stratified by place of residence, age (11 five-year groups from 15-65) and length of employment (16 categories).

In this way the universe which was to be sampled had been reduced to several sub-universes, each of which would now be sampled successively and regrouped to provide a composite sample for the total universe. To sum up, the universe consisted of 2,150 male employees, classified into nine birthplace groups, each of which was in turn analysed into locality groups, age groups, and groups based on length of employment. The size of the sample was set at 550 men.[1]

For the purpose of sampling, each birthplace group was broken down into locality strata according to the number of persons each group had in the seven different localities. There were the full seven strata for the British, four for the Maltese, and two for all the other seven birthplace groups. In each stratum cards were arranged alphabetically and then sampled using random starting numbers. The sampling ratio for British immigrants was one in six, and one in three for continental Europeans, with the exceptions of Italy and the Ukraine, where for various reasons a larger sampling fraction, one in two, was used.[2]

The sample when drawn (the 'Planned Sample') was then analysed into age groups and periods of employment as the total universe had been.

Tests of significance were implemented to compare the sample with the universe in case any bias had been introduced by the sampling procedure. No significant differences between the age distribution or the distribution by lengths of employment of the planned sample and the SEC universe of the overseas born were found.[3] In other words there was no statistical probability that the sample was not representative of the universe as far as the parameters used for sampling were concerned.

In addition to the main sample, here called the planned sample, two subsidiary samples were drawn from the remaining members of the universe, in order to provide replacements for persons who were in the main sample but who had moved out of the Latrobe Valley between the time at which the sample was constructed and the time at which actual interviewing took place. These subsidiary samples were simple random samples, as the high sampling ratios (1:60 for the British and 1:30 for the rest) and the smallness of the cells from which the sample was to be drawn meant that random starting numbers could not be used. Accordingly the requisite number of cards was drawn at random from the different birthplace groups. The subsidiary samples consisted of thirty-six males each.

The size of the two subsidiary samples is an indication of the extent of mobility in the immigrant population under study. At first it was thought that one subsidiary sample would be sufficient to provide a reserve of names for replacements. However, the experience of interviewing made it clear that, in two birthplace groups at least, the number of names in the subsidiary sample was not sufficient to replace the respondents who had dropped out.

TABLE I

Extent of Wastage from the Sample, Classified by Causes in conjunction with Country of Birth

Birthplace	Reason for Replacement				
	Left of own accord	Transferred*	Retired and gone away	Deceased	Total losses†
British Isles	10	1	3	3	17
Netherlands	8				8
Germany	2				2
Malta	3	2		2	7
Italy	6			1	7
Poland	2				2
Yugoslavia	1	1			2
Other overseas-born		2			2
	32	6	3	6	47

* Transferred to another undertaking of the State Electricity Commission outside Latrobe Valley.

† This table makes it clear that the most common cause of a person's dropping from the sample was change of employment; it also suggests that the labour turnover is by no means constant for all groups but varies from one ethnic group to another.

TABLE II

Characteristics of Respondents who Refused to be Interviewed

Refusal No.	Country of birth	Age	Conjugal condition	Locality	Reason for refusal
1	Netherlands	53	Divorced	Moe	'Does not feel like being interviewed'
2	Italy	50	Separated	West Camp	No time; lack of confidence in the project
3	Latvia	48	Married— but wife behind Iron Curtain	Eastern Road Hostel	Suspicious — thinks the interviewer is a Communist agent
4	Ukraine	35	Married	Newborough	ditto
5	Ukraine	35	Married	Newborough	ditto
6	Lithuania	46	Married	Newborough	ditto
7	Lithuania	44	Married	Moe	ditto
8	Latvia	51	Married	Moe	ditto
9	Scotland	39	Married	Newborough	No time. 'Does not feel like being interviewed'

For this reason it became necessary to draw the second subsidiary sample—sub-sample 2.

Table I shows the distribution of persons lost from the main sample and sub-sample 1.

The Obtained Sample

Of the 550 interviews that were attempted 541 were successfully completed. Table II shows the characteristics of men who refused to co-operate in this study.[4]

By using the data from the SEC records it was possible to compare the countries of birth of those who refused to co-operate with the corresponding distribution of the planned sample. This was attempted in Table III, which shows that the largest group of non-respondents came from the Baltic countries. Because of the low frequencies in the group of refusals no attempt was made to apply the chi square test to both distributions. It seems clear, however, that the relatively high rate of refusals among the Baltic people throws some doubt on the validity of any conclusions emerging from this book when applied to the immigrants from Lithuania, Latvia, and Estonia.

Yet another major difficulty was experienced at the interviewing stage when it was discovered that the item 'country of birth' on the records from which the universe was compiled had in some cases been incorrectly stated. This applied particularly to the Ukraine, Yugoslavia, and Malta. It appears that the records underestimated the number of men who were born in any of these countries by listing them as natives of other countries which had also been sampled. By far the largest number of such entries was found among the Ukrainians, who were listed in the records as 'U.S.S.R.' or 'Russia'; many Yugoslavs, too, were recorded under 'Austria', which was the country they had lived in for some years as Displaced Persons or ex-prisoners of war; some Maltese people were recorded as 'British Colony' or 'British'.[5] Typically, while interviewing a person who was listed as 'Russian'—or 'U.S.S.R.-born' we discovered that he was, in fact, Ukrainian or described himself as 'Ukrainian-born'. These discoveries came as a shock, but at that late stage there was very little that could be done to reorganize our universe. Short of a personal check of all 'suspect' birthplaces nothing could be done when the survey was already in progress. All this meant was that for the Ukraine, Yugoslavia, and Malta, the actual sampling fraction was higher than the stipulated sampling fraction. Table III sets out the

TABLE III

The SEC Universe and the Planned and Obtained Samples

Country of birth	SEC universe	Sampling fraction*	Planned sample	Corrected sample	Refusals	Obtained sample	Comparison of age distribution*			Comparison of period of employment†		
							χ^2	d.f.	P	χ^2	d.f.	P
	(1)	(2)	(3)	(4)	(5)	(6)	(7)	(8)	(9)	(10)	(11)	(12)
British Isles	1,099	1 : 6	182†	184	1	183	13·9	9	·10	7·2	9	> ·50
Netherlands	120	1 : 3	44	44	1	43	5·0	4	> ·20	3·2	4	> ·50
Germany	82	1 : 3	26†	28		28	5·9	3	> ·10	6·6	3	> ·05
Malta	218	1 : 3	75†	83		83	10·4	6	> ·10	4·3	5	> ·50
Italy	101	1 : 2	52	53	1	52	7·6	3	> ·05	4·2	3	> ·20
Poland	136	1 : 3	45†	46		46	6·8	3	> ·05	2·4	2	> ·30
Ukraine	42	1 : 2	20†	31	2	29	1·4	2	> ·30	1·3	2	> ·50
Yugoslavia	75	1 : 3	26†	31		31	5·1	3	> ·10	1·2	2	> ·50
Baltic states	71	1 : 3	25†	26	4	22	2·8	2	> ·20	6·1	2	< ·05
Other overseas-born	206	1 : 4	52	22		22	17·9	3	< ·001	14·2	3	< ·01
	2,150		550	550	9	541						

* A certain lack of precision in applying a given sampling fraction to the universe resulted from the fact that a random starting number was used in each of the cells into which the universe was stratified; hence there is no exact arithmetical relationship between the size of planned sample in each birthplace (col. 3) and the sampling fraction (col. 2).

† A discrepancy between the size of the planned sample and corrected sample (col. 4) has arisen from errors in the description of birthplaces in the sampling frame.

various samples side by side with the frequencies that were obtained from the sampling frame (the 'SEC Universe'). The planned sample (col. 3) gives the numbers of names sampled in the manner described earlier in this appendix; col. 4 shows the numbers in what has been termed the 'corrected sample', which contains the actual frequencies as ascertained during the course of interviewing, including the men whose names were included in the planned sample but who firmly refused to be interviewed. The next column (col. 5) shows the numbers of refusals. By subtracting them in corresponding frequencies we get the obtained sample (col. 6).

The obtained sample was subsequently tested for goodness of fit with relation to the SEC universe of the overseas-born males; the same two parameters which were used in the comparison of the planned sample and the SEC universe were used, that is, age structure and period of employment. The results of these tests are fairly satisfactory (see Table III, cols. 7-12). They suggest that with the exception of Baltic states and other overseas-born there are no significant differences between the two populations.

For the Baltic states one test shows that the probability that both distributions were drawn from the same distribution is relatively high (age distribution—col. 9); the second test, however, shows that the Baltic sample could not be considered representative of the SEC universe in respect of period of employment. These divergent results of the tests of significance have confirmed a note of caution which was sounded when discussing the relatively high rate of refusals amongst the respondents in this particular birthplace group.

Little need be said about the disappointing results of chi square tests in the last of our birthplace groupings, 'other overseas-born'. These results are no doubt due to the unfortunate error in the sampling frame which was discussed above. Such a highly significant difference between the composition of the 'other overseas-born' group in the SEC universe and the obtained sample was to be expected in view of the transfer of more than half of the respondents from that frequency to other birthplaces of the corrected and obtained samples.

Appendix C

Confidential

THE AUSTRALIAN NATIONAL UNIVERSITY

DEPARTMENT OF DEMOGRAPHY

THE SURVEY OF IMMIGRANTS IN THE LATROBE VALLEY

JANUARY-MARCH 1959

THE INTERVIEW SCHEDULE

OFFICE USE ONLY:

Locality Group: ....   Interviewer: ....

Code Number: [ ][ ][ ]
              1   2   3

PART I

MIGRANT BACKGROUND AND BASIC DATA

		OFFICE USE ONLY
1.	In what country were you born?	**Age:**
	Subject....................................	[ ][ ]
	· Wife...	S4 W55
2.	What is your year of birth?	**Birthplace and Background:**
	Subject........................	S [ ][ ]
	Wife............................	5 6
3.	Religion	W [ ][ ]
	Subject.......................	56 57
	Wife..........................	
4.*	Subject's Conjugal Condition	**Religion:**
	Single	[ ] 0 [ ][ ]
	Married, spouse in Australia	[ ] 1 S7 W58
	Married, spouse overseas	[ ] 2
	Widowed	[ ] 3
	Divorced	[ ] 4
5.	Last permanent residence in the native country: *(Name the village, town, province)*	**Conjugal condition:**
	Subject...	[ ]
	Wife...	S8

* *Please tick appropriate box thus -* [✓]

245

2.

6.   (i)   What age were you when you left school?

         Subject..........

         Wife.............

Educational Attainment:

S9	W59

   (ii)   Number of years at the following levels of education:

	Subject	Wife
Primary		
Secondary/technical		
University and/or professional		

7.   (i)   What was your father's usual occupation?

         Subject...

         Wife..

Father's Occupation:

S10	W60

   (ii)   Who employed your father?

         Subject...

         Wife..

   (iii)   What sort of work did your mother do?

         Subject...

         Wife..

8.   When did you leave your country of birth?

         Subject............... *(year)*

         Wife   .... *(year)*

9.*   Why did you leave your country?

Migration Decision:

S11	W61

	Subject	Wife
a. To emigrate overseas in search of better opportunities.		
b. Forced to work in Germany during the war.		
c. Fled to escape persecution.		
d. Made homeless by population transfers.		
e. Other reasons *(If other, specify)*		
Subject..		
Wife..		

* *Please tick appropriate box thus -*   [✓]

3.

10. Year of arrival in Australia:

.Subject................(year)

Wife   ....(year)

11. Who paid your passage to Australia?

Passage:

		S.	W.
Full fare	Self		
	Friends or relatives in Australia		
Assisted	I.R.O.		
	Personal Nominee		
	Group Nominee		

S13   W63

12. Why did you choose Australia rather than another country?

Subject...

Wife..

PART II

THE FAMILY IN AUSTRALIA

13.* Do you and your wife have any relatives (other than your children) who live in Australia?

	Subject	Wife
Yes		
No		

If 'yes' specify relationship:

Kin Group:

	SUBJECT		WIFE	
	Relationship	Year of Arrival	Relationship	Year of Arrival
1				
2				
3				
4				
5				

S14   W64

* Please tick appropriate box thus - √

4.

14 (i)* (If prior arrivals) - Did they give you any financial assistance or guarantee of accommodation before you could come to Australia?

	Subject	Wife
Yes		
No		

14 (ii)* (If later arrivals) - Did you give them any financial assistance or guarantee of accommodation before they could come to Australia?

	Subject	Wife
Yes		
No		

Questions 15 to 21 apply to married men only.

15. Country where married.................................

16. Year when married...................

17.* Did you come to Australia together?

    Yes [ ]   No [ ]

18. If 'no', give the year or expected year of your wife's arrival.....................

Years married:

[ ]

S15

19. Children resident with subject or away from home:

Children:

Subject's Columns

Christian Name	Res't(R) or Away(A)	Sex F. or M.	Age at 1.1.59	Country of Birth	Occupation	If student Type of school	R/A	S	A	CofB	Occ.
							16	17	18	19	20 21

Occupation - If none, write S (Student) or B (Below school age) as applicable.

Type of school: P (Primary), S (Secondary), T (Technical College), U (University).

20. *(Read Notes)* Are there any other persons who live in this house in addition to yourself, your wife and your children?

Family size:

Boarder	Sex	Approx. Age	Country of Birth	Relationship to Subject
1				
2				
3				
4				
5				

S22 S23

Birthplace of Boarder No.1:

S24

Please tick appropriate box thus - [✓]

5.

21.   *Fill in after interview*

Subject and wife..   ....

Children resident with subject.............................   ....

Boarders...   ....

Total size of household   ===========

PART III
OCCUPATIONAL ADJUSTMENT

22. *(Subject):*
What was your last permanent job in your native country?...........................

23.*   (i)   Was this the work you wanted to do?

Yes [ ]   No [ ]

(ii) (If 'no') - What was the kind of work you wanted to do?

....

24. *(Displaced Persons only)* .

List the jobs performed after displacement and before emigration to Australia.

No. of Years and/or Months	Type of Employment	Place of Employment
1.		
2.		
3.		
4.		
5.		

* *Please tick appropriate box thus -* [✓]

APPENDIX C

6.

25. *(Subject)*

(See Notes on the Interview Schedule).

Employment in Australia before joining the Yallourn SEC.

No. of years and/or months	Place of employment	Type of work	Reasons for change
1.			
2.			
3.			
4.			
5.			
6.			
7.			
8.			
9.			
10.			

26. *(Subject)*

Employment history with the Yallourn SEC.

Date started	Department	Type of work	Reasons for change

27. *(Subject)*

Have you had any occupational training in Australia since immigration?

Type of training	No. of years and/or months
Trade apprenticeship	
Technical college	
Other (specify)	

7.

28. (*Subject*)

   * Are you satisfied with the physical conditions of your present position?

   Yes [　　]   No [　　]   Undecided [　　] .

29. (*Subject*)

   * Are you satisfied with the rates of pay (including overtime)?

   Yes [　　]   No [　　]   Undecided [　　]

30. (*Subject*)

   (i)* If you had freedom of choice, would you –

   stay in your present job?   Yes [　　]   No [　　]   Undecided [　　]

   choose another job?   Yes [　　]   No [　　]   Undecided [　　]

   (ii) If 'no' or 'undecided', what job would you choose?

   ....

31. (*Subject*)

   If a change is desired, give the reasons why.

   ....
   ....
   ....

32. (*Subject*)

   Do you feel that as a result of your migration your occupational and economic
   position in the world has –   risen? [　　]
                                 or
                                 fallen? [　　]

33. (*Wife*)

   (*See Notes on the Interview Schedule*)

   Employment in Australia to date:

No. of years and/or months	Place of employment	Type of work	Reasons for change
1.			
2.			
3.			
4.			
5.			

   * *Please tick appropriate box thus –* [√]

S

8.

OFFICE USE ONLY

PART IV

STANDARD OF LIVING

(Read Notes)

34.   *HOUSING*

(i)*   TYPE OF DWELLING:

    private house   1

    share of private house   2   Code S 32

    flat   3

    hostel   4

(ii)* TYPE OF STRUCTURE:

    brick, stone, or concrete   1

    wood   2

    fibro   3

    iron   4   S33.

    calico, canvas   5

    other   6   No. of rooms:

(iii) No. of rooms: .... *(excluding bathroom and laundry)*

(iv)   When did you move into your present dwelling? ....yr.   S34

(v)   Where did you live in the Latrobe Valley before you moved into this
       present dwelling?

       Subject:

Years and months	Locality	Type of dwelling
1.		
2.		
3.		

       Wife:

Years and months	Locality	Type of dwelling
1.		
2.		
3.		

(vi)   How did you acquire this dwelling?

    built, or in the process of building, with own resources   1

    purchased or paying instalments for completed dwelling   2

    renting the dwelling   3   S35

(vii)* a. *(If building with own resources)* - How much did the house cost? Or,   Cost of erection:
       if the dwelling is not yet completed, what will be its approximate
       total cost?
                      £...............
                                                                            S36
       b. If the dwelling is not yet completed, how many rooms are to be
       added?
                  No..............

       c. About how much of your weekly wage do you spend on materials and
       labour?
                      £...............
       (NOTE: TRANSFER THIS AMOUNT TO Q.38(v))

* *Please tick appropriate box thus -* | ✓ |

9.

(viii) *(If purchasing the dwelling)* - What was the purchase price? £...............

Purchase price:

□ S37

What deposit was paid initially? £................

How much of the purchase price has been paid off already? £................

(ix)* How did you find the money to build or purchase your house?

bank loan	1
housing commission	2
building society	3
other (specify)	4

Home finance:

□ S38

....

(x) What is the amount of weekly payments of interest and capital?

£.................
(NOTE: TRANSFER AMOUNT TO Q.38 (v))

(xi) If renting accommodation, what is the weekly rent? £..............
(NOTE: TRANSFER AMOUNT TO Q. 38(v))

35. MOTOR CAR OR MOTOR CYCLE

(i) Have you got a car or a motor cycle? Yes □ No □

(ii) If 'yes', state: make...

model..

purchase price of vehicle £...................

M/car-M/cycle:

□ S39

(iii) Was the car or motor cycle new □ or secondhand □ when you bought it?

(iv) Weekly instalment for car or cycle £...................
(NOTE: TRANSFER AMOUNT TO Q.38(vi))

36. CONSUMER DURABLES

(i) Since your arrival in Australia, have you bought the following goods?

I t e m	Yes	No	Indicate here Cash (C); or Hire Purchase (H)	Score
Vacuum cleaner				1
Refrigerator				5
Washing machine				2
T.V. set				5
Radiogram				5
Floor polisher/scrubber				1

Aggregate score ↗

(ii) How much do you pay per week on instalments on hire purchase (including furniture)?

....
(NOTE: TRANSFER AMOUNT TO Q.38(vii))

Consumer durables:

□ S40

* *Please tick appropriate box thus -* □✓

APPENDIX C

10.

37. *FAMILY WEEKLY INCOME*

(i) *(Subject)*
How much is your net weekly wage? (what you bring home) £..............

Subject's wage packet:

S41

(ii) How much overtime would you earn in a week? £..............

(iii) *(If wife is working)* - About how much does your wife earn net each week? £..............

(iv) *(If children are working)* - How much board do your children pay each week? £..............

(v) *(If any boarders)* - How much board do your boarders pay each week? £...........,....

Family income:

TOTAL: £‾‾‾‾‾

S42

38. *FAMILY WEEKLY EXPENDITURE*

(i) How much a week does it cost your household to live each week? £..............

(*Interviewer: The object of this question is to find out how much the family spends on food, clothing, entertainment, fares, drinks, and smokes, etc.; in other words, what is the general weekly expenditure.*)

(ii) How much per week do you and your wife jointly remit to the old country? £........,......

(iii) Weekly contribution to life insurance £..............

(iv) Any other expenses not included in the above categories £..............

(*Following transferred data*)

(v) Weekly cost of dwelling (rent, materials, building costs, payments of interest) £..............

(vi) Weekly instalment on car or cycle £..............

(vii) Weekly instalment on hire purchase £..............

Family expenditure:

TOTAL: £‾‾‾‾‾

S43

39. *SUBJECT'S AND WIFE'S JOINT WEEKLY SAVINGS*

About how much do you and your wife jointly save each week? (including hoardings as well as bank deposits) £..............

Family savings:

S44

40 * *(Subject)*

Compared with your normal living conditions in your native country, do you consider that your present living conditions are:

better ☐

poorer ☐

about the same ☐

* *Please tick appropriate box thus -* ☐✓

11

PART V

SOCIAL PARTICIPATION

N.B. Questions 40, 41, 42, 43, 44 are to be addressed to European Continental and Maltese immigrants only.

41.   *ENGLISH LANGUAGE STANDARDS*

(i)*   Spoken English (*Interviewer's assessment*)

	Subject	Wife	Score
Speaks no English at all			0
Speaks only broken English enough to make himself/ herself understood			1
Speaks colloquial English			2
Speaks good, idiomatic English			3

(ii)* Reading   *(READ THE NOTES)*

	Subject	Wife	Score
Does not read any English			0
Reads newspapers in English but only with difficulty			1
Reads newspapers in English with relative ease			2
Reads books/newspapers with same ease as in native language			3

Total score (i) + (ii)

S [   ]   W [   ]

(*Interviewer*: Add Spoken English (i) and Reading (ii) scores and transfer to box on the margin.)

English language codes:

[   ] [   ]
S45   W66

* *Please tick appropriate box thus -* [✓]

12.

42.   *EXPOSURE TO MASS COMMUNICATION MEDIA*

    (i)   What Australian newspapers are read in this household?

Title	Who reads	Score S	Score W
Dailies:			
Weeklies:			
	TOTAL SCORE		

Score: 1 per paper per person

    Who reads: S (Subject), W (Wife), S & W (Subject and Wife)

    (ii)   Have you ever attended English language classes?

	Yes	No	Years and months	Score
Subject				
Wife				

Score: 0 = no attendance; 1 = under 1 year; 2 = 1 year and under 2; 3 = 2 years and over.

    (iii)   Do you ever listen to English classes by radio?

	Yes	No	Years and months	Score
Subject				
Wife				

Score: 0 = never; 1 = under 1 year; 2 = over 2 years.

    (iv)   Indicate how much you listen to the Australian radio or watch television.

	Never	Only occasionally	Less than ½ hr per day	½- 1½ hrs per day	More than 1½ hrs	Score
Subject						
Wife						
Score	0	1	2	3	4	

13.

43.   (i)*   Do you read newspapers or books in your native language and if yes, how often?

Frequency	Subject	Wife	Score
Never			0
Less than once a month			1
Once a month			2
Once a week			3
Every day			4

S [ ]   W [ ]

Code: [ ][ ]

S47   W68

(ii)   Which foreign language newspapers are read in this household?
       (READ THE NOTES)

Title	Country of publication

44.*   What language do you speak at home?

                    Native language only   [ ] 1
                    Sometimes English, sometimes native   [ ] 2
                    Mainly English   [ ] 3

Code: [ ] S48

45.*   Do your children attend classes in your native language?

       (or - if pre-school children - do you intend to teach them your native language?)

                    Yes, they do (or will) attend   [ ] 1

                    No, they don't attend (or)
                    I am not going to teach them   [ ] 2

                    I don't know what I shall do when my children reach
                    that age.   [ ] 3

Code: [ ] S49

46.   *(READ THE NOTES)*   Do you have many friends here? What countries do they come from?
      Do you work together, visit them, or spend your leisure time with them?

      (i)   Subject.

Form of Association	C. of birth	Score
Work		
Work		
Work		
Visiting		
Visiting		
Visiting		
Leisure		
Leisure		
Leisure		

Code same as score

Work S50   [ ]
Visiting
S51
Leisure
S52   [ ]

* Please tick appropriate box thus - [✓]

14.

46. (cont'd)

Scoring scale:
Mainly subject's compatriots	0
Mainly other immigrants	1
Australians and immigrants	2
Australians only	3.

(*Interviewer:* Allocate ONE score value to each form of association, e.g. work - 0; visiting - 2; leisure - 0.)

(ii) *Wife.*

Form of Association	C. of birth	Score
Work		
Work		
Work		
Visiting		
Visiting		
Visiting		
Leisure		
Leisure		
Leisure		

Code same as score

Work W69

Visiting W70

Leisure W71

Scoring scale:
Mainly wife's compatriots	0
Mainly other immigrants	1
Australians and immigrants	2
Australians only	3.

47.* Do you (and your wife) visit any Australian homes?

	WHERE?			HOW OFTEN?		
	Same neighbourhood	Same town	Elsewhere	Once a week or more	Once a month	Less than once a month
1.						
2.						
3.						
4.						
5.						

48. (i)* Since your arrival in Australia, have you been in touch with any MIGRANT clubs or associations?

Subject.

	Name of Association	As a member	Casual attendance	Are you still in touch?
1.				
2.				
3.				
4.				

* *Please tick appropriate box thus —* [✓]

15.

(ii)* *Wife:*

	Name of Association	As a member	Casual attendance	Are you still in touch?
1.				
2.				
3.				
4.				

49. Since arrival in Australia, have you been in touch with any AUSTRALIAN clubs or associations (trade unions included)?

(i)* *Subject:*

	Name of Association	As a member	Casual attendance	Are you still in touch?
1.				
2.				
3.				
4.				

(ii)* *Wife:*

	Name of Association	As a member	Casual attendance	Are you still in touch?
1.				
2.				
3.				
4.				

50. Do you hold, or have you held, an official position in any of these Migrant or Australian clubs?

(i) *Subject:*

	Name of Association	Migrant(M) or Austn. (A)	Position held
1.			
2.			
3.			

S

53   54

(ii) *Wife:*

	Name of Association	Migrant(M) or Austn. (A)	Position held
1.			
2.			
3.			

W

72   73

* *Please tick appropriate box thus -* ✓

APPENDIX C

16.

51. How often do you go to Church?

	Subject	Wife
(i) once a week		
(ii) about once a month		
(iii) special occasions		
(iv) never		

52. When did you last attend a Church service?

Subject........................

Wife...........................

53. Leisure time activities:

Subject...

....

....

Wife...

....

....

54. What are the things that you miss most of all from the old country?

Subject...

....

....

Wife...

....

....

55. Are you naturalized? (Continental European migrants only.)

Subject: Yes [   ]   No [   ]   Year................

Wife: Yes [   ]   No [   ]   Year................

NO. OF YRS NATURALIZED:

S......

W........

[S74 | W75]

56. (i) When you first came to Australia, did you hope to return home?

Subject.................

Wife...................

(ii) How do you feel about this now?

Subject...

Wife...

LENGTH OF RESIDENCE

S [76 | 77]

W [78 | 79]

INTERVIEWER: 1. Fill in score values in Questions 40, 41, 42, 43.
2. Fill in Interviewer's Report Sheet.
3. Check the answers to ensure that none have been omitted and hand the Schedule in to your Supervisor.

INTERVIEWER'S REPORT SHEET

1. Date of the interview:

2. Time taken for the interview:

3. Number of attempts required to arrange the interview:

4. Have you any reason to suspect that answers given by the respondent are not reliable?

5. What was the attitude of the persons interviewed during the interview?

6. Specify the persons present during the interview:

7. Have you any comments on the parent-child relationships that you have observed during your visit to the migrant's home? Do the children speak the native language of their parents?

8. What struck you most during the interview?

9. What was the general state of the house both inside and outside?

10. Any other information:

Notes on the Interview Schedule

Q. 20. In this question it should be noted that 'boarder' is defined to refer to 'any other persons' living in the house, in addition to the subject, his wife and children. In other words, the 'boarder' may be a non-contributing member of the household (e.g. an aged relative) as well as a person who pays board. In this sense, it differs from the more common definition of 'boarder', which usually refers to a person who pays some money for his keep. 'Boarder' in this Survey is merely a means of classifying other residents of the household. (Question 37 v. asks how much board is paid by these 'other residents'.)

Qs 25, 33. These questions aim to ascertain the degree of employment stability among immigrants, calculated by dividing the number of jobs held under different employers by the number of years the immigrant has been in Australia. Note that we are classifying 'changes in employment', not changes in occupation. That is to say, we are interested not in a person's occupational history so much as in the number of times he has changed his employer. It is for this question irrelevant whether the person has continued in the same trade or occupation (e.g. carpenter, boilermaker, etc.) when he has changed his employment.

Qs 34 to 40. This section deals with such aspects of the Standard of Living as Housing and Income, Expenditure, and Savings. It will be seen that these questions are well-balanced and structured in such a way that the answers should be internally consistent. Surprisingly enough, little difficulty has been encountered in obtaining answers to these questions, although that does not mean that they are not the most difficult questions in the Survey; for most people are initially reticent in answering such questions. It is, however, for the interviewer to encourage answers to these questions once he has established the necessary rapport. The interviewer should be careful to emphasize AT THE BEGINNING OF THE INTERVIEW that the information given will be kept strictly in confidence. There should be no need to reiterate that condition of secrecy here, especially as to begin this section on Standard of Living with an apology or a defence may encourage the interviewee to object to the questions. The interviewer should be careful to note during this section that the answers being given are consistent and should probe any seeming discrepancies.

Q. 41 ii. It may at first seem difficult to devise a means of testing the interviewee's facility in reading English. There are two ways around this difficulty. The first one is that the interviewer should always introduce himself to the person being interviewed with his card showing his credentials as an interviewer in the Survey. Thus the interviewer can make some assessment of his reading ability from the way in which he does or does not understand this card of introduction. The second way of testing English reading ability is by questioning the interviewee on his reading ability, and by combining this answer with his answers to the question on his frequency of reading Australian books, magazines, newspapers, etc., form some reliable estimate of his reading ability. This test may also be supplemented by asking the person to read some part of newspaper or book in the house. This section on English speaking and reading is basically an evaluation on the part of the interviewer.

Q. 43. Following is a list of the more common foreign language newspapers:

		Abbreviation
German:		
Neue Welt	Weekly	NW
Rundschau für Europaische Einwanderer	Monthly	REE
Der Anker	Weekly	A
Polish:		
Tygodnik Katolicki (Catholic Weekly)	Weekly	TK
Greek:		
Elleniki Fori (Greek News)	Daily	EF
Neos Kosmos (New World)	Weekly	NK
Oikogenia	Weekly	O
Phos (Voice)	Weekly	P
Italian:		
La Fiamma (Catholic)	Weekly	F
La Rivista	Fortnightly	R
Dutch:		
Dutch Australian Weekly	Weekly	DAW
De Nieuwe Wereld (New World)	Weekly	N World
Ukrainian:		
Nash Holos	Monthly (?)	NH
Maltese:		
Berqa	Daily published in Malta	B
Other:		
Trade Unionist (several languages)	Monthly	TU

Q. 46. In this question, the interviewer is asked to score the interviewee on associational contacts. There are three categories of associational contact listed here, corresponding to the three main situations in which people are usually found—the work situation, the home situation (i.e. visiting, informal visiting, chats across the fence, borrowing, etc.), and leisure (clubs, sporting activities, local groups, etc.). Although there are three spaces for each of these categories, so that three friends can be listed for each life-situation, only one score is required for each. There are four score-values and so if at work a person had 'Australian and immigrant' friends he would score '2' in work; if he had 'mainly subject's compatriots' in visiting, he would score '0' for that; and if in his leisure activities he had immigrants from other countries as well as his own native country, he would score '1' for leisure. The same system is used for scoring the wife.

Do not forget to fill in the Interviewer's Report Sheet and to check that no questions have been omitted in the interview.

Appendix D

CLASSIFICATION OF OCCUPATIONS

The classifications designed for this study had to serve a multiple purpose of coding: (i) the occupation pursued by the immigrant at the time of the interview; (ii) the last permanent occupation he pursued in his native country; and (iii) the occupation of the immigrant's father. Furthermore, the classification had to be used to compare and reveal changes over time in the three occupations recorded in the interview.

The classification of occupations used in the 1947 census of Australia was adopted with several modifications. First, the Administrative group was amalgamated with the Professional and Semi-professional occupations: the numbers involved in the analysis were not large enough to warrant a distinction between the two groups. Second, Craftsmen and Operatives were amalgamated into one group, the reason being a certain lack of precision in the description of the immigrant's pre-migration occupation and that of his father; added to this was the difficulty of equating the degree of skill before and after migration. Third, the group labelled Service and Protective was ranked No. 5 following and *not* preceding Craftsmen and Operatives in order, to emphasize that persons belonging to that group had an *occupational status* lower than that of the skilled and semi-skilled workers. Finally a new group No. 7—Students—was added.

The classification finally adopted in the study is given below. The underlying idea is that, allowing for groups Nos 1 and 7 (Rural, and Students), which are not represented among the post-migration occupations, the remaining categories represent a scale of ranking from the highest to the lowest occupational status. In the actual analysis (as shown, for example, in Table 19 (c)) only the three composite groups were used: Professional, Semi-professional, Administrative, Clerical and Commercial (Nos 2 and 3), Craftsmen and Operatives (No. 4), and Service and Protective Workers, Unskilled Labourers (Nos 5 and 6).

Occupational Group 1: Rural

Agricultural labourer	Farmer
Dairy farmer	Fisherman
Farm labourer	Forestry worker

264

Gardener
Grape grower
Market garden labourer
Orchardist

Poultry farmer
Smallholder
Timber feller
Vine grower

Occupational Group 2: Professional and Semi-professional, Administrative

Accountant
Architect
Army officer (Regular)
Army officer (Reserve)
Civil engineer
Chemical engineer
Contractor
Draftsman
Engineer

Fuel engineer
Inspector
Manager
Mining organizer
Office manager
Surveyor
Teacher
Technician
Tool draftsman

Occupational Group 3: Clerical and Commercial

Book-keeper
Clerical assistant
Clerk
Local government officer
Office assistant
Public servant

Receptionist
Salesman
Shop assistant
Timekeeper
Typist

Occupational Group 4: Craftsmen and Operatives

Baker
Battery attendant
Battery fitter
Boilermaker
Brass smith
Bricklayer
Cable joiner
Carpenter
Case hardener
Coal conveyor's attendant
Coal dredge operator
Cook
Coppersmith
Crane driver
D.C.C. attendants
Dredge chute attendant
Driller
Electrical fitter
Fitter
Greaser
Loader attendant
Loco driver (elect.)
Machinist, class I
Machinist

Meter tester
O.B. dredge operator
O.B. spread operator
Painter
Patternmaker
Plasterer
Plant attendant (elect.)
Plant attendant (steam)
Plumber
Power grader operator
Pumpman
Railway shunter
Smith
Shovel driver
Tailor
Telephone mechanic
Toolmaker
Toolsmith
Tractor driver
Turbine driver
Turner
Welder
Winch driver

Occupational Group 5: Service and Protective Workers

Camera operator
Chef
Cook
Fireman
Gaoler
Night watchman

Photographer
Policeman
Police officer
Professional soldier
Steward

Occupational Group 6: Unskilled Labourers

Axeman
Bedman
Bitumen worker
Boiler cleaner
Burner
Camp orderly
Chainman
Cleaner
Concrete worker
Dresser
Faceman
Fire pump operator
Furnaceman
Grinder
Hammer driver
Horse driver

Labourer
Laundry worker
Lines assistant
Loader
Pipe layer
Platelayer
Points cleaner
Powder monkey
Sanitary attendant
Sewerage attendant
Stacker
Timberman
Tipper
Tunneller
Waterwork attendant

Occupational Group 7: Students

School student

Student

Appendix E

PROBLEMS OF INTERVIEWING
by EVELYN SNOW

When approaching the immigrants for information many things had to be borne in mind. First, I found that personal appearance was very important. Since a relationship begins from the moment two people set eyes on each other, the interviewer must endeavour to make the first impression as favourable as possible—especially as language differences may make contact difficult. (I found that my clothing often interested my female interviewees, and so was a means of building a closer relationship than the pretext of filling in a questionnaire.)

The next problem was to introduce yourself and explain what was required of the respondent. I found that with people whose English was very limited it was inadvisable to begin by introducing myself by name. Often the person interviewed would think that the name was an English word he should know, and his inability to follow the context of the conversation tended to fluster and irritate him. This was most undesirable for an interviewer trying so hard in the initial stages of an interview to establish a good *rapport*. New Australians tend to become very upset or frustrated when they can't understand or make themselves understood in English, and usually express this irritation in antagonism towards the interviewer—the person who has provoked this feeling of inadequacy—so in all my contacts with the immigrants I tried to convey all my thoughts as simply as possible in order to help the listener and create as little tension as possible.

Once the interviewer has been accepted, and the interview is under way, he must take care that it is he and not the subject who is in charge of the situation. Often the interviewer feels so apologetic about imposing that he exaggerates the degree of friendliness and loses control of the situation. The interviewer must also beware of making any provocative statements or expressing any strong personal opinions—particularly on such matters as politics and religion. Expressing an opinion on politics often arouses suspicion and mistrust and inevitably leads to the destruction of the good relationship which has been established. Politics are of utmost importance to the settlers, particularly former

T

Displaced Persons to whom Communism represents the greatest evil, as they or their families have been the victims of it. For this reason alone, expressing any political opinion can have only poor results.

It is important to consider the background of the persons being interviewed in order to understand their way of thinking and their outlook on life. Since each of the national groups has been affected by different factors, the interviewer's method of approach must vary to conform with the subject's pre-conceived ideas and expectations. Although the approach adopted is modified to suit the conditions found in the actual interview, there are a few general rules—or principles—that I followed in my approach to members of different nationalities.

The attitude of the subject to the questionnaire, and the approach adopted by the interviewer, varies from group to group. I found the Maltese one of the easiest groups to handle. Establishing *rapport* with all my Maltese respondents was a very easy matter: they desired very little information about the survey, or convincing, before expressing willingness to co-operate. I established *rapport* mainly through talking with the children and admiring the house. The easiest contact was made with the husband. The wife played a much less significant role throughout the interview.

It was also very easy to make a good contact with the Dutch, although a quite different method was used. The Dutch required a lucid and detailed description of the survey, its aims and methods, and how the sample was constructed. They took an intelligent interest in the explanations and co-operated enthusiastically when they understood the situation. *Rapport* was established with the Dutch by stimulating and provoking conversations dealing with a great variety of subjects, in which the interviewer and the interviewees participated equally. Of the persons I met during the survey the Dutch seemed most desirous of and able to conduct an intellectual conversation. The wife and husband seemed to play equally important roles. When dealing with the Dutch the interview that is a pleasant conversation will yield better results than an interview manipulated by the interviewer.

There were very few Latvians and Estonians in my sample, so that any conclusions about them would be invalid generalizations. However, I found that the members of these two groups with whom I made contact were very similar to the Dutch in their quick acceptance of my explanation and the willing co-operation that followed. Very little persuasion or convincing was required to obtain all the necessary information. The Estonians spoke particularly good English, so a relationship was easily established, as both husband and wife appeared to enjoy a good conversation. Yugoslavs were equally easy. They demanded an intelligent explanation of the survey, and were then most co-operative. Most of the Yugoslavs in my sample had worked hard in Australia to obtain greater security and attain a higher social level than they had experienced in their own country, so the best way of gaining their favour and co-operation was to encourage them to discuss their achievements and be a good and interested listener. Thus I found that *rapport* was most effectively established with the Yugoslavs when they were given an opportunity to assert themselves.

People from the British Isles had to be approached quite differently. The Scots were relatively easy. After a certain amount of tension and aloofness in the initial stages of the interview, the Scots in all cases became very friendly and co-operative. Usually they resented having to divulge so much personal information to a stranger. Both the Scottish and English settlers were, on the average, older than the other people whom I interviewed, and seemed particularly conscious of my youth. I overcame many of these difficulties with the Scottish people by giving them a very detailed description of the survey, discussing some of the technical aspects of computing and analysing the data, and explaining how the sample was constructed. It gratified the subject that I explained the survey as clearly as I could, and this often allayed some of his fears concerning my extreme youth and competence to be gathering such personal information.

I applied the same technique to the English but without the same success. They seemed to be so wrapped up in themselves that when the purpose of the survey was explained they immediately related it to themselves rather than the population in general, and resented being classed as 'New Australians'. Usually a satisfactory *rapport* was not established until the end of the interview when the value of their inclusion in the survey had been explained at great length. Throughout the interview I was conscious that the subjects were *English*, and I had to make a deliberate effort to avoid such words as 'migrant', 'foreigner' or 'New Australian' lest they felt I was categorizing them as such—which they hate. In all cases of establishing *rapport* with the

English I had to talk of 'newcomers to the district' and 'mixtures of different nationalities'. One Englishman was particularly resentful that I used the term 'New Australian' to describe the immigrants. He claimed that the aborigines were the only 'Old Australians', and that all other people, whether they settled here three generations ago or only three years ago, were equally New Australians.

Perhaps the hardest national groups of all to interview were the Poles and the Ukrainians. The Poles were not so difficult, although they tended to be somewhat suspicious and unwilling to answer questions about themselves. I found the most effective way to allay their suspicions and try to arouse a little confidence was to be as out-going and open with them as possible. This invariably involved answering many questions about my home and family. Only when they had gained a good insight into my background, and were convinced that I was an innocent, naïve, and quite honest person, did they relax and feel that any information I might gain would not be used harmfully. I used the same tactics on the Ukrainians, but their fear of the communists is so intense that they often seemed to feel that it was even more dangerous to trust such a youthful and innocent-looking person than a more overtly crafty one. Usually the only effective means of gaining any Pole's or Ukrainian's trust, or at least co-operation, was to assure him that the priest was aware of the survey and was giving it his full support and approval. To the churchgoing people this is sufficient for full co-operation and even friendship. But there are always the few who feel they cannot trust even the church. For these people there are no rules. Sometimes it was effective to be strong and forceful, but on other occasions a high-handed attitude would have been quite disastrous.

Appendix F

INTERVIEW SCHEDULE USED IN THE SOCIOMETRIC SURVEY

CONFIDENTIAL

THE AUSTRALIAN NATIONAL UNIVERSITY
Department of Demography

THE SURVEY OF THE DUTCH COMMUNITY IN MOE, VIC.
DECEMBER 1960-FEBRUARY 1961

Interview No. ....
Date of first interview ....

1. Name ....

2a. Address ....
....

2b. Housing Commission ....

Private dwelling ....
Sub-tenant ....

3. In what country were you born?
    The Netherlands ....
    Dutch East Indies ....
    Other (specify) ....

4. Year of birth ....

5. What is your religious denomination? ....

6a. Are you married? ....

6b. If yes, what is the country of birth of your spouse?

....

6c. How many children have you got? ....

7. Name your last permanent residence in the Netherlands:—

GRONINGEN	....	N. HOLLAND	....
FRIESLAND	....	S. HOLLAND	....
DRENTHE	....	ZEELAND	....
OVERIJSSEL	....	N. BRABANT	....
GELDERLAND	....	LIMBURG	....
UTRECHT	....		

8a. When did you leave the Netherlands? ....

8b. Year of arrival in Australia

....

8c. Indicate other countries of residence ....

9a. Last permanent occupation in the Netherlands ....

9b. Present occupation in Moe ....

9c. Name your present employer ....

271

10. What age were you when you left school? ....

Sociometric choice:

11a. Name three of your closest friends:—

	(1)	(2)	(3)
Name	....	....	....
Address	....	....	....
	....	....	....
	....	....	....
Country of birth	....	....	....
Age	....	....	....
Occupation	....	....	....
Religion	....	....	....

11b. What three people do you see the most of socially?

	(4)	(5)	(6)
Name	....	....	....
Address	....	....	....
	....	....	....
	....	....	....
Country of birth	....	....	....
Age	....	....	....
Occupation	....	....	....
Religion	....	....	....

Social participation:

12a. Since you have settled in Moe have you joined or made contact with any organization, club, society, etc.?

Yes ....

A.	Trade and professional	....
B.	Church	....
C.	Sporting bodies	....
D.	Social club	....
E.	Political parties	....

No ....

F.	Cultural society	....
G.	Civic or community group	....
H.	Fraternal or mutual aid	....
I.	Other groups	....

(If answer to any of the above is 'Yes', obtain following details:—)

Name of organization, club, society	Type (above)	Date joined	Office held	No. hours spent per month or 'contact' only

12b. How often do you go to church?

Attend on Sundays	....
Attend less than once a month	....
Attend on special days only	....
Never attend	....

13. Are you satisfied with life in Moe?
    (*Probe*: Climate, smoke, economic conditions, housing, opportunities for self and family, friends, recreation facilities.)

14. Interviewer's remarks:
    Subject
    Social situation
    Home

15. Subsequent interviews and observations.

NOTES AND REFERENCES

PREFACE

1 The null hypothesis has been employed in the testing of the statistical material presented in chapters 4 to 9. See 'A note on the Statistical Tests', pp. 44-7.

2 Only a small proportion of the statistical material, consisting mainly of the two-way tabulations (i.e. those that serve to indicate possible statistical relationships between two factors at a time), is presented in the present volume. Most of this material, including the three-way tabulations, can be made available to social scientists upon application to the author.

3 *Democracy on the March*, p. 51.

CHAPTER 1: INDUSTRY

1 Ian F. McLaren, 'The Ruhr of Australia: A History of the Latrobe Valley', *Victorian Historical Magazine*, XXVII, iv, June 1957, pp. 36-8. See also Alan J. McIntyre, 'Gippsland', in G. H. Lawton (ed.), *Longman's Australian Geographies*, No. 10, pp. 6-9.

2 Tracks between Morwell and Melbourne were surveyed in the 1860s and contracts were let in 1872 and 1873. Vic. *Government Gazette*, 1872, pp. 387, 789; and 1873, pp. 1108, 1196.

3 The first discoveries of brown coal deposits in Victoria were made as early as 1857 at Lal Lal near Ballarat, and by 1864 brown coal was being mined and sent to Melbourne and provincial centres for use as an untreated fuel. In its natural state, however, brown coal is not a high-grade fuel, its high moisture content (over 50 per cent) means that in each ton over half is water, and early attempts to utilize it as a raw fuel were unsuccessful. See McLaren, op. cit., pp. 41-2; R. A. Hunt, 'Electricity in Victoria', in G. W. L. Leeper (ed.), *Introducing Victoria*, pp. 153-4; M. G. A. Wilson, 'The Changing Latrobe Valley: The Impact of Brown Coal Mining', *Australian Geographical Studies*, I, i, April 1963, pp. 32-3.

4 Vic. *Parl. Pap.*, Vol. VI, 1891, No. 178.

5 Hunt, op. cit., p. 154.

6 The story of the State Electricity Commission for the period 1918-48 has been published by the Commission under the title *Three Decades*; see also *Monash*, pp. 27-31.

7 The works territory at present occupied and controlled by the Commission at Yallourn covers an area of fourteen square miles.

8 A comprehensive and detailed report on the geology of the brown coal deposits of the Latrobe Valley can be found in D. E. Thomas and W. Baragwanath, 'Geology of the Brown Coals of Victoria', *Mining and Geological Journal*, III, vi (Sept. 1949), pp. 28-56; and IV, i (Mar. 1950), pp. 36-40.

9 R. S. Higgins, G. L. Kennedy, and D. G. Evans, 'The Development of Brown Coal Char as a New Metallurgical Fuel', *Proceedings of the Australasian Institute of Mining and Metallurgy*, No. 195, Sept. 1960, pp. 103-16. See also B. B. Bennet, *Aspects of the Operation and Development of the Lurgi High Pressure Gasification Plant at Morwell, Australia*, paper presented at 8th International Gas Conference, Stockholm, 1961, p. 12.

10 R. S. Andrews, 'Town's Gas Production from Brown Coke', in Leeper, op. cit., pp. 177-9.

[11] The town of Moe has its own Industrial Development Committee which is also represented on the ALVA.

[12] *Advocate*, 16 Dec. 1960.

CHAPTER 2: LIFE AND LABOUR

[1] Charles Daley, *The Story of Gippsland*.

[2] For description of a journey from Melbourne to Sale by coach see Daley (ibid., pp. 80-2), and McLaren, 'The Ruhr of Australia', pp. 39-40.

[3] No population figures are available for the Latrobe Valley in 1911 because that year showed population only by counties and municipalities and small local government areas. The slow growth between 1901 and 1921 probably reflects a general stagnation in economic activities connected with the brown coal development in the Valley after the disastrous fire of 1895 and the closing down of the Great Morwell Mining Company in 1899.

[4] Several of the original pioneers have been traced during the course of this study. They included two Italians, Messrs Girolamo ('George') Doderico and Frank Lovison; two German migrants, Messrs F. Simmons and O. E. Singer; and two Maltese pioneers, Messrs Johnny Mifsud and Frank Manicolo. Of the two Maltese pioneers, Johnny Mifsud has lived in the area much longer than any of the other surviving original migrants. He arrived in Australia in 1920 and after nearly two years on various construction jobs in and around Gippsland he got a job in the new Yallourn Open-cut in 1922. He has lived in Yallourn North ever since. Frank Manicolo arrived in Australia in 1924 and heard from some relatives of Mifsud in Melbourne who suggested he might look for work in Yallourn. He did so and promptly landed a 'pick and shovel' job in the open-cut. Mr Singer, one of the two surviving German pioneers, was one of the group of four German specialists in the production of briquettes who were brought out by the SEC in 1924 as a result of an advertisement placed in the German papers calling applications for four positions in the briquette factory. His compatriot, Mr Simmons, arrived in Australia on the eve of the depression in 1928. He had a variety of jobs before he came to Yallourn as an engine driver in 1931. Mr Lovison arrived in the Latrobe Valley in 1925 and worked in a sawmill before he found work with the SEC. The other Italian pioneer, George Doderico, a native of San Quirino di Pordenone, in the Province of Udine, arrived in Melbourne in 1924 and found work in a quarry near Walhalla. Subsequently he worked on a sawmill near Erica and in 1928 he purchased 228 acres of land from another Italian, Mr Charles Della Torre, who had originally acquired 500 acres east of the Narracan Creek before World War I. Mr Doderico was the first settler to live permanently east of the Narracan Creek, in which is now the East Ward of the Borough of Moe, better known as Newborough. Mr Doderico now lives in Princes Highway, Newborough, not far from where he built his first house in a forest clearing in 1929. He too combined work on the land with full-time employment with the SEC until his retirement in 1959.

[5] The majority of these were enumerated in the Narracan Shire and presumably were mostly employees of the SEC. For example, 99 out of 122 Italians and 58 out of 72 Maltese were enumerated in the Narracan Shire in 1954.

[6] *Census of the Commonwealth of Australia, 30th June 1961*, Bulletin No. 3, Victoria—Population of Cities, Towns and Boroughs, and of non-Municipal Towns.

Life and Labour—*continued*

7 Newborough is not the only example of such an artificial division in Victoria; see A. J. and J. J. McIntyre, *Country Towns in Victoria: A Social Survey*, pp. 21-3.

8 The following account of North Newborough was given in the local newspaper (*Advocate*, 21 Apr. 1958): 'North Newborough is the only isolated area in the Borough; over a thousand people cut off without shops, school, places of work or recreation, where everyone has to go out of the area to do most of the things other people have laid on close at hand. Where everyone must travel in and out of the area frequently, good footpaths are needed above all things, yet there are none. One outlet is by road, battling with motor traffic for a place, a procession of school children, mothers with prams, workers dodging vehicles or walking in dust or mud alongside the road. The other outlet is by a sort of a path across a reserve with a few obstacles thrown in.'

9 This example of a short-lived community effort in a new housing estate is by no means isolated. A common state of standards of judgement and a strong community feeling cannot be expected amongst a population whose social ties with kinsfolk and neighbours have been broken by the process of migration, the task of adjusting to a new house, and the development of new standards of aspiration. Cf. J. M. Mogey, *Family and Neighbourhood: Two Studies in Oxford*, Chapter 6.

10 Newborough forms the East Ward of the Borough of Moe.

11 This figure includes the population of Newborough, which was included in the municipal boundaries of Moe a year later.

12 Under the Latrobe Valley Sub-Regional Planning Scheme of July 1951 restrictions have been imposed on development of Morwell to the south, north, and west, because of the underlying brown coal deposits which may be required for future use.

13 The Gippsland Newspapers Pty Ltd, publishers of the *Advertiser*, reached an agreement, early in 1962, for the purchase of Latrobe Valley Newspapers Pty Ltd, publishers of the *Live Wire* and the *Advocate*. The printing and circulation of these papers will be continued as in the past.

14 C. R. Hoffer in his pamphlet *Interests of Rural People as Portrayed in Weekly Newspapers* writes (p. 4): 'News events about the community convey much more than the actual material appearing in print. By publishing such items the paper tends to reflect and to perpetuate the personal elements which give rural community life cohesiveness and local significance. There is no substitute for the local paper in the performance of this role.' Cf. also Morris Janowitz, *The Community Press in an Urban Setting*, pp. 161 ff.; and Malcolm M. Willey, *The Country Newspaper*.

15 The nuisance of black dust produced by the operations of the SEC at Yallourn, and the objectionable nature of the odour from the APM plant at Maryvale, explain why these industries were considered 'noxious industries' and marked as such on the plans prepared by the Town and Country Planning Board in 1949. See *Future Development of the Latrobe Valley Sub-Region*, p. 15.

16 For example, the Morwell *Advertiser* reported on 8 Dec. 1958 that Morwell Shire Council 'unanimously decried press reports which inferred that the town suffered from air pollution caused by local industry'. On that occasion the council passed a motion to be sent to the Latrobe Valley Development Advisory

Life and Labour—*continued*
Committee pointing out that, through the judicious siting of the SEC and
Gas and Fuel Corporation's plants, the town had less dust and smell than any
other town in this part of the Latrobe Valley.

17 Submission to the State Development Committee Enquiry on the Economic
Development of Gippsland, presented at Morwell, March 1961.

18 *Advocate*, 20 Jan. 1961.

19 'Valley of Power', *A.N.Z. Bank Quarterly Survey*, V, i (Oct. 1955), p. 14.

CHAPTER 3: SOURCES AND METHODS

1 Cf. Paul B. Sheatsley, 'Some Uses of Interviewer Report Forms', *Public
Opinion Quarterly*, Vol. XI, Winter 1947, pp. 601-11.

2 Mr (now Dr) F. L. Jones, then a Research Assistant in the Department
of Demography, A.N.U., was chiefly responsible for drafting the handbook.
Stencilled copies are available from the Department.

3 A complete diary of the survey contains a record of these briefing sessions
as well as other events; it is available for inspection in the Department of
Demography, A.N.U.

4 On examination of all the difficult cases (i.e., refusals, abusive behaviour
of respondents, critical attitude to the survey, and withholding of personal
details, especially one's pre-migration history), I came to the conclusion
that fear is the dominating influence in the minds of the informants. But
fear is not just a vague notion, an afterthought, as it were, of the years of
war, deportations, persecutions, and dangerous living. I am convinced that
in the minds of the subjects fear is very real. Time and again I was reminded
by the subjects of the slogan they learned as children in the Soviet Union.
You can't escape the U.S.S.R. they were told repeatedly. This slogan seems
to have haunted them ever since they escaped from their country. One of my
informants told me that leaflets bearing this slogan were dropped by Soviet
planes as the Ukrainians were fleeing the country with the retreating
German army in 1943. Many recounted hair-raising stories of how the Soviet
Repatriation Mission in Germany raided D.P. camps in the American Zone
in the confused situation of late 1945 to kidnap the Ukrainian people and
force them, as Soviet citizens, to return to the U.S.S.R. Some who could not
reach the American or British zones of Germany were already under armed
guard of Soviet soldiers waiting for transport to take them to Russia; many
escaped but left behind members of their families; all were haunted by the
dreaded slogan.

The fear of returning to the U.S.S.R. did not leave them when they left
Europe. Even the comparative safety of large American troopships chartered
by the International Refugee Organization did not seem to provide the
necessary assurance that at long last they were on the way to freedom.
Another informant recalled what happened in 1948 aboard S.S. *General Omar
Bradley* when the ship was in the Indian Ocean. One night a rumour spread
among the passengers that a Russian agent in the I.R.O. headquarters in
Geneva had cabled the ship's captain and ordered him to sail for Vladivostock
and not for Fremantle. There was general panic aboard and that night
the Ukrainian and Baltic men held an emergency meeting on the deck.
Tempers were running high and the men decided that they would overpower

Sources and Methods—*continued*

the crew and sail for the nearest Australian port. At that point the American captain saw a deputation of the passengers. He was able to explain that the rumour was groundless and convinced everyone that the ship was heading for Fremantle.

A week or so before I arrived in Newborough the newspapers publicized a Soviet request for extradition of an Estonian migrant who lives in Sydney. This case has undoubtedly revived fear and anxiety amongst many of the immigrants, for in the eyes of Soviet law the Baltic peoples and the Ukrainians are still Soviet subjects.

5 The following reports are available for inspection: 'The Migrant Community in East and North Newborough' (Tania Harris); 'Migrant Children and their Problems' (Estelle Carey); 'The Maltese Community in Yallourn North' (Jo Weetman); 'Social Participation and Interviewing in an Immigrant Community' (Evelyn Snow; extracts from this report are given in Appendix E); 'Problems of Migrant Women' (Margaret Wallace); 'English Classes for Migrants' (Rosemary Scouller); 'The Workers' Hostels in Yallourn' (Phillip Boas); 'The Dutch Community in Moe' (Leon Mann); 'The Reformed Church Congregation in Moe' (Estelle Carey); 'The Dutch Family' (Margaret Wallace).

6 See Appendix A. Original life histories are available on the author's files. Identification has been omitted.

7 *Criteria for the Life History.*

8 E.g. the Polish woman and the Maltese trade union official in Appendix A.

9 E.g. the Hungarian tailor, parts of whose story are quoted in Chapter 5; and that of the Dutch woman in Appendix A.

10 Robert Angell, 'A Critical Review of the Development of the Personal Document Method in Sociology, 1920-1940', in L. Gottschalk, C. Kluckhohn, R. Angell, *The Use of Personal Documents in History, Anthropology and Sociology*, pp. 177-233.

11 See Table 6. *Adults* were defined as persons who had ceased full-time education. The term *origin* refers here to ethnic origin and not to birthplace. Thus the Ukrainian population under study included a small number of adolescents who were born in Germany but of Ukrainian parents.

12 As a technique sociometry combines the direct study of group dynamics in which social, cultural, and psychological factors are interwoven, and their measurement. A sociometric test in its classical form was designed to measure various activities operationally defining social proximity and social distance between subjects. 'Sitting together', choice of room-mates, choice of companions for meals, 'walking together', 'visiting other families', are typical examples of this class of sociometric test criteria.

The following are examples of studies using social proximity and social distance criterion: R. E. Wakeley, 'Selecting Leaders for Agricultural Programs', *Sociometry*, Vol. X, Nov. 1947; M. E. Bonney, 'A Study of Social Status on the Second Grade Level', *Journal of Genetic Psychology*, Vol. 60, 1942, pp. 271-305; R. G. Kuhlen and H. S. Bretsch, 'Sociometric Status and Personal Problems of Adolescents', *Sociometry*, Vol. X, May 1947; and N. L. Medalia, 'Unit Size and Leadership Perception', *Sociometry*, Vol. XVII, Feb. 1954, as well as other studies resulting from a U.S. Air Force Contract for the so-called Project Air-Sites, in which Delbert C. Miller and Nakum L. Medalia employed sociometric techniques widely. The criterion of inter-family visits has usually been connected with investigations of whole communities: George Lundberg's

Sources and Methods—*continued*
and Mary Steele's famous study ('Social Attraction Patterns in a Village', Parts I and II, *Sociometry*, Vol. I, Jul.-Oct. 1937 and Jan.-Apr. 1938), the works of Loomis and Davidson on rural communities, and of C. P. Loomis and R. M. Powell in rural Costa Rica (studies published in *Sociometry*, Vol. II, Jan. 1939, and Vol. XII, Feb.-May 1949, respectively) must be mentioned here.

The criterion of the choice of friends and social visiting was used by Leon Festinger, Stanley Schachter, and Kurt Back in *Social Pressures in Informal Groups: A Study of Human Factors in Housing.*

[13] See Appendix G for the interview schedule designed for use in the sociometric survey of the Dutch residents of Moe; a suitably amended schedule was used in the survey of the Ukrainian people in Newborough.

CHAPTER 4: THE SETTLERS' BACKGROUNDS

[1] The percentage of the population of the Netherlands who declared that they had no religion was 17.0 at the 1947 census (K. Ishwaran, *Family Life in the Netherlands*, p. 15). The Dutch sociologist E. F. Hofstee (*Rural Life and Rural Welfare in the Netherlands*, p. 358) suggests that in reality the figure was probably higher, between 20 and 25 per cent. He also argues that the relatively high percentage of people who at a census do not want to be counted among the members of any church does not prove a lack of interest in religious matters but, on the contrary, is a proof of seriousness about them.

[2] The corresponding proportion for all Dutch-born persons in Australia in 1954 was even higher, i.e., 26.6 per cent. This was the highest proportion of all birthplaces listed in the published tables of the census.

[3] Because of small numbers it was necessary to group occupations into four broad classes, combining the professional, administrative, and clerical grades. See Appendix D: Classification of Occupations.

[4] The full significance of these changes in the background and the socio-economic status is somewhat obscured by the fact that 28 men (out of 541 who were interviewed) were attending school immediately before they emigrated to Australia.

[5] Charles A. Price, *Malta and the Maltese: A Study in Nineteenth Century Migration*, pp. 126-7. See also *Report of the Royal Commission on the Finances, Economic Position and Judicial Procedure of Malta*, p. 6.

[6] One Dutch-born immigrant (No. 601) described himself as 'uprooted' because he had come to Australia as a refugee from Indonesia when it was given independence. He chose Australia because it was the 'nearest place' where he could find security and employment. The other respondent (No. 627) was a German by birth who, up to 1951, lived in the Soviet zone of Germany. He escaped to West Germany and in 1956 emigrated to Australia.

[7] For a description of the war-time refugee and forced labour movements see Malcolm J. Proudfoot, *European Refugees: 1939-52*, Chs. 2, 3, and 4.

[8] Cf. R. A. Lochore, *From Europe to New Zealand*, p. 24. The effects of chain migration on the composition of immigrant households in Australia will be examined in Chapter 7.

[9] Charles A. Price, *Southern Europeans in Australia*, p. 134.

[10] Sixteen Maltese men (or 19 per cent of the sample of that birthplace) were 'chain starters'; another thirty-two (or 38 per cent) came to Australia in order to join their relatives; three-quarters of the latter were financially

The Settlers' Backgrounds—*continued*
assisted by their kin. The percentages of 'chain starters' in other birthplaces
are: British Isles, 14; Netherlands, 24; Italy and Greece, 6; Germany, 14;
Poland, 2; Yugoslavia, 16; Baltic states, 29; Ukraine, 3; other central and
east Europe, 5.

11 The actual period of arrival for some groups was even less than the
seven-year period shown in Table 12. For example, all the immigrants born
in the Ukraine, and nearly all born in the Baltic countries, arrived in
Australia between 1948 and 1951.

12 The circumstances under which the Baltic people were evacuated to
Germany and the occupational composition of this group are discussed in
Chapter 5, pp. 75-6.

13 A chi square test comparing Roman Catholic versus non-Catholic
immigrants with regard to the number of children has shown that the two
groups differ at the 5 per cent level of significance.

14 One Maltese couple included in the study had thirteen children; fourteen
of the sixty couples had more than five children.

15 The persistence of fertility patterns has also been noted in a study of
Australian census data. See Lincoln H. Day, 'Fertility Differentials among
Catholics in Australia', *Milbank Memorial Fund Quarterly*, Vol. XLII, No. 2
(Apr. 1964), pp. 57-83. The same phenomenon has been observed in the case of
rural-urban migration by David Goldberg in 'The Fertility of Two-generation
Urbanites', *Population Studies*, Vol. XII, No. 3 (1959), pp. 216-17, and in
'Another Look at the Indianapolis Fertility Data', *Milbank Memorial Fund
Quarterly*, Vol. 38, No. 1 (1960), pp. 23-36.

16 See William Petersen, *Planned Migration: The Social Determinants of
the Dutch-Canadian Movement*, pp. 33-5.

17 Another factor of considerable importance to all 'forced' immigrant
groups was the disruption to family life caused by conditions of slave labour
in Germany, lack of privacy and barrack-like existence in D.P. camps in
Europe, and the separation of husbands and wives, often for a considerable
time after arrival in Australia. See Appendix A (4).

CHAPTER 5: OCCUPATIONAL ADJUSTMENT

1 Using these two groups of occupations, $\chi^2 =$ Very large, d.f. $= 9$, P $< \cdot001$.

2 In addition to the relationship between ethnic origin and occupational
status which has been established in this chapter a chi square test of association
has revealed connection between the subject's rural/urban background and
present occupation. The fact that persons of rural background are under-
represented in the skilled/semi-skilled and higher occupational groups has
been found statistically significant: $\chi^2 = 43 \cdot 1$; d.f. $= 2$, P $< \cdot001$.

3 M. J. Proudfoot, *European Refugees: 1939-52. A Study in Forced Population
Movement*, p. 39. According to this source some 78,000 were transferred
from Latvia and Estonia, and another 50,000 from Lithuania. Among the
Lithuanian ethnic Germans transferred, estimates vary from 15,000 to 35,000
for the number who were in fact Lithuanians and not ethnic Germans.

4 Ibid., p. 40.

5 Ibid., p. 238.

6 The proportion of the Baltic settlers who attained a level of education

Occupational Adjustment—*continued*

higher than primary school was greater than in any other birthplace from central and eastern Europe (see Chapter 4, p. 56).

[7] The immigrants who went straight to Yallourn on landing in Australia were given index value: 'less than 1'.

[8] For example, the Dutch and British immigrants are reputed to be constantly 'chasing after better paid jobs' but the eastern Europeans 'stay put'. (Statements collected by the writer from the Australian people during field work in the Latrobe Valley.)

[9] This, however, cannot be proved by means of a chi square test of association involving all birthplaces tabulated separately, for in five out of twenty cells expected frequencies are less than 5. Contingency tests involving individual birthplaces, with the numbers big. enough to warrant a test, have shown that the following pairs are different at the 5 per cent level of significance: British Isles and Yugoslavia, British Isles and Italy and Greece; the Netherlands and Malta; Italy and Greece and Malta.

[10] $\chi^2 = 1 \cdot 7$; d.f. $= 3$; $\cdot 70 > P > \cdot 50$. The Index of Employment Stability scores were grouped for the purpose of chi square test as in Table 18 and length of residence in five-year groups. The relevant table (No. G.2) has not been published but is available for inspection.

[11] The three inter-connected relationships discussed in this paragraph (i.e. birthplace and Satisfaction/Dissatisfaction, occupational status and Satisfaction/Dissatisfaction, length of residence in Australia and Satisfaction/Dissatisfaction) have been weighted up through the proper statistical procedure of standardization. This procedure has shown that none of the above relationships is purely derivative from the other two and that all have independent existence.

[12] This statistical finding poses considerable difficulty of interpretation. It is quite conceivable that there may be some element in the ethnic background of each group that causes its members to behave identically in some one respect when abroad. One might not be able to isolate those causative elements (and they need not be the same in each ethnic group), but one always has to reckon with their possible presence because 'ethnic background' is a very complex thing containing many elements. For example British migrants might say they are upgraded because occupational mobility is easier in Australia than the U.K.; southern Europeans because wage levels are higher in Australia than southern Europe; Ukrainians because there is more individual opportunity to rise in Australia than in Communist Russia.

[13] See Table 20(c). An interesting departure from the trend shown is a drop in the proportion of 'upgraded' at the duration of residence of ten and under fifteen years. It is suggested that there may be a special reason for that in the composition of the group of early post-war arrivals.

[14] This immigrant was not included in the sample of the SEC workforce. As a resident in the district he came into contact with the research team and gladly responded to the invitation to write a story of the events leading to his settlement in the Latrobe Valley.

[15] Interview schedule No. 181.

[16] Interview schedule No. 362.

[17] The residential qualification of 20 years in force at the time of the survey (1959) was, in 1961, reduced to 10 years.

[18] Interview schedule No. 183.

CHAPTER 6: STANDARD OF LIVING

[1] Just under 30 per cent of the Dutch-born immigrants who were interviewed in the field survey had children who pay board.

[2] In each birthplace the percentage of hostel dwellers is: British Isles, 20·8; Netherlands, 11·1; Greece and Italy, 75·0; Malta, 22·9; Germany, 21·4; Poland, 17·4; Yugoslavia, 19·4; Baltic, 36·4; Ukraine, 3·4; other central and eastern Europe, 47·6.

[3] The proportion of family units with four or more children is highest for Malta (53 per cent), followed by the Netherlands (36 per cent), and the Ukraine (31 per cent) . See Chapter 4, pp. 69-72.

[4] Nearly half the Baltic families have two children and there are none with more than three children. The average number of children per family is 2·08 for the Baltic group, and 2·85 in the Ukrainian group. Just under 60 per cent of all Ukrainian immigrants are house-building or are still repaying the capital borrowed for that purpose; the corresponding proportion of the Baltic group is 32 per cent. The average Ukrainian settler sends £1 2s. 6d. weekly to his family in Europe (see p. 96).

[5] £3 7s. per week, which is the highest level of savings after Germany of all the birthplace groups.

[6] See, for example, J. A. Hempel, *Italians in Queensland: Some Aspects of the Post-war Settlement of Italian Immigrants*, pp. 106-7; also, C. A. Price, *Southern Europeans in Australia*, pp. 185-8, 195-9, 283-4; F. L. Jones, The Italian Population of Carlton (Ph.D. thesis, A.N.U.), pp. 220-2.

[7] Chi square tests have shown that there is no significant statistical association between the level of savings and the country of origin on the one hand and the urban/rural background of the immigrants on the other; (a) weekly savings and country of birth: $\chi^2 = 9\cdot0$; d.f. $= 9$; $\cdot50 > P > \cdot30$ (see Table 21 (d)); (b) weekly savings and urban/rural background: $\chi^2 = \cdot298$; d.f. $= 1$; $\cdot70 > P > \cdot50$. Chi square tests relating to level of savings took account only of persons who do save, and savings were divided into two groups: under £5 and £5 and over.

[8] The proportion of those who do not save is lower among immigrants housed in hostels than among those who live in private housing areas. For example only one-fifth of the residents of Yallourn Hostels have no savings but two-thirds of the immigrants who live in Old Newborough belong to the category of 'non-savers'. The distinction here is between, on the one hand, a group of men who have no family responsibilities or who are trying hard to save up as much as possible in order to bring their wives or fiancées from Europe, and, on the other hand, the residents of private housing areas such as Old Newborough who are still building their houses and paying hire purchase instalments and other debts incurred in the process of settling in.

[9] Length of residence and level of savings: $\chi^2 = 6\cdot6$; d.f. $= 2$; $\cdot80 > P > \cdot70$.

[10] The term 'private house' in this study refers to all categories of housing other than hostels. A further distinction between owner-occupied and rented dwellings will be made to classify private housing according to the method of acquisition.

[11] The duration of residence in Australia is not in all cases identical with the length of residence in the Latrobe Valley. The very great majority of all those interviewed went to live in the Latrobe Valley immediately after arrival in Australia, but some had lived in other parts of the country.

Standard of Living—*continued*

[12] $\chi^2 = 14 \cdot 2$; d.f. $= 2$; P $<$ ·001. The table (No. G.4) is not published but is available for inspection.

[13] The size of standard deviation from the arithmetic mean in most birthplaces suggests a warning against hasty comparisons of average prices.

[14] χ^2 test of association: Purchase price/Urban-Rural. (Purchase price was divided into two groups—under £2,500 and £2,500 and over.) $\chi^2 = 5 \cdot 953$; d.f. $= 1$; ·02 $>$ P $>$ ·01.

[15] χ^2 test of association: Cost of erection/Urban-Rural. (Cost of erection was divided into two groups—under £2,500, and £2,500 and over.) $\chi^2 = 1 \cdot 654$; ·20 $>$ P $>$ ·10.

[16] This is a pointer to a cultural uniformity in the standard of living attained by immigrants once they strike deep roots in the country of adoption. The characteristic will also be noted in the matter of certain consumer durables.

[17] There are no figures for vehicles registered in Australia and classified by sex and age group of owners. The only method of arriving at some comparison with the Latrobe Valley immigrants is to relate the number of motor cars and motor cycles registered to the number of males aged 20 and over. On the basis of this crude method the proportion of Australians resident in Victoria who own a vehicle was 59·8 per cent (30 June 1959, Commonwealth *Year Book*, No. 46, 1960). But even this figure is understated because, although in Victoria all motor vehicles are included in 'motor cars', in all other states 'commercial vehicles' are excluded from the figures for motor cars used for private purposes.

[18] British Isles *v.* Netherlands, $\chi^2 = $ ·164; ·70 $>$ P $>$ ·50; British Isles *v.* Germany, $\chi^2 = $ ·282; ·70 $>$ P $>$ ·50; British Isles *v.* Italy and Greece, $\chi^2 = 24 \cdot 5$; P $<$ ·001.

[19] Some immigrants, who are temporarily unable to purchase a vehicle while shouldering the heavy burden of payments for a house, become conscious of the fact that they are denied the pleasure of owning a motor car. An interviewer recorded the following comment on a 34-year-old Ukrainian who spent £3,000 on a fine house and had just paid off his debts: 'Interviewee made comment that he had never had a holiday. He seemed resentful that English people rented their houses and could afford holidays while he spent every penny on the house' (Interview No. 326). An Estonian immigrant in similar circumstances is 'looking forward to buying a car next year in order to go camping. They intend to go away for the week-end at least every 3 weeks' (Interview No. 324). The magnitude of the financial burden involved in building a house is quite considerable. For example, the average weekly amount currently spent on materials, labour, and repayments of capital and interest charges, amongst Polish-born house-owners, is £5 3s.; the corresponding figure for the Ukrainian immigrants is £4 6s. These figures, of course, do not give any idea of the initial burden in saving enough money to put up a deposit for materials or a house already built.

[20] All interviewers reported that the usual 'tour of inspection' of the immigrant home started from the main bedroom and the children's bedroom, followed by the kitchen and lastly the living-room.

[21] One of our Polish respondents proudly displayed a large living-room with parquet floor, wallpaper, and heavy curtains. The only two items of

U

furniture were a large T.V. set and an expensive refrigerator both flanking the fireplace in the centre of the room!

CHAPTER 7: THE IMMIGRANT FAMILY

1 Table 13 shows the ethnic differences revealed by this analysis. These follow the same pattern as in the case of family size and, if anything, are even more marked. Malta and the Netherlands stand out with the largest households (5·9 and 5·2 persons respectively), and Germany, the British Isles and the Baltic countries for their small-sized units.

2 The numbers of households with boarders (with, in parentheses, those with boarders of birthplace other than that of the head) are: British Isles 13 (4), the Netherlands 5 (1), Italy 1 (0), Malta 8 (1), Germany 2 (0), Poland 4 (1), Yugoslavia 3 (1), Baltic 3 (1), Ukraine 1 (1). The details of this tabulation are not published but are available for inspection in Table D.13.

3 The incidence of extended family in certain ethnic communities, and particular social and occupational groups in Australia, is one of the problems awaiting further research. A good deal of evidence collected in a number of countries has stressed the importance of the extended family in one form or another. See C. M. Arensberg and S. T. Kimball, *Family and Community in Ireland*; J. M. Mogey, *Rural Life in Northern Ireland*; A. D. Rees, *Life in a Welsh Countryside*; M. Young and P. Willmott, *Family and Kinship in East London*; Charles A. Price, *Southern Europeans in Australia*; F. L. Jones, The Italian Population of Carlton: a Demographic and Sociological Survey.

4 Cf. W. I. Thomas and F. Znaniecki, *The Polish Peasant in Europe and America*, Vol. I, Ch. 2, and Vol. II, Ch. 3.

5 The very real meaning of this relationship struck the writer especially during the sociometric survey of the Ukrainian community in Newborough. See Chapter 9, p. 171.

6 Conflict between the members of a family has been mostly studied in terms of differences in conceptions of roles. See Robert C. Angell, *The Family Encounters the Depression*; Ruth Shoule Cavan and Katherine H. Ranck, *The Family and the Depression*; Reuben Hill, *Families under Stress: Adjustments to the Crises of War, Separation and Reunion*; Mirra Komarovsky, *The Unemployed Man and his Family*.

7 Interview No. 364. It is possible that the desertion of Mr C. by his wife was in part because of the loss of occupational status as a result of migration. Before the war he was his own master and had other men working under him. Now he hasn't even got a tradesman status and has admitted that he is very unhappy about it. At his age there is little prospect of a change. The man Mrs C. ran away with is a very successful garage proprietor in a country town of Victoria and could have been the image of her husband twenty years earlier.

8 Pp. 1847-9.

9 Thornstein Sellin, *Culture Conflict and Crime*, p. 78. See also Harold Ross, 'Crime and the Native-Born Sons of European Immigrants', *Journal of Criminal Law and Criminology*, Vol. XXVIII, July-August 1937, pp. 202-9; Irwin L. Child, *Italian or American: The Second Generation in Conflict*; S. N. Eisenstadt, 'Delinquent group formation among immigrant youth', *British Journal of Deliquency*, Vol. II, No. 1, July 1951.

10 Cf. Thomas and F. Znaniecki, op. cit.

11 Herman R. Lantz, *People of Coal Town*, p. 156. These findings are also

The Immigrant Family—*continued*
borne out by a report on a mining community in England: see Norman Dennis, Fernando Henriques, and Clifford Slaughter, *Coal is Our Life: An Analysis of a Yorkshire Mining Community*, Chapter V.

CHAPTER 8: COMMUNITY PARTICIPATION

1 See question 41, interview schedule, Appendix C. The assessment of spoken English was based on the experience of the interviewer; a reading test which was given in each case consisted of a cutting from the Moe *Advocate* describing the arrival of the team of interviewers on 20 January 1959 and the start of the survey. This helped to familiarize the immigrant with the objectives of the survey and made it possible for the interviewer to assess the fluency with which the passage was read.

2 More light on this point will be thrown in the next section of this chapter which examines friendship patterns at work and leisure.

3 $\chi^2 = 29 \cdot 7$; d.f. $= 1$; $P < \cdot 001$.

4 English language standard by age groups: chi square tests for comparison of any two age groups:

20-34 v. 35-49: $\chi^2 = 5 \cdot 0$; d.f. $= 1$; $\cdot 05 > P > \cdot 02$.

20-34 v. 50 and over: $\chi^2 = 5 \cdot 5$; d.f. $= 1$; $\cdot 02 > P > \cdot 01$.

35-49 v. 50 and over: $\chi^2 = \cdot 688$; d.f. $= 1$; $\cdot 50 > P > \cdot 30$.

The last test conceals the fact that there is a much greater proportion (37 per cent) in the 50 and over age groups of men who speak very little or no English as compared with both the other age groups where the corresponding proportion is much smaller (about 10 per cent).

5 $\chi^2 = 3 \cdot 5$; d.f. $= 2$; $\cdot 20 > P > \cdot 10$. The tabulations showing the distribution of various indices of social participation in conjunction with length of residence in Australia are not published in the text. They are available for inspection, and for working purposes have been grouped in the 'G' series of tables.

6 See question 42, interview schedule, Appendix C. The answers to this question were subsequently scored and aggregated. The aggregate score of exposure to mass communication media was coded and tabulated in conjunction with several major characteristics of the population under study.

7 $\chi^2 = 13 \cdot 2$; d.f. $= 2$; $\cdot 01 > P > \cdot 001$. Another factor which was assumed to be associated with the extent of exposure to mass communication media is length of residence in Australia. A chi square test has shown, however, that this association cannot be established: $\chi^2 = \cdot 701$; d.f. $= 2$; $\cdot 80 > P > \cdot 70$.

8 In all, thirty-seven weekly and monthly periodicals were listed covering a whole range of interest from the illustrated magazines with the more popular appeal (such as those listed above) to the more specialized publications such as *Stamp News*, *Current Affairs Bulletin*, and *Popular Science*.

9 A study of the local press readers in several suburbs of Chicago found that there was complete absence of any association between the person's ethnic origin, urban/rural background, amount of education and what the author has called 'the basic readership index'. See Morris Janowitz, *The Community Press in an Urban Setting*, pp. 128-30.

10 See question 43, interview schedule, Appendix C; and Table 26.

11 About 25 per cent of the Polish and Ukrainian immigrants, however, never read books or newspapers in their native languages.

12 $\chi^2 = 0 \cdot 3$; d.f. $= 1$; $\cdot 70 > P > \cdot 50$.

Community Participation—*continued*

[13] $\chi^2 = 20 \cdot 8$; d.f. $= 1$; P $< \cdot 001$.

[14] A monograph that deals with the role played by migrant press in Australia and discusses figures of circulation and other 'vital statistics' of the foreign language press is being prepared in the Department of Demography of The Australian National University by Miriam Gilson and Jerzy Zubrzycki.

[15] The low proportion of Yugoslavs who speak their native language at home is consistent with their ranking on other indices of social participation, e.g. native language reading and intentions regarding teaching native language to their children (see Table 26). This seems to put the Yugoslavs apart from the other east European groups.

[16] $\chi^2 = 8 \cdot 5$; d.f. $= 1$; $\cdot 01 > $ P $ > \cdot 001$.

[17] $\chi^2 = 0.717$; d.f. $= 1$; $\cdot 50 > $ P $ > \cdot 30$.

[18] Chi square test shows that there is no significant difference between length of residence in Australia and the teaching of native language to children: $\chi^2 = 5 \cdot 9$; d.f. $= 2$; $\cdot 10 > $ P $ > \cdot 05$.

[19] The Ukrainian Youth Association is a nation-wide organization which was formally incorporated in 1952. The following extract from Articles of Association describes its aims:

'(*a*) To organize the Ukrainian youth in Australia and to afford to its members the means of social intercourse, mutual assistance, cultural and moral improvement and recreation within their national organization. (*b*) To promote all forms of sport and physical development of its members; to introduce educational recreation and cultural lectures in English and Ukrainian; to promote plays and concerts; to inculcate good Christian citizenship; to stand for the Ukrainian national ideals. (*c*) To obtain and furnish information or otherwise acquaint its members with Australian institutions and the Australian way of life. (*d*) To foster Ukrainian culture and tradition among its members. (*e*) To spread amongst its members information on matters affecting their lives and interests, and to publish such papers, periodicals, books and other literature as may seem conducive to any of these objects. (*f*) To consult, co-operate and combine with other associations and persons in Australia or elsewhere having similar objects or principles or whose co-operation may be beneficial to the Association or any of its objects. (*g*) To allot or allocate money for the furtherance of any of the objects of the Association.

'4. Members of the Association shall be persons of Ukrainian descent who shall pay such entrance fee and subscribe such sums as may from time to time be approved by the Association in General Meetings.'

[20] A large proportion of 'Not stated' in the visiting and leisure categories made tests of significance impracticable in the whole of this section.

[21] The British have a relatively high proportion of men who associate mainly with other British immigrants. This is understandable in view of the relatively large numbers of British-born immigrants in the SEC workforce; this gives the British a greater chance of associating with other British at work than the less numerous groups.

[22] The actual tabulations are available for inspection, in Series G, Tables 21, 22, 23, unpublished.

[23] Trade union membership was not included in this analysis because in a sense it is not voluntary; the principle of 'closed shop' is strictly enforced in the SEC and all employees have to belong to a trade union.

[24] This proportion of 'non-joiners' may seem very high, though there is no

Community Participation—*continued*

study of Australian society which would serve as a yardstick for comparison. Several American studies have found that members of the lower classes (in which most of the Latrobe Valley immigrant population belong) appear to have fewer associational relationships than the members of the middle classes. In one of the pioneer studies Mirra Komarovsky found that 68 per cent of men in the unskilled category did not belong to any associations ('The Voluntary Associations of Urban Dwellers', *American Sociological Review*, Vol. XI, 1946, p. 686). Another investigation conducted by Floyd Dotson in New Haven showed that three-fifths of the working-class men studied did not participate at all in formally organized associations ('Patterns of Voluntary Association among Urban Working Class Families', ibid., Vol. XVI, 1951, pp. 688-9). See also W. A. Anderson, 'Family Social Participation and Social Status Ratings', ibid., Vol. XI, 1946, p. 256, and Genevieve Knupfer, 'Portrait of the Underdog', *Public Opinion Quarterly*, Vol. XI, 1947, pp. 103-14.

25 According to S. N. Eisenstadt, assimilation is thought to occur most rapidly and completely if the immigrant establishes primary ties, as well as more formal associational relationships, with the members of the receiving society. Hence the extent of participation as well as the composition of the immigrant's interpersonal network is very important to the study, and ultimately to the understanding, of the process of adjustment ('The Place of Elites and Primary Groups in the Absorption of New Immigrants in Israel', *American Journal of Sociology*, Vol. LVII, 1951, pp. 222-31). A recent Canadian study concerned with the problem of the composition of the immigrant's interpersonal network or reference group uses Merton's concept of 'status homophily', which he defines as 'observed tendencies for similarity between the group affiliation of friends or between their positions within a group' (R. K. Merton and P. F. Lazarsfeld, 'Friendship as Social Process', in M. Berger (ed.), *Freedom and Control in Modern Society*, pp. 21-2).

26 No attempt will be made here to list and describe *all* the ethnic bodies in the Valley. Most associations will be listed but only some will be fully described as examples of either category.

27 The Dutch Australian Club in Morwell also caters for mixed membership. A local paper described the programme of a 'Wind-Mill' night: 'Folk dancing by Morwell pupils of Mrs Minneboo; gymnastics in continental style; Dutch singers leading in community singing, sketches, and vocal and musical items will comprise the first part of the programme. There will be a Tea Garden and Herring Stall and a Continental as well as Australian supper will be available. St Nicholas will put in an appearance at the function. A ball will start after supper and continuous dancing will be led by two orchestras' (*Advertiser*, 30 Oct. 1958).

28 Ministers of several denominations visit the district from Melbourne. The chaplains (priests) we interviewed included a Lithuanian Catholic, a Slovene Catholic, a Ukrainian Catholic who conducts services in the Greek Rite, a Ukrainian Orthodox, a Dutch Catholic and a Polish Catholic.

29 The welfare functions of the Dutch Social Club continue to be performed by the Comedy Club, as seen in the following item in the local press: 'The Dutch fraternity and their friends in our midst put on a play at St Kieran's Hall on Friday night. Entitled "The Little Apostle", it was in Dutch for the benefit and enjoyment of the older members who cannot understand or speak much English.

Community Participation—*continued*

'Mr Sturk, President of their "Comedy Club" play group, explained that they had made it a rule to produce one purely Dutch play every so often, as old people found it very difficult to master a new language, and this was one means of keeping them happy, with a little glimpse of their old home life now and again.

'Out here several years himself, Mr Sturk acts as interpreter for many of his Dutch compatriots, as well as a general information bureau, and their Social Club was originally formed with the idea of raising funds for those amongst them, not long here, who were in needy circumstances due to ill health or some other misfortune.

'During the few years they have been operating, considerable funds have been raised for this purpose, as well as for helping local charities' (*Advocate*, 8 Dec. 1959).

[30] Interview with Councillor E. ('Ted') Scott, Newborough, 14 Mar. 1961.

[31] *Advocate*, 8 Feb. 1962.

[32] The term horizontal social mobility is used by W. Lloyd Warner in *Democracy in Jonesville*, pp. 146-7.

[33] In addition to subjective factors which have not been probed in this study, there are two objective factors that may help to explain this puzzle. Immigrants from the Baltic states and northwest Europe have two things in common: a predominantly urban residential and occupational background and a relatively high level of educational attainment. Possibly these factors play a decisive part in this nexus.

[34] This example of a German electrical mechanic and his wife serves to illustrate this point: "The couple seem well adjusted and are very happy in Australia. They both speak fluent English and get on very well with Australian neighbours; he wants to make Yallourn North his permanent home and will not return to Germany—'only for a visit'. Yet the man and his wife are reluctant to seek naturalization; if they change citizenship it will only be in order to obtain a staff job in SEC" (*Interview No. 222*).

[35] This was true of the Ukrainians, a large percentage of whose members belong to voluntary organizations, but they are mostly Ukrainian and not Australian associations.

[36] This included things like lack of live theatre shows, closing of cinemas on Sundays, and 'city life'.

[37] A study of a group of British immigrants in a Western Australian town showed that between half and two-thirds of the women, as compared with a quarter and a third of the men who were interviewed, had bouts of home-sickness (Alan Richardson, 'The Assimilation of British Immigrants in a West Australian Community—a Psychological Study', *R.E.M.P. Bulletin*, Vol. IX, Jan.-June 1961, p. 41).

[38] This is no more than an impression of the present writer, supported by observations of other members of the research team. Systematic research into this aspect of adjustment is badly needed in Australia. Dr R. T. Appleyard, of the Department of Demography, A.N.U., is at present studying this factor in a survey of British immigrants in Australia.

[39] The migration of eastern and southern European peasants around the turn of the century to the urban industrial centres of the United States provides a well-documented case of the creation of a number of institutions

Community Participation—*continued*

(e.g. mutual aid societies, credit institutions, national churches) to provide for the needs of people whose occupational pursuits had been radically changed. On this point see Stanley Lieberson, 'A Societal Theory of Race and Ethnic Relations', *American Sociological Review*, Vol. XXVI, December 1961.

CHAPTER 9: SOCIAL PARTICIPATION AND GROUP AFFILIATION

1 Cf. George Homans's celebrated description of the functions of primary group membership in *The Human Group*, p. 457. For the application of this notion in a study of a community see J. A. Barnes, 'Class and Committees in a Norwegian Island Parish', *Human Relations*, Vol. 7, Feb. 1954, pp. 39-58.

2 Of the twenty-one Ukrainians who received no choices six, including four adolescents, gave only non-Ukrainians as friends; two others were 'social isolates' because they gave and received no sociometric choices. That group of eight can therefore be described as being completely outside the Ukrainian community. The remaining thirteen persons seem to be on the fringe of the Ukrainian community in that, while they indicated at least one Ukrainian choice, they nevertheless received none.

3 Forty of the hundred and fifty-eight people who receive no choices by Dutch in Moe gave only non-Dutch as friends, thirteen gave no choices and received none, and thirty-two others gave no Dutch friends in Moe.

4 The detailed tabulations are available for inspection in unpublished Table S.1.

5 *Present occupation of males of Dutch origin in Moe and of Ukrainian origin in Newborough (Percentages)*

Occupation	Dutch ($N = 229$)	Ukrainian ($N = 46$)
Rural	1·3	
Professional	3·9	
Commercial:		
(a) Clerical	4·4	
(b) Retail establishments:		
(1) Self-employed	4·8	
(2) Employee	7·0	2·2
Domestic	2·2	
Craftsmen	38·0	13·0
Operatives	29·7	67·4
Labourers	8·3	17·4
Retired	·4	

6 For details see unpublished Table S.6.

7 Possibly religion could also be a criterion of homogeneity in the Ukrainian community. It will be shown later that the Orthodox-Greek Catholic division is not as far-reaching and fundamental as the differences between the main religious groups amongst the Moe Dutch (see also Plate 8).

8 This resulted in a frequency distribution in which the value of the Index (X) ranges from 0 through fractions to 1. The mean value of X and standard error were computed for both the Dutch and Ukrainians, with the following results:

Social Participation and Group Affiliation—*continued*

	X	SE
Dutch		
(N = **393**)	·677	·0184
Ukrainian		
(N = **79**)	·660	·0344

9 This is confirmed by a t-test which shows no difference between the two populations at the 5 per cent level.

10 See pp. 173-5 for further comments on the religious doctrines of the Reformed Church and the composition of the Moe congregation.

11 The Index of Clannishness applied to each denomination gave the following results:

Dutch	X	SE	N
Reformed Church of Australia	·856	·0302	**60**
Presbyterian	·725	·0365	**91**
Roman Catholic	·657	·0322	**124**
All other denominations	·473	·0790	**25**
No religion	·597	·0414	**93**
Total	·677	·0184	**393**
Ukrainians			
Orthodox	·616	·0658	**30**
Greek or Roman Catholic	·701	·0362	**48**
Total*	·660	·0344	**79**

* Includes one who gave religion as 'Assembly of God' and made no Ukrainian choices in a total of four choices. Results of t-tests at the 5 per cent level:

	Presbyterian	R.C.	Other	No religion	Total Ukrainian
Reformed Church v.	Different	Different	Different	Different	Different
Presbyterian v.		*	Different	Different	*
Roman Catholic v.			Different	*	*
Other v.				*	Different
No religion v.					*

* No difference can be established.

12 On the average nearly half of the friendship choices made by both Orthodox and Catholic were *kum* relationships (49 from a total of 107 in the case of Orthodox, and 83 from a total of 181 for Catholics).

13 An examination of sociometric choices by province of last permanent residence was made using an index similar to that described on p. 171 and in n. 8. First, a frequency distribution was obtained showing Dutch choices in Moe from the same province as a proportion of total Dutch choices in Moe; next, an expected value was computed for each province to take account of the different numbers available for choice; finally, an observed mean was compared with the expected mean for each province. On this basis it was possible to identify the provinces where the proportions of in-group choices are the greatest.

14 The choices considered here had to be only those of Dutch persons living in Moe, as it was only for these that province of last permanent residence was known. Hence the x values in the frequency distribution were obtained by

Social Participation and Group Affiliation—*continued*
taking Dutch choices in the same province as a proportion of all Dutch choices in Moe. A t-test on the difference between observed and expected means showed significant differences at these levels: Limburg: difference significant at the 1 per cent level; Friesland, North Holland, South Holland, North Brabant: difference significant at the 5 per cent level; Groningen, Overijssel, Gelderland, Utrecht: no significant difference at 5 per cent level.

An analysis of reciprocal sociometric choices in three of these provinces gives a good indication of the closeness of ties amongst the immigrants from the three provinces. The people from Limburg are quite outstanding in this regard: 17 of 22 'Limburgers' (as they are called locally) made a total of 30 Dutch choices in Moe and were chosen by 17 (or 57 per cent) of these; 12 'Limburgers' made a total of 19 Limburg choices in Moe and were chosen by 16 (or 84 per cent) of these. It is of interest, too, that all Limburg choices were given and reciprocated by Roman Catholics. In the North Brabant group 18 of 25 persons of that province of origin made a total of 40 Dutch choices and were chosen by 16 (or 40 per cent) of these. Eleven persons from North Brabant made a total of 13 North Brabant choices and were chosen by 8 (or 62 per cent) of these. The immigrants from Friesland numbering 45 made a total of 69 Dutch choices in Moe and were chosen by 25 (or 36 per cent) of these. Their 21 Friesland choices were reciprocated by 9 persons (or 43 per cent) of that group. The majority of those who reciprocated Friesland choices were members of the Reformed Church in Moe. As stated above, the analysis of reciprocal choices is confined to the residents of Moe and underestimates the true extent of Dutch choices by leaving out of account Dutch choices in the neighbouring towns of Newborough, Yallourn, and Morwell. For example, many Limburg people in Moe gravitate to Morwell, which seems to have a large number of people of that origin. The annual Limburg Ball (on Shrove Tuesday) in Morwell is well patronized by the Dutch people from all over Gippsland.

15 Many Dutch and other writers stress the distinctiveness of the Catholic south (the provinces of North Brabant and Limburg). This is seen mainly in the sphere of values. For example, William Petersen shows that, in spite of the fact that the two Catholic provinces are the most industrialized, the Catholic Church's 'full social programme . . . was successful in mitigating the personal and social disintegration that has often accompanied industrialization elsewhere' (*Planned Migration: The Social Determinants of the Dutch-Canadian Movement*, p. 95). The strength of Catholicism in North Brabant and Limburg as a way of life is seen in the relatively high birth-rate, stability of family life, and the vitality and power of the various social, welfare, and cultural institutions established by the church.

16 An old tag preserves recognition of this affinity: 'Bread, butter and green cheese, is good English and good Fries' (Great Britain: Naval Intelligence Division. Geographical Handbook Series. *Netherlands*, p. 80).

17 Ibid.

18 The speech of the Frisians belongs to the West Germanic group of languages; the Low Franconian dialects, the Brabant-Franconian and the Limburg-Franconian, represent the Low Germanic speech of the Francs. The spread of these dialects coincides with the limits of the invasion of the Salian Franks in the fourth and the fifth centuries. North Brabant, Limburg, and

Social Participation and Group Affiliation—*continued*
the adjacent parts of Belgium lie on the frontier between Germanic and Romance speech in Belgium today.

[19] A similar finding with respect to the acquaintanceships of farmers of different religious denominations in the Netherlands was reported by a Dutch sociologist A. K. Constandse in two separate studies: 'Sociale Hierarchie in Kamerik', *Mens et Maatschappij*, Vol. 29, No. 5 (1954), pp. 294-307; and 'Acquaintanceships of Farmers in Newly Colonized Areas', *Sociaal Kompas*, Vol. VI, No. 2 (1959), pp. 69-74.

[20] The mean values (with standard error in parentheses) for the various denominations are as follows:

Reformed Church	$(N = 60)$	·644	(·047)
Roman Catholic	$(N = 124)$	·587	(·033)
Presbyterian	$(N = 91)$	·375	(·035)
Other	$(N = 25)$	·190	(·053)
No religion	$(N = 93)$	·446	(·045)

[21] Of 187 Roman Catholic choices in the same denomination 33 (12·3 per cent) are Australian. Of 102 Roman Catholics who made choices in their own denomination 29 (28 per cent) included at least one Australian Roman Catholic in their choices.

[22] Only 4·9 per cent of Reformed Church adherents never attend church. Corresponding percentages for other churches are: Roman Catholic 11·0, Presbyterian 37·5, Other 29·6.

[23] The doctrinal basis of the church is strict adherence to what are called *De Drie Formulieren van eienigheid der Gereformeerde Kerken in Nederland* (The Three Formulas of Unity of the Reformed Churches in the Netherlands). These consist of *Heidelberg Catechismus* (The Heidelberg Catechism), *Belijdenis des Geloofs der Gereformeerde Kerken in Nederland* (The Confession of Faith of the Reformed Churches in the Netherlands), and *De Dordtsche Leerregels* (The Rule of Doctrine of Dordrecht). The last of these documents consists of five articles against the Remonstrants drawn up in 1618 and 1619.

[24] Petersen, op. cit., pp. 186-93. In addition to overseas migration by Orthodox Calvinists there was some movement to France, particularly the Yonne Valley southeast of Paris. This particular settlement was started in 1936 by a Dutch farmhand who rented a farm for himself and then other farms for his relatives and friends. A man of remarkable zeal and energy, he started a bilingual school and a Calvinist church. A French sociologist, G. Lecarpentier, writing in 1949, described the community of 400 as very closely knit; he also found no instances of intermarriage ('Les Agriculteurs Hollandais dans l'Yonne', *Population*, Vol. IV, Jan.-Mar. 1949, pp. 163-8).

[25] Rev. T. L. Wilkinson, *The Reformed Churches of Australia: their Origin, Necessity, Beliefs and Activities* (Publications on Reformed Faith and Practice No. 2), p. 6.

[26] This group includes one past office-bearer and a founder of the church (No. 259) who resigned his office on account of ill-health.

[27] It is possible that these structural attributes of primary groups are different in the Reformed Church as compared with the Ukrainian group and that this difference can be related to the theological factor—the emphasis on judgement and individualism in Calvinist theology. In the absence of spontaneity the only way that the Moe Reformed Church can exist is by emphasizing the uniformity of attitudes and norms (as well as the hostility to

Social Participation and Group Affiliation—*continued*
other churches), to make up for the inevitable dysfunction of the stress on
individual salvation. This attitude results in a denigration of the mediating
function of the religious group and stands in direct contrast to the beliefs
of the Catholic and Greek Orthodox Churches.

28 Many observers have commented that there is often a connection between
fundamentalist religion (such as the Reformed Church) and authoritarian
tendencies within groups with low social status. See S. M. Lipset, *Political
Man: the Social Bases of Politics*, pp. 106-7; Bryan Wilson, 'An Analysis of
Sect Development', *American Sociological Review*, Vol. XXIV, 1959, p. 8; and
Sects and Society: the Sociology of Three Religious Groups in Britain.

29 This tendency of the foreign churches to retard the social integration has
been observed by many sociologists. See, e.g. W. Lloyd Warner and Leo Srole,
The Social Systems of American Ethnic Groups, pp. 160, 217; J. J. Mol,
'Churches and Immigrants: A sociological study of the mutual effect of religion
and immigrant adjustment', *R.E.M.P. Bulletin*, Supplement 5, Vol. 9, May
1961, pp. 29-31; J. Zubrzycki, *Polish Immigrants in Britain: a Study of
Adjustment*, pp. 121-33; Nicholas Tavuchis, *Pastors and Immigrants: The
Role of a Religious Elite in the Absorption of Norwegian Immigrants*.

30 One further method, not mentioned in the text, has been the analysis of
choices within neighbourhoods. The difficulty of identifying such units, particularly in the less-developed areas of Moe and Newborough, has made it
impossible to reduce the pattern of sociometric choices in this regard to a
statistical statement. The overall picture that emerges, however, suggests that
sociometric choices involving Australian people are invariably neighbourhood
relations ('next-door neighbours' or 'people across the road'). Sociometric
choices involving a person's compatriots are based on several considerations of
which physical proximity is only one and certainly not the dominant factor.
This suggests that, in an analysis of social relationship in places where several
ethnic groups live side by side, it is necessary to take into account other factors
in addition to physical distance, viz. ethnic origin, religion, kinship ties, and
even the district or the actual place of origin (i.e. their former neighbourhood
ties). Robert E. Park refers to this phenomenon as a 'situation in which the
physical distances and social distances do not coincide, a situation in which
people who live side by side are not and—*because of the divergence of their
interests and their heritages*—cannot, even with the best of good will, become
neighbours' (*Human Communities*, pp. 89-90; my italics). Frank L. Sweetser Jr.
makes the same point when he writes that there are 'two distinct concepts that
bear the same label "neighbourhood": the real neighbourhood of the ecologist
and the primary group neighbourhood of Cooley' ('A New Emphasis for Neighbourhood Research', *American Sociological Review*, Vol. VII, 1942, pp. 525-33).
The studies in Moe and Newborough suggest that the two neighbourhoods do
not coincide spatially. For an example of the opposite view which identifies
primary groups with ecological neighbourhoods see, e.g., Leon Festinger and
Stanley Schachter, *Social Pressures in Informal Groups: a Study of Human
Factors in Housing*; and Leo Kuper, *Living in Towns*, especially Chapter VI,
'Social relationships in Braydon Road'.

CHAPTER 10: CREATING COMMON VALUES

1 The work of a group of social psychologists at the University of Western
Australia is the best example of a series of co-ordinated studies of this angle

Creating Common Values—*continued*
of immigrant adjustment. These publications are listed in the bibliography, marked with an asterisk.

2 The range of research already carried out by Australian social psychologists, demographers, historians, and economists in the field of immigration constitutes a firm foundation on which specific, comparative studies of areas such as the Latrobe Valley could be undertaken. These publications are listed in the bibliography, marked with a dagger.

APPENDIX A: NOTES

From Haarlem to Moe
1 The English translation follows as closely as possible the style and form of the original Dutch document. Its sincerity is unmistakable and this could also be seen in the enthusiasm and promptness with which it was written.

2 The regulations then in force under the Assisted Passage Scheme of the Netherlands Government restricted the amount of Dutch currency that could be taken out of the country in 1952.

3 Dutch National Anthem.

4 The Dutch word literally translated is 'toilet milk'.

5 This is a rough translation of the Dutch word *gezelligheid*, though it gives only an approximate idea of the full meaning of the word.

The Story of a Maltese Trade Union Official and Political Organizer
1 This story, written in English by a Maltese electrician, is reproduced as it was written, except that spelling errors have been corrected.

2 New part of the Valetta metropolitan area.

3 The history of the split in the Malta Labour Party is roughly as follows. In July 1949 the Commander-in-Chief of the British Mediterranean Fleet decided to dismiss 1,200 Malta naval dockyard employees who were no longer required. Naturally this raised a storm in Malta, since this number represented a large portion of the workforce on the island and the dockyard is the chief source of employment. Dr P. Boffa (Labour Prime Minister), Mr D. Mintoff (Deputy Prime Minister), and Mr E. Ellul (Commissioner-General in London) met the British Colonial Secretary (Mr Creech Jones) in London to discuss the situation. During the talks, Mr Mintoff, completely on his own initiative, issued a statement saying that if the British government continued to postpone a decision on Malta's claim to direct Marshall Aid and that if an inadequate reply were given to representatives, the Maltese government would ask the people of Malta in a referendum to renounce their allegiance with Britain and 'Throw in their lot' with the U.S.A. or any other country which would offer economic aid in exchange for the use of Malta as a base. The Maltese Cabinet amended this so that the last part of the statement referred to the U.S.A. only, but Mr Creech Jones demanded that the threat be withdrawn before he would continue discussions. Upon Dr Boffa's withdrawal of the statement, Mr Mintoff resigned from the Cabinet. Dr Boffa succeeded in winning a vote of confidence on his action in the Maltese Parliament with the aid of minority parties, but in October was defeated on a motion of censure by the General Conference of the Maltese Labour Party. With his supporters he formed the Independent Labour Party which became the Malta Workers' Party. Labour was defeated by the Nationalists in the general election of September 1950 but in 1951 the Malta Workers' Party was included in the government formed

by Borg Olivier, the Nationalist leader, and despite dwindling support, continued in this position. At the 1953 election only Boffa, Colombo, and Coles were elected, and the defection of Coles to the Maltese Labour Party at the end of 1954 caused the downfall of the government and the end of the M.W.P. At the ensuing election of February 1955 the M.L.P. led by Dom Mintoff gained an absolute majority of seats over the Nationalist Party and no minority party candidates were elected. (J.Z.)

From the Agony of War and Slave Camp to Freedom and Peace in Australia

1 The following life record was written by a Polish woman now resident in Moe. It is given in full, for it provides a truthful and sincere account of the terrible years spent by this woman and her family under the German occupation of Poland, followed by the misery of a slave labourer's existence in Germany. It emphasizes the feeling of complete personal degradation and loss of security experienced by many Displaced Persons. The striving towards the security and stability of employment, together with the possession of a home of one's own in Australia, have been shown to be striking characteristics of the Displaced Persons. The story of Mrs Lydia M. is an apt illustration of these features.

The original was written in Polish and is reproduced here in an English translation; sub-titles and occasional footnotes were added.

2 A clandestine newspaper.

3 The reference here is to the defeat of the overwhelming forces of the Red Army by the small Polish Army in August 1920.

The Story of a Latvian Engineer

1 The original version of this life history was written in Latvian and is reproduced here in an English translation. The writer has an outstanding record of leadership in community affairs in the Latrobe Valley.

APPENDIX B: SAMPLING PROCEDURE AND NON-RESPONSE

1 The decision to limit the size of the sample to 550 was purely arbitrary. The limiting factor was the estimated time available for each interview and the number of interviewers.

2 The higher sampling ratio for Italy and the Ukraine was used for several reasons. For Italy, it was thought that a higher sampling ratio would yield a large enough number to enable the analysis of this group by regions of origin. Such an analysis would have enabled several research workers at The Australian National University, currently engaged in the study of Italian migration, to compare their regional distributions with mine. This plan was abandoned in the course of the analysis of the data because the information collected relating to the district of origin in Italy proved to be unsatisfactory. For the Ukrainians it was also hypothesized that an analysis by region of origin would throw some light on the differences of behaviour between those who before World War II were domiciled in Poland and those who lived in the U.S.S.R. Hence it was thought desirable to introduce a sampling ratio large enough to yield at least twenty respondents. In the end this decision proved highly embarrassing, for due to the confused state of the SEC records from which the names were compiled the number of Ukrainians was found to be greatly in excess of the number so listed.

3 Birthplace by age: $\chi^2 = 21\cdot8274$, d.f. $= 36$, P > 90. Birthplace by length of employment: $\chi^2 = 21\cdot3589$, d.f. $= 36$, P $> \cdot90$.

4 An account of the difficulties encountered in interviewing the immigrants is given in Chapter 3 and Appendix E.

5 Nearly all the countries which were incorrectly given as birthplaces for the purpose of sampling were included in the residual group 'Other overseas-born'.

BIBLIOGRAPHY

Official Sources

Commonwealth of Australia

Commonwealth Bureau of Census and Statistics, Census 1954 and 1961.
——, *Official Year Book of the Commonwealth of Australia.*

Victoria

Final Report of the Royal Commission Appointed to Inquire as to the Best Means of Developing and Promoting the Coal Industry of Victoria, *Parliamentary Papers*, Vol. VI, No. 178, 18 Dec. 1891.
Town and Country Planning Board, *Future Development of the Latrobe Valley Sub-Region*, Melbourne, 1949.
State Electricity Commission, *Monash*, Melbourne, 1961.
——, *Three Decades*, Melbourne, 1949.

United Kingdom

Naval Intelligence Division. Geographical Handbook Series. *Netherlands*, London, 1944.
Report of the Royal Commission on the Finances, Economic Position and Judicial Procedure of Malta, London, H.M.S.O. (Cmd. 6090) , 1912.

Books and Articles

Anderson, W. A., 'Family Social Participation and Social Status Ratings', *American Sociological Review*, Vol. XI, No. 3, June 1946.
Andrews, R. S., 'Town Gas Production from Brown Coke', in G. W. Leeper (ed.), *Introducing Victoria*, Melbourne, 1955.
Angell, R. C., 'A Critical Review of the Development of the Personal Document Method in Sociology, 1920-1940', in L. Gottschalk, C. Kluckhohn and R. Angell, *The Use of Personal Documents in History, Anthropology and Sociology*, New York, 1945, pp. 177-233.
——, *The Family Encounters the Depression*, New York, 1936.
†Appleyard, R. T., 'The Economic Absorption of Dutch and Italian Immigrants into Western Australia', *R.E.M.P. Bulletin*, Vol. 4, July-Sept., Oct.-Dec. 1956.
Arensberg, C. M., and Kimball, S. T., *Family and Community in Ireland*, Cambridge (Mass.), 1940.
Barnes, J. A., 'Class and Committees in a Norwegian Island Parish', *Human Relations*, Vol. 7, Feb. 1954.
Bonney, M. E., 'A Study of Social Status on the Second Grade Level', *Journal of Genetic Psychology*, Vol. 60, 1942, pp. 271-305.
†Borrie, W. D., 'The Growth of the Australian Population with Particular Reference to the Period since 1947. Part I. The Role of Immigrants', *Population Studies*, Vol. XIII, July 1959.
†——, *Italians and Germans in Australia: A Study of Assimilation*, Melbourne, 1954.
†——, and Zubrzycki, J., 'Employment of Post-war Immigrants in Australia', *International Labour Review*, Vol. LXXVII, Mar. 1958.
†——, et al., *The Cultural Integration of Immigrants*, Unesco, Paris, 1959.

297

Breton, R., and Pinard, M., 'Group Formation among Immigrants: Criteria and Processes', *Canadian Journal of Economics and Political Science*, Vol. XXVII, No. 3, 1960.

Cavan, Ruth S., and Ranck, Katherine H., *The Family and the Depression*, Chicago, 1936.

Child, I. L., *Italian or American: The Second Generation in Conflict*, New Haven, 1943.

Constandse, A. K., 'Acquaintanceships of Farmers in Newly Colonised Area', *Sociaal Kompas*, Vol. VI, No. 2, 1959.

————, 'Sociale Hierarchie in Kamerik', *Mens et Maatschappij*, Vol. 29, No. 5, 1954.

Daley, C. S., *The Story of Gippsland*, Melbourne, 1960.

Day, L. H., 'Fertility Differentials among Catholics in Australia', *Milbank Memorial Fund Quarterly*, Vol. XLII, No. 2 (Apr. 1964), pp. 57-83.

Dennis, N., Henriques, F., and Slaughter, C., *Coal Is Our Life: An Analysis of a Yorkshire Mining Community*, London, 1956.

Dollard, J., *Criteria for the Life History*, New York, 1949.

Dotson, F., 'Patterns of Voluntary Association Among Urban Working Class Families', *American Sociological Review*, Vol. XVI, 1951, pp. 687-93.

Eisenstadt, S. N., 'Delinquent Group Formation among Immigrant Youth', *The British Journal of Delinquency*, Vol. II, No. 1, July 1951.

————, 'The Place of Elites and Primary Groups in the Absorption of New Immigrants in Israel', *American Journal of Sociology*, Vol. LVII, 1951, pp. 222-31.

Festinger, L., Schachter, S., and Back, W. (with chapters by C. Bauer and R. W. Kennedy), *Social Pressures in Informal Groups: A Study of Human Factors in Housing*, New York, 1950.

Goldberg, D., 'Another Look at the Indianapolis Fertility Data', *Milbank Memorial Fund Quarterly*, Vol. 38, No. 1, 1960.

————, 'The Fertility of Two Generation Urbanites', *Population Studies*, Vol. XII, No. 3, 1959.

Hempel, J. A., *Italians in Queensland: Some Aspects of the Post-War Settlement of Italian Immigrants*, The Australian National University, 1959.

Higgins, R. S., Kennedy, G. L., and Evans, D. G., 'The Development of Brown Coal Char as a New Metallurgical Fuel', *Proceedings of the Australasian Institute of Mining and Metallurgy*, No. 195, Sept. 1960.

Hill, R., *Families under Stress: Adjustments to the Crises of War, Separation and Reunion*, New York, 1949.

Hoffer, C. R., *Interests of Rural People as Portrayed in Weekly Newspapers*, Special Bulletin 298, Michigan State College, Agricultural Research Station, Section of Sociology, East Lansing, Feb. 1939.

Hofstee, E. W., *Rural Life and Rural Welfare in the Netherlands*, The Hague, 1957.

Homans, G., *The Human Group*, London, 1951.

Hunt, R. A., 'Electricity in Victoria', in G. W. Leeper (ed.), *Introducing Victoria*, Melbourne, 1955, pp. 153-4.

Ishwaran, K., *Family Life in the Netherlands*, The Hague, 1959.

Janowitz, M., *The Community Press in an Urban Setting*, Glencoe (Ill.), 1952.

†Kmenta, J., 'Economic Mobility of Immigrants in Australia', *Economic Record*, Vol. XXXVII, Dec. 1961.

Knupfer, Genevieve, 'Portrait of the Underdog', *Public Opinion Quarterly*, Vol. XI, Spring 1947.

Komarovsky, Mirra, *The Unemployed Man and His Family*, New York, 1940.

———, 'The Voluntary Associations of Urban Dwellers', *American Sociological Review*, Vol. XI, No. 6, Dec. 1946, pp. 686-98.

Kuhlen, R. G., and Bretsch, H. S., 'Sociometric Status and Personal Problems of Adolescents', *Sociometry*, Vol. 10, May 1947.

Kuper, L., *Living in Towns*, London, 1953.

Lantz, Herman R., *People of Coal Town*, New York, 1958.

Lecarpentier, G., 'Les Agriculteurs Hollandais dans l'Yonne', *Population*, Vol. IV, Jan.-Mar. 1949.

Lieberson, S., 'A Societal Theory of Race and Ethnic Relations', *American Sociological Review*, Vol. XXVI, Dec. 1961.

Lilienthal, D. E., *TVA: Democracy on the March*, New York, 1953.

Lipset, S. M., *Political Man: The Social Bases of Politics*, London, 1960.

Lochore, R. A., *From Europe to New Zealand*, Wellington (N.Z.), 1951.

Loomis, C. P., and Davidson, D., Jr., 'Sociometrics and the Study of New Rural Communities', *Sociometry*, Vol. 2, Jan. 1939.

———, and Powell, R. M., 'Sociometric Analysis of Class Status in Rural Costa Rica—A Peasant Community Compared with an Hacienda Community', *Sociometry*, Vol. 12, Nos. 1-3, Feb.-Aug. 1949.

Lundberg, G., 'Social Attraction Patterns in a Rural Village: A Preliminary Report', *Sociometry*, Vol. 1, Nos. 1-2, July-Oct. 1937.

———, and Steele, Mary, 'Social Attraction Patterns in a Village', *Sociometry*, Vol. 1, Nos. 3-4, Jan.-Apr. 1938.

McIntyre, A. J., 'Gippsland', in G. H. Lawton (ed.), *Longman's Australian Geographies, No. 10*, Melbourne, [n.d.], pp. 6-9.

———, and McIntyre, J. J., *Country Towns in Victoria: A Social Survey*, Melbourne, 1944.

McLaren, I. F., 'The Ruhr of Australia: A History of the Latrobe Valley', *The Victorian Historical Magazine*, Vol. XXVII, No. 4, June 1957.

Medalia, N. L., 'Unit Size and Leadership Perception', *Sociometry*, Vol. 17, Feb. 1954.

Merton, R. W., and Lazarsfeld, P. F., 'Friendship as Social Process', in M. Berger (ed.), *Freedom and Control in Modern Society*, New York, 1954.

Mogey, J. M., *Family and Neighbourhood: Two Studies in Oxford*, Oxford, 1956.

———, *Rural Life in Northern Ireland*, London, 1947.

Mol, J. J., 'Churches and Immigrants: A Sociological Study of the Mutual Effect of Religion and Immigration Adjustment', *R.E.M.P. Bulletin*, Supplement 5, Vol. 9, May 1961.

†Oeser, D. A., and Hammond, S. B., *Social Structure and Personality in a City*, London, 1954.

Park, R. E., *Human Communities*, Glencoe (Ill.), 1952.

Petersen, W., *Planned Migration: The Social Determinants of the Dutch-Canadian Movement*, Berkeley and Los Angeles, 1955.

Price, C. A., *Malta and The Maltese: A Study in Nineteenth Century Migration*, Melbourne, 1954.

†———, *Southern Europeans in Australia*, Melbourne, 1963.

†———, *The Method and Statistics of 'Southern Europeans in Australia'*, Canberra, 1963.

†———, (ed.), *The Study of Immigrants in Australia, Proceedings of Conference*

on *Immigration Research Convened by the Department of Demography, The Australian National University*, Canberra, Aug. 1960.

Proudfoot, M. J., *European Refugees 1939-52: A Study in Forced Population Movement*, London, 1957.

Rees, A. D., *Life in a Welsh Countryside*, Cardiff, 1950.

*Richardson, A., 'The Assimilation of British Immigrants in Australia', *Human Relations*, Vol. 10, 1957, pp. 157-66.

*———, 'The Assimilation of British Immigrants in a West Australian Community—A Psychological Study', *R.E.M.P. Bulletin*, Vol. IX, Jan.-June 1961.

*———, 'Some Psycho-social Characteristics of Satisfied and Dissatisfied British Immigrant Skilled Manual Workers in Western Australia', *Human Relations*, Vol. 10, 1957, pp. 235-48.

Ross, H., 'Crime and the Native-Born Sons of European Immigrants', *Journal of Criminal Law and Criminology*, Vol. XXVIII, July-Aug. 1937.

Sellin, T., *Culture Conflict and Crime*, New York, 1938.

Sheatsley, P. B., 'Some Uses of Interviewer Report Forms', *Public Opinion Quarterly*, Vol. XI, Winter 1947.

Sweetser, F. L., Jr., 'A New Emphasis for Neighbourhood Research', *American Sociological Review*, Vol. VII, 1942, pp. 525-33.

*Taft, R. A., 'Ethnic Stereotypes, Attitudes and Familiarity: Australia', *Journal of Social Psychology*, Vol. 49, 1959, pp. 177-86.

*———, 'A Psychological Model for the Study of Social Assimilation', *Human Relations*, Vol. 10, 1957, pp. 141-56.

*———, 'Is the Tolerant Personality Type the Opposite of the Intolerant?', *Journal of Social Psychology*, Vol. 47, 1958, pp. 397-405.

*———, 'The Shared Frame of Reference Concept Applied to the Assimilation of Immigrants', *Human Relations*, Vol. 6, 1957, pp. 45-55.

*———, and Doczy, A. G., 'The Assimilation of Intellectual Refugees in Western Australia: with Special Reference to Hungarians', *R.E.M.P. Bulletin*, Vol. 9, No. 4, Oct.-Dec. 1961, and Vol. 10, Nos. 1-2, Jan.-June 1962.

Tavuchis, N., *Pastors and Immigrants: The Role of a Religious Elite in the Absorption of Norwegian Immigrants*, The Hague, 1963.

Thomas, D. E., and Baragwanath, W., 'Geology of the Brown Coals of Victoria', *Mining and Geological Journal*, Vol. III, No. 6, Sept. 1949, and Vol. IV, No. 1, March 1950.

Thomas, W. I., and Znaniecki, F., *The Polish Peasant in Europe and America*, 2 vols., 3rd ed., New York, 1958.

'Valley of Power', *A.N.Z. Bank Quarterly Survey*, Vol. V, Oct. 1955.

Wakeley, R. E., 'Selecting Leaders for Agricultural Programs', *Sociometry*, Vol. X, No. 4, Nov. 1947, pp. 384-95.

Warner, W. L., *Democracy in Jonesville*, New York, 1949.

———, and Srole, L., *The Social Systems of American Ethnic Groups*, New Haven, 1945.

Wilkinson, T. L., *The Reformed Churches of Australia: Their Origin, Necessity, Beliefs and Activities*. Publications on Reformed Faith and Practice No. 2, The Reformed Publishing Committee, Parramatta, N.S.W. [n.d.].

Willey, M. N., *The Country Newspaper*, Chapel Hill, 1926.

Wilson, B., 'An Analysis of Sect Development', *American Sociological Review*, Vol. XXIV, 1959, pp. 3-15.

———, *Sects and Society: The Sociology of Three Religious Groups in Britain*, London, 1961.

Wilson, M. G. A., 'The Changing Latrobe Valley: the Impact of Brown Coal Mining', *Australian Geographical Studies*, Vol. I, No. 1, Apr. 1963.

Young, M., and Willmott, P., *Family and Kinship in East London*, London, 1957.

Zubrzycki, J., *Polish Immigrants in Britain: A Study of Adjustment*, The Hague, 1956.

——, *Immigrants in Australia: A Demographic Survey based upon the 1954 Census*, Melbourne, 1960.

Manuscripts

Bennet, B. B., Aspects of the Operation and Development of the Lurgi High Pressure Gasification Plant at Morwell, Australia, Paper presented at 8th International Gas Conference, Stockholm, 1961.

‡Boas, P., The Workers' Hostels in Yallourn.

‡Carey, Estelle, Migrant Children and Their Problems.

‡——, The Reformed Church Congregation in Moe.

†Craig, J. I., Assimilation of European Immigrants: A Study in Role Assumption and Fulfilment, Ph.D. Thesis, The Australian National University, 1954.

‡Diary of the Survey, 19th Jan.-28th Feb. 1959.

‡Harris, Tania, The Migrant Community in East and North Newborough.

Jones, F. L., The Italian Population of Carlton: A Demographic and Sociological Survey, Ph.D. Thesis, The Australian National University, 1962.

‡Mann, L., The Dutch Community in Moe.

‡Scouller, Rosemary, English Classes for Migrants.

‡Snow, Evelyn, Social Participation and Interviewing in an Immigrant Community.

Submission by Advance Latrobe Valley Association to the State Development Committee Inquiry on the Economic Development of Gippsland, presented at Morwell, March 1961.

‡The Survey of Immigrants in the Latrobe Valley, Victoria, Jan.-Mar. 1959.

‡Interviewers' Handbook.

‡Wallace, Margaret, The Dutch Family.

‡——, Problems of Migrant Women.

‡Weetman, Jo, The Maltese Community in Yallourn North.

* indicates the publications of a group of social psychologists of the University of Western Australia, referred to in Chapter 10, n. 1.
† indicates the research referred to in Chapter 10, n. 2.
‡ held in Department of Demography, The Australian National University.

INDEX

Advance Latrobe Valley Association, xiv, 9-10, 23, 28-31
Advocate (Moe), 23, 36, 44, 276
Advertiser (Morwell), 23, 36, 44, 276
Age group, x, 22, 29, 35, 44, 67; and English language standard, 132
Age structure, *see* Age group
Australian Paper Mills, Maryvale, 8, 22

Baltic states, settlers born in, x, 40, 51, 185, 233-4; age structure, 67; Displaced Persons in Germany, 235-6; education, 56, 90, 91; English language (facility), 129, 132; mass communication media, 134; migration to Australia, 67, 75-6, 236-7; native languages (children taught), 140-1; naturalization, 157; occupational adjustment, 87; period of residence in Australia, 67; political refugees, 141; size of family, 69; social participation (withdrawal), 163; standard of living, 90, 91, 95, 100, (housing) 100, 101
Bonegilla Migrant Centre, 83-4, 237
British Isles, settlers born in, 11, 12, 26, 28, 56, 81-3, 185, 188-92; family problems, 83; friendship pattern, 142; membership of associations, 144, 146; occupational adjustment, 75; period of residence in Australia, 67; size of family, 69; standard of living, 90-1, 106, (housing) 97, 100, 102, (motor vehicles) 104
Brown coal mining, ix, 3-8, 34, 274

Chain migration, *see* Family migration
Children of settlers, 112-13, 116-23; bilingual, 118-20, 140; choice of occupation, 123-4; conflict (norms of behaviour), 116-18, 123, 124; employment opportunities (Latrobe Valley), 28-32, 120-1, 124, 185
Conceptual framework, 34
Consumer durables, 90, 105-7
Contra Club, 147

Country Women's Association (C.W.A.), 154
Cultural participation, *see* Participation, community

Delinquency, juvenile, 117-18; *see also* Family, under stress
Demographic characteristics of settlers, 67
Displaced Persons, 28, 60, 69, 101, 227-9; withdrawal from social participation, 115
Distribution of Population Committee, 30
Doukhobors, the, 109
Dutch-born settlers, 13, 16, 26, 28, 56, 185, 193-202; friendship patterns, 142; mass communication media, 134; membership of associations, 144, 146; native language (reluctance to teach children), 140; naturalization, 157; religion (response to questions), 279; size of family, 69, 71; social participation, 167; standard of living, 91-2, 95, (housing) 97, 102-3, (interior decoration of houses) 107-8, (motor vehicles) 104
Dutch community in Moe, 43, 150-2, 168-82; Index of Clannishness, 171, 289-90; province of origin, 172; religious affiliation, 173-80; social class composition, 170, 289; Social Club, 150-1, 165, 287; social integration, 168-71

Employment stability, *see* Occupational adjustment
English language classes, 40, 133-4
Estonian-born settlers, *see* Baltic states, persons born in
Expenditure levels, *see* Standard of living

Family, x, 111-26; extended (in Europe), 111-12, 284; migration, 13, 58, 60-6, 111-12, 277; size, 69, 71-2; under stress, 113-18, 120-5, (integrating forces) 118-23, 125-6, (inter-

Family—*continued*
generation conflict) 116-18, 124, 284
Field survey, 37-41; *see also* Interview Schedule, Interviewing
Fertility, *see* Family, size of
Friendship patterns, 142, 144
Foreign language church, 180; *see also* Reformed Church of Australia, Ukrainian Orthodox Church

Gas and Fuel Corporation, 7, 28
Gereformeerde Kerk, see Reformed Church of Australia
German-born settlers, 11, 13, 26, 28, 56; friendship patterns, 142; mass communication media, 134; native-language publications (reading of), 138-9; naturalization, 157; occupational adjustment, 75; original settlers in Latrobe Valley, 275; standard of living, 91, (housing) 97, 100, (motor vehicles) 104
Gold mining, 4, 11
Good Neighbour Council, 153, 156
Great Morwell Coal Mining Company, 4, 5
Greek-born settlers, x, 58, 64, 165; friendship patterns, 144; informal associations, 146; mass communication media, 134; membership of associations, 144; native language (reading publications in), 138, 139, (teaching children) 140; occupational adjustment, 75; process of migration, 58, 64-5; standard of living, 90-2, 95-6, (motor vehicles) 104

Hazelwood SEC installation, 33-4, 185
Homesickness, 158-60, 198
Hostel dwellers, 97
Housing, 18-19, 39, 97, 100-3, 106-8; cost, 100-1; credit for, 101; mortgage payments, 96; purchase price, 100; temporary, 101, 102
Housing Commission of Victoria, 20, 21, 43, 100
Hromada, see Ukrainian community in Newborough
Hungarian-born settlers, 60-2

Income of settlers, *see* Standard of living
International Refugee Organization (I.R.O.), 60, 61, 76

Interview schedule, 34-7, 41, 90, 245-63
Interviewing, 37-9, 242, 267-70, 278
Isolates, social, *see* Participation, community
Italian-born settlers, x, 11, 13, 26, 51, 185; friendship patterns, 144; English language standard, 129; informal associations, 146-7; mass communication media, 134; membership of associations, 144; native language (reading publications in) 138, (teaching children) 140; occupational adjustment, 75; original settlers in the Latrobe Valley, 275; process of migration, 60

Kinship ties, *see* Family migration
Kum relationship, 112-13, 171

Language, 118, 285; and community participation, 134; barrier, 119-20; spoken at home, 118-19
Latvian-born settlers, *see* Baltic states, settlers born in
Legion of Mary in Newborough, 154
Life history method, 42, 187-8
Lithuanian-born settlers, *see* Baltic states, settlers born in
Live Wire, 23, 36, 44, 276
Lutheran Church in Newborough, 149

Macarthur, James, 3
Maltese-born settlers, 11, 13, 16, 26, 51, 57, 77, 160; foreign-language publications, 138; native language (teaching children), 140; occupational adjustment, 75; process of migration, 58, 63, 86-7, 202-9; rural background, 58, 75; size of family, 69, 71, 95, 111; standard of living, 95, (housing) 100, 107
Maltese community in Yallourn North, 40, 58, 63, 77, 111, 112, 148-9
Masculinity, 13, 26, 28
Monash, Sir John, 4-5, 18, 125
Morwell Power and Fuel Undertaking, 7
Motor vehicles, ownership of, *see* Standard of living

Naturalization, ix, 40, 156-8; *see also* Participation, community

Newborough Public Hall, 20, 155
Newspapers: Australian, 135-8; foreign language, 138-9, 285; readership of, 135-9
Non-response, see Sampling
Null hypothesis, see Statistical tests

Occupation, x, 44, 264-6; pre-migration, 56; present, x, 56
Occupational adjustment, x, 73-89, 280
Old Order Amish, the, 109
Orthodox religion, 51

Participation, community, 129, 164-6; and naturalization, 156-8; factors responsible for, 129, 132-5, 138-42, (language spoken at home) 139-40, (mastery of the English language) 129, 132-4, 138, (mass communication media) 135, 138, (teaching of language to children at home) 140-1; friendship patterns, 142, 144; membership of voluntary associations, 144, 146-56; withdrawal from, 158-64
Period of residence, 13, 16, 35, 63, 67, 78, 91, 95, 96, 185; and English language standard, 132; and friendship patterns, 144; and reading of native language newspapers, 138
Personality characteristics of settlers, 185
Pilot survey, 35
Polish Association in the Latrobe Valley, 140, 148
Polish Association in Victoria, 140
Polish-born settlers, 13, 16, 39, 51, 185, 211-23; Displaced Persons, 69, 223-9, (en route to Australia) 229-31; English language standard, 129; friendship patterns, 142, 232-3; mass communication media, 134; native language (reading publications in), 138, (teaching children) 140, 141; naturalization, 157; occupational adjustment, 75; political refugees, 141; size of family, 69, 71; standard of living, 96, (housing) 100, 101, 231-2, (motor vehicles) 104
Pre-migration background, x, 52, 56-8, 135, 138
Press: Australian, 135, 138; foreign language, 138-9
Primary group affiliation, 43, 287, 288, 293

Reformed Church of Australia and New Zealand, 51, 173, 290, 291; congregation in Moe, 154, 171, 173-81; Committee of Management, 170; degree of clannishness, 171, 290; functions of Minister and Elders, 174; inter-generation conflict, 116-17; kinship ties, 112; Ladies' Guild, 175; social participation, 168-9; sociometric choices, 177-9; Sponsoring Committee, 176; Youth Group, 175
Refugee camps in Europe, 60-2, 69, 228-9, 235-6, 277
Religion and immigrant adjustment, 44, 51, 69-70, 171, 180, 292-3
Rotary Clubs, 23, 40, 152
Russian-born settlers: emigration to Australia, 88; occupational adjustment, 88-9; social participation (withdrawal), 163

Sampling, 33-4, 43, 239-42, 244
Saturday schools, 140-1
Savings, see Standard of living
Scandinavian-born settlers, 11
Soccer teams, 149-50
Social participation, see Participation, community
Sociometric survey, 42-4, 168-70, 173, 177, 289-91
Standard of living, x, 90-110; consumer durables, 105-7; income and expenditure levels (ethnic groups), 90-1, 95, 96; motor vehicles, 103-4; savings, 96; see also Housing
State Electricity Commission of Victoria (SEC), 4-5, 24, 28, 33, 38, 44, 88, 97, 191, 192, 198, 199, 237, 239-40
Statistical tests, 44-7, 274
Strzelecki, Paul, 3

Ukrainian Association in Victoria, 141, 168
Ukrainian-born settlers, xi, 16, 40, 67, 112; English language (standard of spoken), 115; membership of Ukrainian associations, 144, 167; native language (reading publications in), 138, (teaching children) 140-1; naturalization, 157; occupational adjustment, 75; political refugees, 141, 170; standard of living, 95-6, (housing) 101, 102, 107, 109

Ukrainian community in Newborough, 43, 167-9, 181; Index of Clannishness, 171; religious adherence, 171, 180-1; social class composition, 170, 289; social integration, 168-70

Ukrainian Orthodox Church, 171, 181

Ukrainian Youth Association, 141, 142, 286

Wage levels, *see* Standard of living

Yugoslav-born, xi, 183-4; membership of voluntary associations, 144; occupational adjustment, 78; standard of living, 91, (housing) 97, 100

Y.M.C.A., 40, 237